Children, health and the social order

Children, health and the social order

Berry Mayall

Open University Press
Buckingham · Philadelphia

Open University Press
Celtic Court
22 Ballmoor
Buckingham
MK18 1XW

and
1900 Frost Road, Suite 101
Bristol, PA 19007, USA

First Published 1996

A catalogue record of this book is available from the British Library

ISBN   0 335 19282 3 (pb)   0 335 19283 1 (hb)

Library of Congress Cataloging-in-Publication Data
Mayall, Margaret Berry, 1936–
      Children, health and the social order / Margaret Berry Mayall.
         p.   cm.
      Includes bibliographical references and index.
      ISBN   0-335-19283-1 (hbk.). — ISBN   0-335-19282-3 (pbk.)
      1. Children. 2. Child development. 3. Child psychology. 4. School children —
   Health and hygiene. 5. Education, Primary.
      I. Title.
   HQ767.9.M385   1996
   305.23—dc20   95-37675
                                                                              CIP

Typeset by Type Study, Scarborough
Printed in Great Britain by Biddles Ltd, Guildford and King's Lynn

Contents

Acknowledgements

I have been helped by many people and organizations in the work towards this book. I am grateful to the Nuffield Foundation for a grant to work on the Greenstreet study. The ESRC funded the Health in Primary School study (Research grant ROOO 234476), on which my colleagues Gill Bendelow and Pamela Storey have collaborated; to it and to them my thanks are overdue. The Institute of Education provided seed-corn money to help me develop work on the status of health in education; and to carry out work on school dinners with Sheila Turner and Melanie Manthner. The Institute also granted me study leave, which enabled me to work solidly on this book for a time.

I am very grateful to the staff of the schools we have worked in, and to all the children and parents, for talking with us about daily life at home and school. In the interests of anonymity all names have been changed.

My colleagues, Sara Tibbs and Deborah Hickey, helped me greatly with interviewing and I am especially grateful to Gill Bendelow and Priscilla Alderson for commenting on an earlier draft of the book.

one

Introduction

This book is about childhoods: how they are experienced and understood by children and adults. Since children's and adults' experiences and understandings differ and conflict at some points, children may be expected to find points of tensions in their attempt to live a reasonably satisfactory daily life. This book has developed out of a range of research studies which have looked at children's early years, through adult eyes and, latterly, through children's own accounts.

Some of the issues involved in studying the daily lives of children are touched on here. Children's lives are lived through childhoods constructed for them by adult understandings of childhood and of what children are and should be. Most of children's actions are therefore influenced by adult views; children, like others, are not free agents. Inter-relationships between agency and structure need to be addressed, in trying to understand children's childhoods. Further, since children, up to and through the early school years, live mainly within the care of women, who themselves act under the greater power of social policies constructed largely by men, we are faced with not only intergenerational issues, but gender issues (Alanen 1992, 1994), and with power relationships structured into the triangle of men, women and children.

The stance of the observer and researcher must also be addressed. If one is not a child, can one and should one attempt to understand and convey what children's experiences are? Are there some specific difficulties in collecting data with and from children? What purposes are served by so doing? Researching children and childhood can look like and often has looked like the study of a strange tribe, of non-persons, on whom, however, great hopes are based, as the next generation of adults. Issues in researching children are taken up later in this chapter (pp. 12–19).

Just as the researcher–researched relationship must be worked at, so too must the basic stance to be adopted. The study of children has traditionally been focused on individuals, making their way through a series of stages towards mature adulthood. This psychological gaze has been both adultist and individualistic. This book, in line with some recent developments in sociological research, attempts to consider children as a social group with specific relationships to other social groups, such as parents and teachers; as a group, their inter-relationships with socio-economic factors are specific too. The approach taken here lifts children, conceptually speaking, out of the traditional association with family, in order to consider how, as a group, they relate to the people they live with and to the staff of the schools they attend.

In the attempt to take a sociological view of children and of childhood, more issues emerge to be tackled: it becomes necessary to attend to the gendering and adulting of sociology itself (see Chapter 3). The feminist research enterprise has drawn attention to how sociology as developed in the century or so up to the 1960s was structured by its concern to understand society seen from the standpoint of men (e.g. Oakley 1985a; Smith 1988). Men's work in institutional settings was its focus, and in complement sociologists emphasized a sharp division in social life between the public and the private domains, assigned women to the private, and accepted their beings and actions there as natural and unproblematic. The cognitive, rational, impersonal world of men in the public sphere was contrasted with the intuitive, emotional, inter-relational world of women in the private sphere. Women have challenged all of this: the division of social life into two separate and unequal domains, the ascription of naturalness to women's lot, and the designation of certain innate characteristics to women and their lives.

Strikingly, the founding fathers of sociology excluded children and childhood as suitable topics for consideration and their descendants continue to do so. Defined as non-adult objects of socialization, and as non-contributors to social wealth, they have been invisible to the sociological gaze. The process whereby sociology traditionally excluded women, through deeming them theoretically uninteresting, similarly accounts for the exclusion of children. Through the designation of children as socialization projects sociology has both naturalized children and written them out of the sociological script. Feminists too, in the interests of freeing themselves theoretically and practically from the home and domestic responsibilities, have until recently not considered children as a social group; some have regarded them as one cause of women's oppression (see Oakley 1994 for discussion). The slow process of giving children and childhood sociological recognition has begun through the construction of a 'sociology of childhood'. The first, base-line tenet here is the idea of children as a social group, on whom social forces operate to condition the character of childhood as lived. For instance, social policies on the family, housing, education and health have, whether purposefully or not, had powerful impacts on childhood experience (see Chapter 2). The standpoint here is to conceptualize children as agents, with specific angles, as a social group, on the institutions and adult groups they interact with. Such a standpoint allows one to consider the balance between child and adult contributions within the interaction, and within the broader social context. Children's interactions with teachers at school, for instance, are powerfully structured by wider adult understandings of what schools should do.

The above suggests that adults have viewed children as inadequate versions of themselves. The larger view is that adulthood itself derives its definitions as opposites to those it ascribes to childhood. Children are those people assigned to that category by adults, and so adulthood and childhood are relational concepts. One of the principal adult-defined constituents of child–adult relationships is adult power and authority. Yet, as women who care for children on a daily basis know from experience, there is a continuously shifting balance between the control they exercise over children's daily lives, the empathy they feel and the care that they give to children (who need food, warmth and comfort) and the more equal relationships of companionship: sharing daily experiences, and responding to the same stimuli as they traverse their daily round. It has been suggested that men remember less of their childhoods than women do (see Ward 1990: 1); one reason may be that few men but most women experience (albeit at second-hand) childhood again in the company of children. The dismissal of children from the minds of sociologists may derive not only from their concern for the public social order, but also in part from rejection of their poorly remembered past. It seems probable that men are more likely to construct children and childhood as different from adults and adulthood than women who, through living with children, are more likely to stress both continuity and similarity. Indeed it is noticeable that those male sociologists who first began to pay attention theoretically to children pointed to their experiences of living with children as evidence of how they gained new understanding of childhood (e.g. Denzin 1977).

In considering childhood as structured, mediated and experienced by adults and children, we have to consider the linkages between generation and gender. As things stand, in Western 'advanced' societies, it is mainly women who do the hands-on care of children, at home, at minders, in nurseries and playgroups and schools, up to the age of 10 or 11. Girls and boys experience women as the principal adults in their daily lives; and women themselves, like children, are controlled largely through the patriarchal social order in their public and domestic lives. In the home, pre-school and school – the principal sites of children's daily lives – social expectations and norms intersect with the knowledge and behaviour of women to structure the experiences of children, and to define the limits and opportunities of childhood (see Chapter 4). It has to be said that there is very little research information about children's daily experience of gendered and generational daily life. The aim in this book is to study the available data in order to explore childhood within sociology.

An important theme running through the book is the linked status of children's bodies and children's minds – in theory and in policy, in homes and schools. The newly fashionable sociology of the body has again been developed from an adultist standpoint and has virtually excluded children from consideration (see Chapter 5). Psychology and sociology have colluded to provide a structure of belief that makes natural objects out of children's bodies, that devalues them and therefore that cannot study linkages between bodily and cognitive experience. Classically, in developmental psychology, children's minds, but not body–mind links, have been the principal topic studied (see Chapter 3). The traditional sociological standpoint, handed down by Durk-heim (1961: 17–19), also focuses on cognitive and moral training, with the school as the appropriate agency for training the child to meet societal demands. In these scenarios bodily experience is theoretically uninteresting; it comes under health, rather than within psychology or sociology, and health care is the natural assignment of mothers at home, and of health services for surveillance and cure. Furthermore, traditionally, children's minds have been looked at from the vantage point of adult perspectives; it has been cognitive imperfections and not competences that have been centrally at issue. But we may turn this round and argue that children should be judged competent members of society unless cases suggest otherwise and we may then also grant that they have abilities and interests to judge the social circumstances in which they live their lives (Alderson and Montgomery 1995).

So a central topic for study is children's linkages between the bodily and the cognitive. Just as women have challenged the presentation of science and knowledge as factual, and have indicated how it is rooted in men's understand-ings (e.g. Rose 1986; Harding 1992), so we stand at the beginning of considering children's knowledge and its contributions to human understand-ings. In early childhood, bodily and cognitive knowledge surely must be closely linked. Acquiring control over urination, learning to use a spoon, learning to walk, all these attract praise from the people on whom one depends for social worth. Learning these bodily skills and being praised for these accomplish-ments, gives children a specific knowledge of the importance of their bodies in the social worlds they inhabit. Learning social rules about behaviour also attracts loving approval, through which they learn consciousness of how bodies impact on social relationships and customs. Common-sense experience tells us that children, like other social groups, both enjoy achievement and value it highly; they delight in achievement of bodily control, of physical skills and, as time goes on, of skills highly valued by adults – such as reading and writing and calculating. Judy Dunn's work on the development of children's social and moral understanding suggests that both the emotional and the cognitive are contributory factors (Dunn 1988: 186–9). Studies of children's views on achievement and on linkages between emotional and cognitive experience and understanding can help us to understand not just the conditions of childhood experience and learning, but those of people in general: how the emotional and cognitive interact to structure people's experience and understandings through life.

The organization by adults of children's daily experiences in time and space constitutes an important set of structures through which, as adults, we teach ourselves that they are different from us (see Chapter 6). For instance, we assign social significance to the chronological age of children – so under-5s are deemed essentially the province of mothers and the health surveillance system – with bodies as a central focus, while over-5s are the property of schools and education services – with corresponding focus on minds. Within school, children's allowed activities are also structured by age, according to age-related schema about developmental needs: as part of the curriculum infants may play, juniors may not. The spatial siting of children in specific institutions provides justification for demarcating children and childhood as different and unequal. In Western societies, childhood can be seen as characterized by protection and exclusion (Engelbert 1994). Children are supposed to be under the eye of adults in places and times designated by adults: the home, on the street, in school. They are excluded from adult-oriented places and times: cinemas, family festivities, traffic-dominated neighbourhoods, workplaces and so on. Through this corralling of childhood, we learn to think children are other. So powerful is the normalization of these divisions of children from adults, that when they dislike the places and times we consign them to, we judge them at fault, rather than the environment. It has been widely reported that children's own time free of adult supervision has been drastically reduced in recent years in industrialized countries, in response to adult fears about adult behaviour in public places (e.g. Ward 1990: esp. 184–91). Under these circumstances, it becomes common-sense knowledge that children are different, because they need to be shielded, by adults, from adults (just as men shield women from men). Thus the biological dependencies of early childhood become compounded with socially constructed dependencies (Lansdown 1994).

Including children in considerations of the social order requires rethinking that social order (see Chapter 7). We have been brought up to conceptualize the public and the private as theoretically distinct domains of social life, where work is defined as that which is paid for and carried out in the public domain and activity at home is thus defined as not work. Women have forced reconsideration of these distinctions. Women propose and show that what they do is productive and reproductive work; and that their work takes place in and across the private and the public. Women work paid and unpaid at home in childcare (as mothers and as minders); they work unpaid in institutions (as helpers at school, as volunteers in hospitals) as well as in paid work. For women, the home is not the site of leisure, nor of comfort and support, since they work there to ensure the care and comfort of children and men. They cross these theoretical divides too in taking with them their bodies, minds and emotions from the 'natural, emotional and non-cognitive' domain of the home into the 'constructed, rational and cognitive' worlds of the workplace (Martin 1989: 197). Incorporating children into sociological consideration has similar impacts on thinking about the public and the private. They too work both at home and in institutions – and little of their work is paid; they too take their bodies, emotions and minds with them, and meet with varying recognition of these constituents of their being, at nurseries, schools, shops and sports centres.

Conceptualizing children as agents also forces reconsideration of the division of labour: who does what work, and what status is attached to the work and the doers of it. Women's work with their children then may be seen not only as a top–down socialization enterprise, but also as a collaborative enterprise where children both need help, care and protection, and act as learners and doers in the social worlds they engage with. At school, though teachers may, for practical and theoretical reasons, wish to hold on to their authority, the construction of children as active in the enterprise of learning and in the social world of the school has implications for the education service as a whole and for teachers' contributions within it. Furthermore the work, paid and unpaid, that children do (at school, at home, at jobs in the locality) suggests they are net contributors to social life rather than merely costs on parents and the state (Qvortrup 1991; Morrow 1994). Women's work both in the home and the school has low social status because it is women's work, defined as natural and therefore easy. But if children are regarded as active, participating in the acquisition of knowledge and of social relationships, emphasis is thrown on the present as well as the future of children's lives. In turn, women's work with children may be understood not as easy preparatory activity, but as collaborative, interactive work with people to make something worth while of their lives both now and for the future.

Finally we can draw from the above a further point to be discussed in this book: alliances between children and mothers. The point under discussion here is that children, so far from being objects, may be regarded as people working in alliance with their mothers; theoretically, too, with their teachers. Children can be seen as people constructing and reconstructing the social order of the home (Solberg 1990) and the school (e.g. Björklid 1986). We can take this further and suggest that children, in alliance with both women and men, can be seen as working to develop and strengthen their abilities to face the social worlds constructed for them, and the wider social worlds into which they will move. These are intergenerational gendered alliances. In particular, the work of women needs consideration, as agents in helping girls maintain the strength of their voices as they meet the challenges of a male-dominated social order (Brown and Gilligan 1992: 220–32).

But beyond the help that children may get from women in their social worlds, it is clear that their rights as people will not be met without larger measures. Though the United Nations has established a Convention on the Rights of the Child (1989), it is up to individual nations (the UK signed in December 1991) to implement it. As the Children's Rights Development Unit (1994) has painstakingly documented, and the UN (1995) has endorsed, the UK has a long way to go. The principle of children's rights is unrecognized in most areas of social life, and implementation is, in complement, not on the public agenda. Even the principle of listening to children's views is barely recognized. Research for and with rather than on children has a part to play here. Some of the measures that might upgrade children's rights are discussed in Chapter 7.

This book, then, offers explorations of some large topics. These explorations can only be a partial, early-stage contribution to the very large enterprise of rethinking sociology to include children's understandings. The aim is to contribute to developing ideas within sociology, and by considering children's social positioning to think about how children's lot might be changed.

Learning from research

At this point it is relevant to say something about my research history, since the themes and topics of this book derive partly from those experiences. I came late into the world of social science research. During the years when young women were first propounding revolutionary feminist ideas, I was a full-time mother, except for a few precious hours when, as I put it, I kept myself sane by doing a bit of teaching. These were the Bowlby years, when mothers told each other they must stay at home with under-3s to ward off maternal deprivation. Of course another kind of maternal deprivation took its place. I read Hannah Gavron on *The Captive Wife* (1966) with very great empathy; but I also found it hard to empathize entirely with some of the proposals reputedly advanced by the women's liberation movement, as reported in the *Guardian*: 24-hour crèches and women's liberation from childcare. For though I was bored, depressed and angry with my designated and unremitting lot as the sole childcarer, I had absorbed and to an extent identified with the message that a few hours a week at playgroup (a new idea in the middle 1960s) was enough for her and for me, because the kinds of knowledge you acquire of your child through living the days with her is uniquely useful in caring for her.

When she went to primary school at 5, I went back to college, and acquired social administration and social work qualifications. One surprise there was that no one else in my year of 25 students wanted to focus on children. Adult and youth mental illness and deviance were all the rage. It seemed that children's daily lives and services for children, then as now, had low status. But when I qualified, I found a job in a new research unit – the Thomas Coram Research Unit – which was interested in children, and the issue of children's rights to adequate services was uppermost in our minds as we studied minders, day nurseries, nursery schools and voluntary-sector initiatives (Hughes *et al.* 1980). Two other points struck me very forcibly at the time.

The first was that mothers interviewed about their lives with their children, and about their use of and wishes for certain services, looked at those services from the children's point of view. Though many mothers were in desperate social and financial straits, and urgently needed daycare to help them manage, they thought first of their child's welfare, judged the adequacy of the placement and moved their children out swiftly if it failed to satisfy them. This was a very striking reminder of the close affinity between mothers' well-being and that of their children, and of the respect mothers had for their children's well-being.

The second point was that mothers and daycare staff talked very differently about children; and the experience of hearing their views, and of seeing the two sorts of people in action, alerted me for the first time to the idea that children and childhood might have varying meanings for adults. For childminders, children presented a management issue; they had to organize a group, keep the peace and carry out the many tasks involved in the care of babies and young children; concurrently they also had to manage their home: do the shopping and cooking and cleaning. So whether or not the child 'settled' easily, and was 'good' were relevant issues. Nursery nurses, whose job entailed mainly childcare in a setting where others provided the food and cleaned up, spoke much less in management terms; we postulated that their training might lead them to adopt more individualizing approaches to the children. Few mothers talked in management terms; it was the child's individuality and achievements that drew forth comment. Mothers were more likely than minders or nursery nurses to say their child was difficult − presumably, we thought, because the relationship between child and mother was more individual and interactive than that with daycare staff. Though these data could be interpreted in many ways, at the least they suggested that the same child could call forth different descriptions and judgements in different settings: social context and adult remit and child−adult relationship were relevant (Mayall and Petrie 1983: ch. 6).

The next study I was involved in focused in more detail on mothers' ideas about childcare, in particular on the health care that mothers give their under-3s. This study − *Keeping Children Healthy* − was part of a Social Science Research Council (SSRC)-funded programme of research on child health and education. Its impetus was the Black Report (issued in 1980) − which provided evidence of inequalities in child health by social class. The study focused on children's access to health and to health services, through the parents' care. We took two small areas of inner London, socially mixed in character, and identified all the first children aged 18−36 months, living in two-parent families; the sample included both white, indigenous families and three ethnic minority groups (Mayall 1991). We interviewed the main caregiver, in most cases the mother (135), and the principal issues explored were: the characteristics of maternal and paternal child health care; how material and social factors affected their practices; and how useful were health services in helping them in their tasks.

Again this work provided some striking lessons (Mayall 1986). Firstly, it pointed to the complexity of health care at home: how mothers' knowledge of physical, emotional and social factors contributed to their understanding of their child's health status; and how this knowledge fed into their health-related decisions. Child health care was not a simple matter of health belief leading to action; it derived from the complexities of experiential learning, and was structured by social policies, and by the material and social contexts within which mothers worked.

Secondly, mothers' accounts suggested differences between 'lay' and 'professional' perspectives on the functions and value of child health services, and on appropriate action for children: issues here were mothers' concern for individual child welfare versus health professionals' public health remit; and the related debate between the two sides about meanings of 'responsible' health-care behaviour.

Under the same programme of studies on children, health and education, the newly renamed Economic and Social Research Council (ESRC) funded a further study: the Under-Twos Study, conceived as a follow-up to Keeping Children Healthy. The aim was to take fuller account of two factors which could be important in determining children's health status – ethnicity and contacts with health services (Mayall and Foster 1989). This qualitative study was designed to include an inner London multi-ethnic sample of households. All the 33 households had a first child aged 21 months. We aimed for three interviews at monthly intervals, in order to tap into the varieties of daily experience and use of services. In all families the mother was interviewed; where fathers were resident or involved with their children – 24 cases – half agreed to be interviewed. On the health worker side the study included a random sample of 28 health visitors working in the health clinics and GP surgeries used by the mothers for their children, and a comparison sample of 20 health visitors working in a county district health authority. The health visitors too were interviewed three times, at monthly intervals. We also interviewed the 11 clinical medical officers who worked in the community child health services alongside the inner London health visitors.

The principal issues studied, through exploration of the daily lives and work of mothers and health staff were: the character and relative status of paid and unpaid women's health care knowledge; the character and acceptability of health staff preventive work with mothers, and benevolence versus control as issues on both sides; paid and unpaid women's power to shape their work with and for children; and power relationships between the two sides.

This study deepened our understanding of the types of knowledge held by mothers and health professionals, and showed clearly the gulf between experiential lived learning and book learning. It provided detailed exploration of the workings of the 'psy complex': how intervention into the home is implemented, how the two sides regard this intervention and how mothers negotiate with health visitors and doctors. It also reinforced understanding of the socio-economic factors bearing on the daily lives of mothers and their children, and in particular the difficulties faced by ethnic minority mothers in arriving at a satisfactory way of life in the hostile environment of inner London.

These studies provided some basic themes for further research: varying models of childhood and childcare; the status of women's knowledge; links and relationships between the public and the private; and the division of labour between women. More recently I have been involved in three further studies which explore these issues, but in relation to the daily lives of children once they reach school age. These include a detailed study of daily life in one school; a study of food, and especially school dinners, at another school; and a study of health-related policies and practices in English and Welsh primary schools. The impetus for these studies was the understanding, gained from earlier work and from the newly emerging international interest in childhood as a social phenomenon, that children's own experiences and understandings deserved a hearing. Listening to children as well as to adults is essential in the study of children's daily lives. In particular, school provides an interesting social environment, with specific characteristics compared to features of children's social environments in the pre-school years: the compulsory nature of attendance; the professional training of teachers; and the division of labour for the care and education of the children within the school. In brief, I wanted to move beyond the consideration of adult understandings (mothers, daycare and health staff) about and for children, and to incorporate children's own understandings. As I envisaged it, a triangular set of relationships and tensions needed study: with children, mothers and staff (health and education) as the points of the triangle.

In the following paragraphs I give some detail about the main studies which I draw on during the course of this book. The principal study referred to is the Greenstreet study, with the Health in Primary Schools and Bluelane studies used to fill out some points.

In the Greenstreet study (funded by Nuffield Foundation, 1991–3) (Mayall 1994a), I explored some of the themes that had been important as regards pre-school children and their families, but moved up the age-range to focus on school-age children, who travel between the home and the school on a daily basis, and experience the care of two sets of women: mothers and school staff. The aim was to study children's understanding of their experiences at home and school. I drew the sample from one school, collected data from them at school, and interviewed their mothers at home.

This was a small-scale study, carried out over two terms in 1991 in one socially mixed London primary school. The school was over-subscribed and all the parents interviewed were enthusiastic about it. The school was housed in post-war buildings: classrooms arranged in blocks of four; a library; a resources room; and an administrative block (the head's and secretary's office, staff-room with kitchen area, medical room, supervisor's room (with first aid and small kitchen)). There was also a large hall used for gym, assemblies, dinners, parent-run jumbles and teas, and other meetings. Outside there were two asphalt playgrounds, for infants and juniors. There was a one-storey building housing a nursery class with its own playground. In the junior playground was a two-storey wooden hut, used as an after-school centre. At the time of the study, there was a reception class for children aged 'rising 5' to 6, and one class for each year-group, seven classes in all. As well as class teachers, there were four supervisors/helpers, responsible for dinner-play supervision, and for helping in class. In the reception class, help was also provided by a part-time teacher, and by two local (unpaid) women. By comparision with many schools responding to our postal questionnaire (see below), this school was well equipped and staffed.

All the children in two classes, the reception class (22 children aged 5–6) and class 5 (30 children aged 9–10) were studied. I collected data from the children, through interviews with teachers (six) and non-teaching staff (the secretary, four helpers, the head) and the school nurse; and through interviews at home with a random selection of mothers of some of the children (12 reception and 10 class 5). Equal numbers of mothers of boys and of girls were included.

The principal topics explored with all these people included: children's daily lives in and across the social worlds of the home and the school; the division of labour between children, parents, school and health staff for the health care of the children; the character of the caring work of parents and school staff; and how this was structured by the social setting.

The Health in Primary Schools study (funded by the ESRC, 1993–5) builds on the Greenstreet study. It aims to consider how health is conceptualized and treated in primary schools. It has taken place at two levels. A 1 in 20 random sample of primary schools in England and Wales has been targeted, and data collected from 620 schools (62 per cent of those mailed) through a brief postal questionnaire (Social Science Research Unit 1994). Case studies have taken place in six varied schools to explore the questionnaire topics in more detail. In each school data have been collected from 6- and 10-year-olds, their teachers and other school staff; also through group discussions and questionnaires with parents. Data from these case studies will be reported on elsewhere, but data from the questionnaire are used in this book. Topics for both the questionnaire and case studies include: the character and perceived appropriateness of the school building and grounds for the welfare of the children; how the physical care of the children is attended to and by whom – in particular, what schools do about safety, illness, accidents and food at school; how health education is included in the formal and informal curriculum of the school; and the contribution of the school health service to the health care of the children.

In the Bluelane study (funded by Institute of Education 1993), my colleagues Sheila Turner, Melanie Mauthner and I, concentrated on a small but critical aspect of the school day – the school dinner – and studied children's beliefs about food both in general and in relation to food at school (Mauthner *et al.* 1993). The study was concerned with factors that structure the character and consumption of the midday meal at school, and with children's views on food at school (together with some comparisons with food at home). The fieldwork for the study was carried out by Melanie Mauthner during one term in an infants school in a socially deprived and ethnically varied area of a midlands city. She spent time in the school as a participant observer with two classes: of 5–6 and 7–9-year-olds; and collected data with the children through drawings, discussions and small group interviews; and talked informally with the class teachers and other staff. An important part of the work was participant observation of dinner-time at the school.

So this book draws on a number of studies I have been involved in. All of them have to do with intersections of health with education issues. They pursue a number of themes across the studies and across the years. They are all concerned with knowledge – how it is acquired, through experience, through interactive encounters, through more formal learning; and with the status of knowledge held by certain groups. A second theme is how mothers' and children's daily lives work out, given that the welfare of each is dependent on that of the other, and given that mothers and children live their daily lives in a social world hostile to their interests. A third theme is consideration of how women and children cross and recross the public and the private; how women communicate with each other in connection with children's welfare, and how children and women negotiate the division of labour, including the status of children's activities and viewpoints.

The earlier studies collected data from adults. This was in part because the children concerned were very young (under 3 years old), but it must also be said that at the time researchers were less tuned in to collecting data from and with children than they are now. The most recent three studies have tried to put children centre stage, and in all three data have been collected directly with children.

Researching with and for children

As described in the above section, this book draws on research studies I have been involved in. The book as a whole is an attempt to incorporate children into sociological thinking, and this has required carrying out an academic exercise: reviewing the literature; discussing the arguments; and making suggestions about how we may push forward thinking about children as social actors in social contexts. Much of the book perforce takes a stance far removed from children's expression of their lived experience. Yet it was critical to incorporate children's spoken and written accounts of their daily lives into the argument of the book. This is because some of the argument is based on what they say. They are conceptualized here as competent reporters of their experience. The standpoint taken is that giving them 'a voice' (Gilligan 1993) means more than recording their views; it means attending to them and taking them seriously, as part of sociological discourse. Further, the aim of doing the research and of writing it up is to work for children, rather than on them: to describe their circumstances in order to clarify these, with a view to considering social change.

This position is likely to lead to conflict with some sociologists, on two main grounds: that empirical data is irrelevant to constructing an argument; and that, anyway, children are not competent reporters. It is a basic position in this book that empirical studies are essential contributions to thinking at theoretical levels. The construction of an argument needs to be sensitive to its quality of fit – a theory has to be measured against the experiences of those it purports to describe. There needs to be an interaction between the theory and the experience, each building on and refining the other. Thus Wright Mills (1967: 74) argues 'that any systematic attempt to understand involves some kind of alternation between (empirical) intake and (theoretical) assimilation, that concepts and ideas ought to guide factual investigation, and that detailed investigations ought to be used to check up on and re-shape ideas'. In this case, too, the use of children's own words as one means of considering their social positioning, can provide a corrective to the biases of adult views. For, as Frances Waksler (1991b) says: 'Adulthood is a perspective, a way of being in the world, that embodies a particular stance towards children, a stance that allows adults to deal with children in everyday life, but that limits sociological understanding.'

Until recently, children as reporters and witnesses have tended to be excluded from empirical research studies, which have instead used mothers as informants on their children. I have myself had research proposals turned down on the grounds that no useful data could be collected with people under the age of 12. In recent seminars on childhood research, participants return again and again to methodological problems they perceive as inherent in doing research with children, given children's proposed failings and inadequacies: as cognitive incompetents, children are routinely wrong and misunderstand; they have insufficient experience to understand and interpret what they see and experience; they are likely to confuse fact with fiction; and may give the answers they think adults want rather than report accurately. On these grounds, they are not interesting commentators, and those who listen to them and report their sayings lay themselves open to the charge of naivety. The replies to these points come under two categories: most of the points apply to adults too; and if children have different understandings from adults, then that is interesting in itself. Adults, like children, vary in their knowledge and experience; on topics important to them, both groups are likely to have knowledge, thought and wisdom, as researchers have found in the case of children with serious health conditions (e.g. Bluebond-Langner 1978), and as is shown in children's discussions of the merits and demerits of school. All of us could probably do with more experience and knowledge, we interweave fact and fiction both consciously and unconsciously and tell interviewers what we think they want to know.

Collecting data

The above points about the data children provide leave open the specifically difficult issue in research with children: power relationships. It is inescapable that in a range of ways children's voices may be affected by the power inequalities between them and the researcher, and that this presents an even more formidable difficulty than it does in research with adults. A first and critical topic is consent.

Consent includes consent at the outset and consent along the way. But children do not have an independent voice: at the outset of research it is hard to side-step the pathways controlled by adults to children, since they manage children's lives and act as gatekeepers to children. An interesting example is given by Moore (1986: 89), who contacted children through a school and then asked individual children to show him their favourite play places; in one instance a mother turned up and suspiciously asked what he was doing with her daughter. At Greenstreet, I had to get permission from the head and through her from class teachers. Once installed in the classroom, the researcher has acquired status as someone accepted by the teacher. The class teacher in each of the two classes (reception and class 5) discussed with me how to introduce me. With the 5-year-olds, she introduced me as a helper and someone who was interested in children's ideas about health. With the older children, the teacher suggested I introduce myself and tell them about research more generally. So I explained the research: on children's, parents' and teachers' ideas about health, and that I hoped to write a book about it. This led immediately to a suggestion from some of the girls: could they take part in writing the book. I had to explain that it would take time to sort through the data. However, I said I could feed the data back to them for discussion. So, for instance, when they wrote notes on ways they kept themselves healthy, I quickly analysed the answers and further discussed them with the class as a whole. When in pairs several raised the topic of food at school as problematic, and most showed their concern that life should be interesting, I reported these points back to them, for further discussion. Yet these activities do not constitute a good response to their interest in participating in writing up the research. Though having more time would help, there is also the problem that a year later the children may have grown out of their then stated views; they move on but the data are fixed in amber. In the case of the 9-year-olds, they had dispersed to secondary schools by the time I had reached some understanding of what they said to me. Further, some aspects of interpretation will depend on knowledge they do not have access to. And further, the school staff themselves may not wish for continued participation in the research a year or two on. However, conferences for children to discuss research data and the writing of books with them remain targets for future research projects.

Consent implies putting oneself in the hands of the researcher and her agenda. Erica Burman (1994: 144) gives an example which indicates that power belongs with the researcher, whether child or adult: she reversed the usual roles, by asking the children to interview her, and found herself uncomfortably aware that she could not challenge their agenda without breaking through the voluntary character of her agreement to be interviewed. Even the most open or free data collection session is structured by the researcher. However, I sought consent for each activity. In both classrooms I negotiated with the teacher when it would be appropriate to collect data with the children. First I spent two or three days just as a general helper in the class, partly to observe and partly so that the children would feel at ease with me. The teacher then decided how to slot my work in with the classwork. She would say to children, would you like to go with Berry. Under these circumstances, children generally said yes – though occasionally one would say no, they didn't feel like it or were too busy. Of course, going with me meant a change of scene – out of the classroom, and a change of activity; and children seemed generally to enjoy talking into tape recorders and playing back, discussing real life topics, writing food diaries. In particular they seemed to relish discussing school with someone who was not in authority there.

The researcher's status in school is at best ambiguous: people aim for the 'least-adult role' (Mandell 1991) but are bound to fail. Barrie Thorne, for instance, who made serious attempts to get inside the social worlds of children, through participant observation, occasionally found herself treated with suspicion (are you a spy?) and also found herself drawn into adult collusion (exchanging knowledgeable glances with the teacher) and adult activity (helping to care for children) (Thorne 1993: ch. 2). In my case, I was one of several adults who took part in class activities: mothers helped out in class, and the helpers came and went during the day. As an older woman, I may have looked somewhat like a granny, which perhaps served to distance me from the authority structure of the school, run by younger women. On the other hand, constrained by time, I had to get through an agenda: to collect data both from the children and from staff within the timetable I had proposed and had accepted. So I had to behave in a purposeful way, engaged in my adult activity.

Like Allison James (1993: ch. 1), it seemed to me that children must be experiencing me as more than one person during the research, as a non-official friendly person, as adult with her own agenda, and as class helper. I received unofficial pieces of information: children talked to each other, it seemed, openly; they spoke critically of school and home, and showed me bruises, cuts and grazes which they did not report to the staff. But children also recognized that I had my own purposes when they asked, why are you asking us these questions? And they turned to me as a class helper: one who tied shoe-laces and mopped up accidents. Like other helpers, I took part in the day's educational activities too: listened to reading; helped with maths cards; and played board games. Children's consent to research thus takes place within a context of understandings: this adult has school approval and takes part in some recognizable school activities; but she is positioned at a distance or at an angle to school – she wants to know what children think of it.

The least-adult role, as I have suggested, is hard to sustain in the face of one's complex set of roles in school. Like others, I tried at least to position myself as separate from the authority structure of the school and to be, in some respects, a person on their own level. Thus, for instance, I sat with the children when the teacher was talking with them. I went with them on their daily round. I sat (uncomfortably) on low chairs to hold group discussions. More theoretically I tried to see school life through their eyes. Perhaps the strongest card was to try to address and maintain in the foreground their own agendas; this is not common practice in schools and so was both a means of distancing myself from school agendas and a way of getting children's confidence. In complement, I tried to make it clear that I was not there to moralize: what they said did not call forth adultish comment. I also tried to be responsive to their perspectives on the data collection sessions: letting them choose their companions; keeping sessions short; and ending the session if they got restive or bored. The teachers and I made sure that children always talked with me in twos and threes, rather than alone; this redressed power imbalances to some extent, and it allowed them to discuss topics with each other.

During my weeks in the school, I explored a range of ways of collecting data. Some of it was observational, with field notes written up at the end of the day. But in the time available I could not rely solely on observation. With the 5-year-olds I asked them to draw me pictures of ways they kept healthy, and talked with each about their drawing. Some of them also drew pictures of playtime and dinner-time. I put the drawings together as a book, and went through it with them during the story-time session at the end of the day; and left it for them on their book shelves. I also talked with the children in pairs, in the library if it was free or, failing that, in a corner of the classroom; I asked them to tell me about what they did first thing in the morning; and on another occasion what they liked best and least about school and would change if they could; similarly what they enjoyed and disliked about being at home. These were just outline topics. The children themselves broadened discussion to include social relationships and responsibilities at home and school, constraints on the maintenance of health at school, and the importance of food and play at home and school.

With the 9-year-olds, I started by getting them to write a list of the things they did to stay healthy and gave them back an analysis of these lists. Then we had a whole-class brainstorm: where does health care take place – I filled in a flip chart with their suggestions. Then I asked the children in groups of three or four to talk with me about divisions of responsibility for health care. The teacher and I collaborated on a writing project: on Monday mornings they started a 'silent writing book': for half an hour they wrote about topics suggested in broad outline: me and my family; being at home; when I was ill; being at school. This project ran into some difficulties, since the children's ability and interest in writing varied so widely, especially by gender; however, it did provide useful data. Since food emerged as a major concern, I asked the older children to fill in a diary of their food consumption yesterday, on a chart, listing food items, where consumed, who provided/bought it, and who put it together/cooked it. I discussed these diet sheets with them to fill in the picture of the day and to enquire how they evaluated the day's food. I talked with the children, again in small groups, about what aspects of their daily lives they found most interesting, and most boring. Since I had by then begun to look at the 5-year-olds' data, I had some ideas about differences between experience at 5 and 9, in the infants and juniors. So I asked the 9-year-olds to reflect on their school experience now and then; this was fruitful since they found it interesting to compare, and it also acted as a form of triangulation, comparing the two sets of data. Thus the 5-year-olds showed in action, as well as in their talk, their enjoyment of playing during class time, and the 9-year-olds, talking about school life now and then, remembered their enjoyment of play in those early school years: when they participated in activity, and achieved by doing. All the conversations were taped and transcribed, for each of the activities. Of the 30 children, varying numbers participated in each activity, since a few would be away from school, and a very few said they were too busy or unwilling. These two classes provided plenty of data, which, alongside other work, I analysed during the next year. During this time, through established contacts, I was able to go back and collect some more data, in people's homes, where my colleagues (Sara Tibbs and Deborah Hickey) and I carried out some interviews with mothers and their children. We briefed the mothers and asked them to take the lead in conversation with their children, and this proved a good way of collecting data, since the children were relaxed and confident on their home ground, talking with the person they knew best.

Interpretation

As I have indicated, the aim of talking with children, mothers and school staff was to collect data on topics of direct interest to them: daily life. I also assumed that their experience and knowledge was represented in their accounts and should be respected. In this book I have relied mainly on children's own accounts for quotation, but contextualized them with some comments from the interviews with adults.

The varying methods of data collection allow for some comparison or triangulation. As noted in the last section, I could compare 9- and 5-year-olds' accounts of life in the infants. My observation of the school day could be compared with people's accounts. I was also able to check my developing understanding of what children said, both by going back and checking it out with the same children, and by later interviews – which provided fuller data on topics such as health maintenance at school, food and play. Data from other studies has also been used both to help me understand, and to provide comparisons. There is much fuller information on school lives than on home lives for this age-group, and research in families is essential (though difficult) if we are to understand children's social positioning once they reach school age.

Interpretation of both home and school life ideally requires study of the varying perspectives of the different participants. It is notorious that most studies of home life have relied on mothers' accounts and that they are asked to speak for children. The social positioning of women as home-makers and of children as subsumed within the home and the family is compounded by the fact that women are the main informants on the home and on children's lives there; we know almost nothing of fathers' views on childcare and family life. Whereas in the 1960s and 1970s researchers such as the Newsons worked within the assumption that mothers were the appropriate informants on childcare, more recently changing perceptions among researchers have been challenged by gendered assumptions within families. Thus in the Greenstreet study, the aim was to complement children's accounts with those of both fathers and mothers. But though a few fathers agreed in principle, only two (out of 22 resident fathers) made themselves available on the appointed day or evening. Studies of family life which aim to study both parents either have to accept second-best – where fathers refuse – or exclude those families, which also biases the sample and data. The first option was chosen in a recent household-focused study of health behaviour among young people, where 55 per cent of the young people and 55 per cent of mothers, but only 31 per cent of resident fathers agreed to be interviewed (Brannen *et al.* 1994).

In considering the import of children's accounts, I have tried to move back and forth between the empirical and the theoretical: to consider children's views in tension with the structuring provided by adult views on children and childhood, and with the social norms, in turn, contextualizing these. In addressing the central question: how are children socially positioned? it has been relevant to consider the contributions of theory to understanding the empirical data, and of the data to understanding theory.

This book makes no claim to cover the range of childhoods in Britain; it does not address the most highly privileged, or those children commonly regarded as victims or as threats. It considers children attending a popular school in a socially mixed but not extremely deprived or privileged area of London, and adds in some information from a study of children living in a very deprived area (the Bluelane study) and from a national survey; it compares these three sets of data with those from other studies. Nor does the book claim to include comprehensive studies of children's lives: for instance I have not delved into the children's home lives to explore the full complexities of social relationships, nor studied individual social problems and dysfunctions – though I heard about some. The aim of the book is to think about lived childhoods, in general; and the focus of the book is on features common to children's lives, in particular socially constructed and experienced features. These are used in order to reflect on children as a social group, how they fit into sociological debates, and what difference including that group makes to such debates.

Finally, as to the topics discussed and the plan of the book, it has to be said that at the outset, though I aimed to study children's daily lives wherever they were spent, this aim was not fully achieved. I had envisaged initially that children might conceptualize daily life as the space and time of their social group, however much adult control impinged on their days. So I hoped to hear about children's own social order, including their experiences across and beyond adult-controlled contexts of home and school, with a conceptual emphasis on children's own domains. They did talk in these terms; in discussing their daily lives children, as a social group, had a specific 'take' on life, as I hope to demonstrate. But the restriction of children's lived lives, as they describe them, largely to the home and the school has also restricted the research enterprise and the resulting book. They talked little about time and space away from adult supervision; it seems that though children valued such freedom, they had little of it. Children's accounts of their experiences – largely at home and school – shape the book: it has to focus on those two contexts, though their own values and activities, including those operating at a tangent from adult social worlds, are distinctive. This end product may reflect how children's ideas are structured by adults'. But it may also be an imaginative limitation on my part; and no doubt another approach would lead to another story of where and how children's lives are lived.

Plan of the book

The book moves through a series of linked topics to approach children's experiences of their social positioning. Chapter 2 starts on the process of problematizing childhood and children's lives in childhood. The chapter examines how children's childhoods are structured through established and developing understandings, social policies and divisions of labour. Children's well-being in the social worlds they inhabit is the particular focus of the empirical studies that underpin discussion in this book; and Chapter 2 explores some features of the politics of child health that determine children's lives: child health policies; the status of health in education; adults' and children's knowledge of child health care; the division of labour in childcare; caring and control as women's work; and resources available to ensure children's health.

Chapter 3 moves on from this broad view of the political and material conditions of childhood, to study how the ideas of influential theorists in psychology and sociology have shaped child-related policies and the lives of children. It is argued that developmental psychology, based on positivist and universalist goals with a biological basis, has dominated theorizing about children and profoundly influenced policies towards them. Further, the psychologists' designation of children as developing non-people and as socialization projects has allowed sociologists to write children out of their scripts. Until recently children have been naturalized – that is, they have been regarded unproblematically as the object of women's natural caregiving and socializing work first in the home and, on reaching school age, at school. In the last ten years, however, vigorous attempts have been made in both large-scale and small-scale sociological work to reconsider the social and political status of children and childhood. This work has endeavoured to extract children from their naturalized positioning as individual objects of socialization, and has conceptualized them as a social group, who participate in the construction of social life. Childhood itself, in this newer work, has been problematized through study of how it has been socially constructed, across time and space. Notable here have been the international macro-level work carried out under the project called Childhood as a Social Phenomenon and the detailed empirical studies informed by these new approaches.

Chapter 4 continues the study of factors affecting children's lived experience; it considers the knowledge held by some of the influential groups of people who play a part, on the ground, in conditioning children's daily lives, that is, parents and teachers. The chapter considers the developing view among psychologists that children's abilities are better viewed positively – in terms of their strengths and achievements, than negatively – in terms of their weaknesses and failings. Building on feminist work, which has shown how knowledge is structured according to gender, and which ascribes value to women's experiential knowledge, this chapter reflects on the character of children's own experiential knowledge. I argue that children contribute to the work of building and maintaining the social order of the home through their assumption of responsibility for self-care, through their work in helping to maintain the home as a health-promoting environment and through their participation in the construction and reconstruction of relationships. The chapter moves on to the world of the school, where it is noted that the child-centred theory which powerfully structures both teacher knowledge and the social order of the school allows little place for children's own contributions, inhibits their ability to look after themselves and restricts their contributions to the social order.

These three chapters provide a framework in terms of policies, adult theory and knowledge for consideration of how children experience their daily lives at home and school and beyond or outside the two contexts. Chapters 5 and 6 focus directly on these experiences. In Chapter 5 the bodily and cognitive experiences of children are considered, and the dualism separating them and connections between the two are discussed. It is argued that the moral order of the home respects the bodily as well as the cognitive in children, and indeed sees the first as inextricably interlinked with the second; childcare and child participation involve both. Tensions at school between attention to the bodily and cognitive are considered in the light of policies, theoretical constructs of children and childhood and the individual knowledge of the women who care for the children. I suggest that the tendency within the school's moral order to separate out the bodily from the cognitive is not only uncomfortable for the children, but possibly counter-productive in academic terms.

Chapter 6 takes up children's experiences in relation to two main sorts of time: adult time, that is, time ordered in adults' interests; and adults' classification of children according to age and stage. It considers the powerful structures imposed by adult time: routines, timetables, constraints, goals; how children manage within these structures; how far they are negotiable; and how far the home and the school offer permeable structures of rules and social relationships. The implications for children's experiences of adult categorization according to chronological and assumed developmental age are considered. The value commonly placed on children's own time in spaces unsupervised by adults, is discussed in order to consider children's own valuation of both freedom and the right to participate in social worlds as people with valuable contributions to make.

Chapter 7 takes up the themes and topics adumbrated in the first part of this chapter, for discussion in the light of the journey through the book. The idea of children as a social group is considered in the context of the social condition of children in Britain, and at micro level in relation to the experiences and views of the children studied. I note their view that the home and the school provide more and less permeable moral orders respectively, wherein children can make their voices heard, and their view that whilst freedom is to be valued, so too is participation – and on both counts they are subject to over-control by adults. The chapter further explores linkages between ideas about relation-ships between bodies and minds in the context of the conceptual and service splits between health and education. A central topic in Chapter 7, as in the book, is the cross-cutting influences of gender and generation; for instance the relationships and experiences of girls at home and school differed from those of boys; and women's importance as the adults in children's lives in both settings is further explored. These points lead on to discussion of the divisions of labour between adults and children, girls and boys in and across the domains of home and school, and the evidence for alliances or collaborative activity between women and children is considered. The book ends with discussion of children as citizens and of ways in which their rights may be recognized in policy and practice.

two

The politics of child health

A distinctive feature of the book is its emphasis on children as actors, who participate in social worlds, and take a share in the work of homes and schools. The book regards children as a social group whose members express their own views – both as individuals and as members of the social group – on services, relationships and social issues that concern them. Of constant concern throughout the discussions that follow are the social contexts within which they live out their daily lives. Children's daily lives are structured by social policies formulated and implemented without consulting them, for they have no voice to speak for their own interests. Indeed these policies can be seen as inextricably intertwined with assumptions about the rights and duties of parents, and the superior knowledge and abilities of adults to order children's lives. This chapter considers features of the political context which conditions childhood, under the following headings:

- child health policies;
- the status of health in the social worlds of education;
- child health care: adults' and children's knowledge;
- the division of labour;
- caring and control as women's work;
- resources for child health.

Child health policies

Though health professionals often present the characteristics of a healthy child to us 'lay' adults and children, and in particular to mothers, as factual and incontestable, it is an important assumption of this book (though not a new one) that child health is not a neutral, factual concept; notions of child health are constructed out of essentially political considerations. As has been said, 'The truth is that medicine, professedly founded on observation, is as sensitive to outside influences, political, religious, philosophical, imaginative, as is the barometer to the changes of atmospheric density' (Oliver Wendell Holmes, quoted in Kennedy 1983: 6).

What the medical profession, the nursing profession and other allied professions choose to study, highlight, test for, survey for, define as worthy of their attention, will be determined by a range of social and economic factors, including their own interests. These will include issues of public health, understandings of the appropriate respective inputs of doctors, nurses and other professionals as against mothers, fathers and other 'lay' people, models of what childhood is and how it should be lived, managerial and professional concern to measure service-delivery and cost-effectiveness. A well-worked example is the effort expended by psychologists, and taken up with enthusiasm by the medical, nursing and social services professions, on promoting the proposition that child health is ensured only if mothers are constantly with their young children (Davin 1978; Doyal 1983: chs 4 and 6; Walkerdine and Lucey 1989).

The school health service (SHS) provides an example of how health service provision is structured by considerations other than those of a thorough-going attention to policies and practices that would improve children's health. Professional views, congealed over time, have been critical to the development of the SHS, and at least three factors are implicated: split responsibility at all levels, worries about duplication of services, and models of childhood.

Firstly, since 1948 (when the NHS Act 1946 was implemented), health and education have come under separate ministries, and from ministerial level down to school level, the two services have operated in parallel rather than collaboratively. Though pious pleas for liaison and collaboration are frequent, to date these depend on local and individual initiative, rather than on planned policies and strategies. Services for children are therefore fragmented. Important information held by school staff may never reach health staff and vice versa. Further the goal of the service has been largely defect-spotting, with children referred on to curative services if necessary. This has meant that traditionally, and still today, whole classes of children file through for rapid inspection. This fragmentary and cursory service is poorly designed and implemented to contribute to the maintenance and promotion of children's health.

Secondly, given the existence since 1948 of the freely available general practitioner service and the community child health services, professionals have questioned the need for a school health service. Duplication of service has been a concern. And, along with other preventive health services, the SHS has always been a poor relation of curative services, with low levels of provision. Yet school staff and parents regard an available, accessible, on-site school health service as important for them (Mayall 1994a). In practice, provision varies widely, as the SSRU national survey indicates (SSRU 1994: 41–2). For instance the doctor visited only once a year in 19 per cent of schools; but four or more times in 28 per cent of schools. Even more marked was variation in nurse visits: in 24 per cent the nurse visited once a term or less, whereas in 17 per cent she visited once a week.

Thirdly, the service, as so far provided, has conceptualized children as the objects of professional scrutiny, and as dependants of their parents; until very recently there has been little understanding of the notion that children themselves might be viewed as the clients and users of the SHS. These models seem to be in process of change, perhaps partly in response to the Children Act 1989: both the Health Visitors' Association and the British Paediatric Association have recently drawn attention to these points and to children's rights (HVA 1988; BPA 1992). But in the new NHS market forces are currently important in dictating policy. For it is presently proposed (and implemented in some areas) that the SHS offer a more selective service than before (Richman and Miles 1990). Yet it can readily be argued, from the children's point of view, that an SHS should offer a responsive service to them, available on a more frequent and regular basis than it often is at present, so that children can use it as a health care resource for information and advice. This is indeed the view put by mothers (Mayall 1994a). And children's welfare demands not fragmented but integrated thinking and services. There has been some movement here: in some areas, a more comprehensive and responsive system is provided through health interviews, which allow for more equal and leisurely interaction between the child and the professional.

Inevitably, the power of the medical profession to make decisions about what is important, appropriate and relevant to their discipline and practice raises issues of knowledge, interest and responsibility. People with knowledge and occupational interests acquired during professionalization find themselves faced with 'lay' knowledge and in turn 'lay' people have to negotiate with professionals the status of their knowledge and their interests. The respective responsibilities of professionals and those they meet will always provoke moral debating issues: what constitutes responsibility both in principle and in behaviour? what is the appropriate division of responsibility? These concerns about knowledge and responsibility between the two sets of adults are further complicated if children are included in, as actors with knowledge, health concerns and a sense of responsibility. Yet the debates have been conducted between the various sets of adults. No one has seen fit to ask the children their views, and there is little information on parental views. These issues are taken up in Chapter 6 (pp. 135–7), where the workings of the SHS at Greenstreet are discussed.

The status of health in the social worlds of education

Health at school – nutrition, fresh air and exercise

The points made above about the school health service relate to larger considerations about the status of health within the education system. These are indeed large considerations, which require a book on their own, but it is instructive to look, even briefly, at the history of this topic, in order to illuminate the present situation. Nutrition and exercise have been key issues on which decisions have had to be made by providers of the education service. Running through the first 100 years of state education have been their intertwined goals: remedial action, social training and educational improvement; with varying emphases at various points in the history. Framing these concerns have been debates on the proper division of responsibility between parents and the state for children's welfare.

The early history of state education indicates how the physical health of the nation's children was forced on to the political agenda once the poorest were incorporated into the schooling system, from the 1870s. Basically, schooling could not proceed effectively if children had poor health; if they were starving, someone had to feed them (Hurt 1979: esp. chs 5 and 6; Hendrick 1994: esp. ch. 3), otherwise state financial input into schooling would be wasted. Educationalists and medical men struggled with the unwelcome proposition that even though blame for children's poor health could be assigned to mothers, public agencies would have to intervene in the interests of efficiency (Lewis 1986; Cunningham 1991: esp. ch. 8). The first, most urgent requirement from the 1870s onwards was to feed the children, and as Hurt demonstrates, battles raged on two main issues: would the provision of meals create a dependency culture amongst feckless parents, and if meals were provided, who should provide them. These two factors – the unwillingness of policy makers on principle to share nutritional responsibility with parents and the vexed question whether voluntary agencies or local authorities should provide – ensured that the most meagre meals were provided and only to the most needy (Hurt 1979: ch. 5). The urgent physical needs of children, exposed by the inception of state education, ensured that children's bodies, as well as their minds, were on the educational agenda by the turn of the century. Yet resistance to catering for children's nutritional needs was slow to overcome during the first 40 years of the century; by 1939 school meals were provided by about half of local authorities, but free dinners and milk to only 2.8 per cent of school-age children (Bryder 1992); the war years shifted the balance somewhat: meals based on minimum nutritional requirements were provided free to eligible children and at cost price to others (Coles and Turner 1992). The 1944 Education Act, enacted in the heyday of enthusiasm for the welfare state, reiterated the education service's role in promoting the physical welfare of children, through the statutory responsibility laid on LEAs to provide meals of a certain nutritional standard and milk.

State intervention to improve the bodily status of children took other forms: pronouncements on physical education and on the fresh air movement both demonstrate an intertwining of aims – the remedial, the social and the educational. In the early days, the stated aim of the physical exercise curriculum was both therapeutic – to restore children to an acceptable level of health, and educational – to develop qualities of 'alertness, decision, concentration and the perfect control of mind over body' (Board of Education 1905: 9, quoted in Kirk 1988: 55). The claims of fresh air to strengthen the bodies of slum children are traced by Linda Bryder, who shows how in open-air schools the rules of school life included: 'respect for order and food and sleep, love of sunny, moving air and pure water, dutiful habits, gentle manners, the power of keeping silent, the self-control of ordered play, the concrete practical lessons which really develop brain agility in a way that books alone never do' (Stevens Burrow 1915, quoted in Bryder 1992). An important goal in the nursery school movement was to train children as exemplars for health education in the home; for instance Margaret McMillan (1930: 85) wanted schoolchildren to go out, clean, healthy and alert, to offer their mothers a vision of what good child-rearing could do. Linda Bryder notes that probably it was the food provided in the open-air schools, rather than the air, that improved children's health, but food was more expensive than air. The abandonment of special schools for particularly needy children was accompanied by the growth of the idea that all schools should offer an open-air regime. The post-war years of optimism and expansion promoted the building of primary schools designed for healthy living (Maclure 1984), with large light airy classrooms and space for outside activity.

It is likely that continued willingness within education services during the first half of the twentieth century to address children's health (Webster 1983) was part of a pattern of social movements which highlighted the importance of the physical capital of the nation: the impact of the death rate in World War I and the eugenics movement, combined with unemployment in the 1930s. A key document on primary education in the aftermath of that war is the Hadow Report on the primary school (Board of Education 1931), which, in proposals for the curriculum, discussed first, and thereby gave pride of place to, physical care. The Committee promoted 'the claims of a physical culture which includes physical training and efficiency but goes beyond these, since it includes also training in comely posture and movement upon social occasions' (1931: para. 76, pp. 93–4). These broadly therapeutic aims – linking physical to social acceptability – were set out more fully in the 1933 Board of Education Syllabus for Physical Training in Schools; and the provision of open-air recreational facilities was enacted in the 1937 Physical Training and Recreation Act. However, in the reorganization of education under the 1944 Education Act, responsibility for physical education was transferred from health to education, from the Chief Medical Officer to the Senior Chief Inspector of the Ministry of Education; and, it is alleged, the emphasis since then has been on justifying physical activity less on remedial or therapeutic grounds, as on moral, intellectual and cognitive grounds (Bray 1991). This educational justification continued to be advanced, as the later DES publication *Movement* shows; it claimed that physical education was 'an integral part of the education process' (DES 1972: 8) arguing that it should promote versatility, sensitivity and 'the ability to apply skill and control in purposeful creative and imaginative situations' (DES 1972: 3–22, esp. 14).

Since the late 1960s, the linked histories of the two topics – nutrition and physical activity – encapsulate concurrent, interacting processes: towards emphasis on cognitive achievement, and towards the contraction of the education service. The 1980 Education Act enacted governmental withdrawal from responsibility for children's physical welfare within the education system, by repealing the 1944 LEA duty to provide meals, and replacing this with discretion to provide, though children from poor families still had to be provided for. It also devolved nutritional standards from national to LEA level. The evidence since then is that children's diets at school have worsened (DHSS 1989). Other political changes in the 1980s have indicated that school meals will not improve: the 1988 Education Act put financial management in the hands of schools, and the concurrent contraction in funding of the primary education service suggests that economy measures, including those affecting nutrition, will continue (*Guardian*, 8 November 1994: 8). These changes are not only nutritional, but also social. The 1944 concept of the school meal as an integral part of the educational day, was replaced by a valuation of the school meal in economic terms. In complement to this policy change, children's experience of their school day must have changed. The common pattern when I went to school in the 1940s and 1950s was for the whole school to sit down together to eat a midday meal; nowadays, many children bring their own food, or go out of school to the local shops at midday. For children, there will now be no understanding that the education service takes responsibility for what they eat. This responsibility has been replaced by individualistic health education projects aimed at changing children's behaviour.

Current government edicts have the effect of stressing the cognitive way above the physical, as the object of state enterprise. Indeed the purpose of government policy is to make school strictly instrumental to the economic demands of the state. The introduction of the National Curriculum and testing, combined with larger classes consequent on financial stringency (*Guardian* 21 December 1994: 6), is the context within which teachers report that their time is limited more than ever to getting through tasks set by government (Sparkes 1992). In addition, the increased power of governors is likely to lead to priority being given to the cognitive over the physical, in order to please parents (Sparkes 1992). Currently, physical education is not a core subject (English, maths, science), but one of seven foundation subjects, and achievement in these subjects is to be assessed. Official thinking on physical education has moved from emphasis in *Movement* (DES 1972) on the individual child's needs, wishes and abilities to the testing of children's performance by pre-determined standards of achievement (Office for Standards in Education (OFSTED) 1993). Further, it has been proposed that formal games be given higher status within the physical education curriculum (football, hockey, tennis, netball) – though these were abandoned by many teachers years ago as too competitive and as unpopular with children. Indeed, some schools have sold off their playing fields in order to improve their financial position.

Both nutrition and exercise are important areas of life for children, who recognize it if schools give them a poor service (see pp. 123–35). Children's adverse comments on dinner-time (Mauthner *et al.* 1993; Mayall 1994a) are not stereotyped responses; they reflect poor provision. Wendy Titman (1994: 55–63) reports that children regard the playground as part of the school (whereas teachers often think of school as the buildings and the activities within them). She finds that children read the physical environment of the school as a set of symbols that show how adults judge children's social value; if children experience the playground as unpleasant they believe the school staff both know this and do not care. However, the parlous state of many school playgrounds and the poor opportunities for play and exercise provided in many primary schools are attracting attention among teachers, partly through environmental concern (Titman 1994). In the SSRU survey (1994: 13–15) a fifth of respondents rated the playground space as poor and 44 per cent rated play equipment poor. However, pioneering efforts are being made to work towards better physical and social environments at school, in some cases with the enthusiastic participation of the children (Blatchford and Sharp 1994).

The politics of state education is working to increase the separation of the physical from the cognitive and to promote the cognitive above the physical. The data reported in this book provide a commentary on these points; they suggest that children do not regard themselves as merely cognitive agents; nor do they split their understanding of themselves into bodies and minds. Their accounts suggest identity as embodied persons, where hand, brain and heart interlock (Rose 1986), and not as 'Cartesian minds that happen to be located in biological matter in motion' (Harding 1992).

Education and health – divided they rule

If one were planning services for children from scratch, one might decide on a Children's Department to oversee the provision of a unified service across health, welfare and education. However, history has intervened. In the early years of state education in the UK, the visible effects on children of extreme poverty forced educationalists to take account of health issues; but the provision of 'free' health services under the welfare state has encouraged the development of education and health services as separate and independent operations. Currently these services do not operate with regard to the whole child, but are split at ministerial levels as to function: into schooling/education functions, health functions and welfare. This is striking for all ages of children. Thus for the youngest children who spend time during the day with minders or at nurseries, responsibility for the children's welfare lies with the Secretary of State at the Department of Health; at service level it is split between social services (welfare, standards) and health services (monitoring of health). On the other hand children at nursery school or the nursery class of a primary school come under the Secretary of State at the Department for Education.

The minds and bodies of primary schoolchildren are divided up between the Department for Education and the Department of Health (which oversees the school health service), and that split in responsibility extends down to local education and health services, run in parallel rather than in collaboration. Social services too have an interest in primary-age children with special needs, and in children deemed to be at risk; but children's welfare may also be supervised by education psychologist services – employed by the education authority.

Divisions of labour between health and other services have frequently been identified as inefficient and leading to ineffective services. Yet these divisions are deep and difficult to overcome. This is indicated by the stream of reports urging collaboration: as in *The Health of the Nation* (Department of Health 1992), work on school health services (British Paediatric Association 1993; 1995), and work on health and social services for children (Audit Commission 1994). It is notable in these reports that collaboration between these health and social services is stressed (for these services used to be under one ministry), whereas drawing the education service into the network of collaboration is soft-pedalled.

The established compartmentalization of life into discrete services is bolstered by a whole range of factors: the priorities and agendas of individual services; inertia; hierarchies; time constraints; and political pressures (e.g. Handy 1985). Within the health service, the establishment of an internal market means that tightly defined priorities and programmes of work will be geared to specifically 'health' issues, rather than leaving space for working across agency and topic boundaries. And within health services, the focus of work is geared around promotion, prevention and cure, with boundaries around each of these, and with most of the money going to cure. Within the education service in recent years, the pressures of government programmes of change have required staff at all levels to focus their attention on such matters as the National Curriculum, testing of children, local management of budgets and cuts in central funding.

The social positioning of children within education and health services is conditioned by these splits between their remits and concerns. Because the health service aims at public health and so provides a quick inspection service at fairly rare intervals, it is not geared to listening to children's concerns. Nor is it designed to collaborate with teachers to provide a holistic service taking account of interactions between children's bodies and minds. Teachers, employed to help children learn, also claim to care for the whole child (Steedman 1988; Burgess and Carter 1992); yet, as children find, they relegate hands-on physical care to non-teaching staff – women with lower status. Children's experiences reflect the adult-oriented division of labour.

Child health care: adults' and children's knowledge

Much of the important daily work people do to maintain their health has low status in the eyes of health and education service providers. These are the activities of ordinary life, of adjustment and restoration, based on one's knowledge of what suits one's own body and being. People, including children, acquire health-related knowledge through informal learning at home, and both formally and informally in educational establishments; they use their knowledge to promote their own well-being, in the context of and in interaction with social and physical features of their environments.

Mothers' care of their babies offers a visible example of the detailed activities people engage in to maintain their health; we can see these activities because, in the case of babies, they are enacted on and for another person. Mothers adjust their actions, in order to restore and improve their babies' experience, minute by minute. Such activities include: modifying the warmth of the baby's clothing and covering; altering how the baby is held; offering nourishment; providing movement, through rocking and walking about; offering visual stimuli; auditory comfort through soothing words and gestures (Dunn 1977). Mothers also acquire through careful and prolonged observation and em-pathetic understanding, knowledge of signs their baby provides of changes within and from her usual state of well-being; such signs may presage illness, or may be symptomatic of response to external stimuli and events, or may signal some developmental change (Mayall 1986) (see Chapter 5).

As children get older, more competent and voluble, they work in collabor-ation with mothers: a mother's knowledge of changes in her child's well-being and of appropriate action operates in tandem with her child's own acquired knowledge and wish to take over self-maintenance activities. In the main study to be reported on in this book, children themselves (aged 5 and 9) report on how they manage the ordinary health maintenance and adjustment activities of daily life – eating, drinking, excretion, warmth, exercise – in the social worlds they live in and interact with: at home and at school – where children also seek to maintain their health and well-being, but where the social controls and expectations provide a more rigid framework.

Children learn about adult understandings of the importance or lack of importance of health issues through their experience of daily life at school. In the day-to-day activities of the school, health has mixed status, and the messages children receive about how school regards health-related behaviour and health knowledge are unlikely to be co-ordinated. Health education is not part of the core curriculum, though, confusingly, described as essential to it (National Curriculum Council 1990a: 1) and so may receive variable attention in schools. The informal health curriculum – inscribed in policies and practices about exercise, play, school dinners, snacks, social norms for behaviour – also educates children about school views on health maintenance and promotion. Other messages are conveyed to children through the characteristics of the school health service, the state of the building, playground and equipment, and staff knowledge and behaviour when children feel ill or have an accident.

Thus the health-related knowledge children acquire at school is conditional on the character of a range of services, systems and traditions rooted in history, but putting forth strong living branches. It will be important in this book to consider children's own experiences of the school day: how health and welfare issues intersect with learning and teaching issues; to whom they turn for help; what is the status of their welfare; and whether their voices are attended to. It will also be relevant to study how parents and school staff, with their different ideas about children, childhood, schooling and health issues, interact and collaborate across the public–private divide to affect children's well-being at school.

Lay and professional knowledge about health and health care stand at tangents to each other. Professional knowledge is structured by the very service divisions which they themselves perpetuate. Professionals in the health service are encouraged to think of their work as preventive or curative or promotional. Ordinary people, including children, carry out a continuum of activities that span these divides: ranging through health maintenance, adjustment, care, treatment and cure to health promotion. Teachers represent an interesting case between these two positions: they are taught that they have specific educational skills, and that health is the province of a different service, but they also believe in the value of whole-child care and education. Caring for children is what they say they do, but it has to take place within the central academic goals and social norms of the school, which may inhibit health care. Conversations with children – reported in this book – reveal children's concern for their own bodily and emotional well-being, their understandings of links between the two, and their attempts to maintain and restore their well-being in the face of the opportunities and constraints of social contexts, including the knowledge and behaviour of the adults who both care for them and control them.

The division of labour

A major theme in this book is children's relationships to and participation in the division of labour. Integral to the considerations of this theme are the control of both women's and children's daily lives through the established structures of male domination.

As Stacey (1980) documents, the broad concept of the division of labour was developed in the early days of sociology to describe and analyse human social arrangements in complex societies. It allowed early theorists the opportunity to explain as natural the existing gender divisions in society and to perpetuate those divisions, which maintained their own powerful positions. Sociological men, looking around them at their workplaces, and basing their theory on the natural superiority of men to women, posited the public domain of work as the centrepiece of the social order, where men contribute through their work to the advancement of the social good, the gross national product and the support of the family. In turn, the home is regarded as the private domain, where the natural character and tendencies of women are deployed in the care of children and men. The family is dependent for survival on the man's contribution, but also contributes through reproduction of the species to the social order. The power of this vision of the social order to structure not only women's lives, but also their thoughts is evident in the late nineteenth-century UK suffrage movement, where the aim for many was strengthening women's position in the home rather than releasing them from it (Wilson 1977: 112–15); an enthusiasm shared by some US suffragettes (Turnaturi 1987).

Key themes in the demonstration by men of their natural superiority have been rationality and individuality. As Leonore Davidoff's (1990) analysis shows, the ascription of these to men, but not to women and children, is accomplished by defining the concepts through reliance on the already gendered organization of society; given the societies considered, only men could be deemed to be rational and individual. 'Rational individuals through their free status and power of knowledge were independent of other men's will or influence. And the public domain was defined by the presence of such individuals' (Davidoff 1990). Thus, she notes, the very meanings of rationality and individuality are gendered. They also exclude children of both sexes. For children as dependants lack individuality as free citizens, and lack rationality, defined by adults as the property of adults.

The social control of women comprises both control in the interests of individual men in the family, and control in the interests of the state – for women are to reproduce appropriately socialized citizens. If women take up paid employment they are largely to be restricted to work which does not interfere with their reproductive activities; and which is in keeping with their natural characteristics: caring, human service or people work, such as teaching, social work, nursing, catering, cleaning, laundry work. And they will work to the instruction and in the service of their male superiors (e.g. Mitchell 1971; Rowbotham 1973a; Smith 1988; Elshtain 1993). Women's work with children will include both care and control, and that control will serve to reproduce the social order. Within this context, Stacey's analysis (1980; Stacey and Davies 1983) draws attention to a critical feature of classical division of labour theory: its assumptions about children and childhood, in relation to socialization by women within the family.

Just as assignments of social position by gender were not recognized as problematic until women pointed them out, so stratification and thence exclusion by age was not recognized as problematic for sociology until very recently (1970s). Indeed nineteenth-century sociology was able to look to the developing Child Study field for support for its assumptions. That there was a burgeoning interest in what childhood was and how it should be lived in the second half of the nineteenth century seems clear (Hendrick 1994). Whatever its causes – moral panic over juvenile crime, the new visibility of the nation's children in state education, the need for a healthy army – impetus was provided through the evolutionary movement and the studies by some influential men in the USA (such as G. Stanley Hall) and in the UK (such as Darwin). This interest in childhood focused on twin pillars in the organization of the discipline of psychology: socialization and developmentalism (see Chapter 3).

It was clear therefore that if the primary function of the home was reproduction of the species, the first agent for socialization was the mother. According to Christina Hardyment (1984: ch. 3), a proliferation of babycare books at the turn of the century told mothers how to do it; their childcare work should be based on both social goals and current knowledge of how children develop. The aim was to provide young people fit to take their place first in schools and thence in adult social worlds, according to gender. It was convenient, to say no more, for sociology to harness socialization theory to their assumptions about how women should live their lives. Children were not regarded as interesting as people, or theoretically, to men; the task of making them so lay with women at home, through early socialization. Just as one may read through sociology books up to the 1960s – and beyond – and find no recognition of the structurally distinct position of women (see Oakley 1985b: 72–3), so the social group of children has continued to be ignored (see Chapter 3).

One of the main purposes of this book is to reconsider the division of labour, taking account of children as a social group. Throughout the following chapters, a range of issues are addressed: how do children and their parents, understand and negotiate on such matters as knowledge, responsibility and functions or duties in respect of childcare? What are the tensions inherent in adult socialization activities and child-led learning and behaviour? What contributions do children make to families and to the private domain? Given that the daily lives of school-age children (and of many pre-school children) cross the private and public domains, what can we say about the extent of children's identification with the home and with other social contexts, such as the school? Do they identify with their own social group – children – in domains that are separate from, operate across or intersect with the public and private domains of the workplace and the home?

Caring and control as women's work

Integral to considerations of the division of labour is the topic encapsulated in the phrase 'women's work'. This includes both caring and control. A major issue for women in their work in both the private and public domains is how to balance caring and control; how to engage in both; and why to choose which emphasis at which point. These are concerns for children too: in which mode is this woman behaving to them just now? With what goals in mind? What is the balance in her mind between care and control? A major issue for children is how far they can make their own voices heard and negotiate a reasonably comfortable daily life, in tension with the care and control exercised by women.

Caring is women's work, assigned to them in theoretical discourse, allocated in ideology and practice, through the mechanisms of policy and service structures (Finch and Groves 1983). Even at the time in the nineteenth century when theoretical frameworks proposed natural linkages between women, caring and the domestic domain, and social policies restricted women's opportunities for other public domain work, these linkages were experienced as false for most women. In Victorian England, 'working women' worked, and so, by the late nineteenth century, did many women with any education (Holcombe 1973). A minority of middle-class women fitted the discourse. And many women contested their restriction in the home by developing movements to resist domination (Rowbotham 1973b). But much of the work done by women, now as then, is 'people work' (Stacey 1980), which comprises the physical and emotional labour of caring for people, caring about them, and modifying their bodies and minds towards socially approved norms.

People work is likely to be experienced by the subject and the object as conflictual, for it comprises not just care, but control. In the service of the social order of the home, and in the service of the state, women work to civilize, regulate and construct children's bodies and minds. At home, both caring work and socialization in the name of private and public moral norms requires women to control their children. In their work as teachers, nurses and social workers, women are required to work for state agendas, to regulate the bodies and minds of children, mothers and patients in socially acceptable ways and towards societal goals. Women paid to do people work also acquire, through training, allegiance to professional goals and norms which may over-ride care considerations.

Children find themselves in the hands of two sets of women, the paid and the unpaid, who work towards the socialization of children, in the service of the state, both holding knowledge and responsibility relevant to combining control with care. Stacey and Davies (1983) have promoted the concept of the intermediate domain between the public and the private, where the two sets of women – the paid and the unpaid people workers – meet to negotiate the status of their knowledge and the division of labour and responsibility. The regulation of mothers in the interests of the reproduction of adequate citizens is a principal aim underpinning state employment of health visitors, with social workers at the sharp end for the regulation of the more deviant mothers and families (David 1985; Davis and Brook 1985). Essentially, community nursing, social work and teaching may be understood as reflecting a specific set of relations between the family and the state: that the first serves the latter (Langan 1985); and also an optimistic view – that parents' beliefs and practices can be modified to suit professional beliefs (see Parton 1985: ch. 2).

Concurrently with the establishment of these views during the implementation period of the welfare state, we have seen the decline of more radical traditions in women's paid work on social and health issues. In the health area, we hear little nowadays about women's struggles to work against social, economic and political structures to establish a better deal for mothers, children and families (Doyal 1983 on women and health; Robson 1986 on health visiting). The teaching profession too, which in the 1960s and 1970s had a radical wing (e.g. Rubinstein and Stoneman 1970; Holt 1975) has lost some of its cutting edge, though alternative agendas continue to be discussed (Meighan 1986). At the chalk-face in the 1990s, most teachers have enough to do in holding some semblance of a line in the face of governmental assaults on standards in education. They are not likely to advance more proactive arguments for education as a resource and constructive opportunity for children. In social services departments, where 'radical' work, focused on local communities, has long had a place alongside individualistic approaches in work with families, individualistic child protection work is taking up most of social workers' time (Audit Commission 1994).

Foucauldian arguments on alliances between women and the state propose a framework where the caring work of women is subordinated to the patriarchal control function, under the authority of the larger male-dominated social structures governing both the public and private domains (cf. Walkerdine and Lucey 1989). Donzelot's (1980) analysis within this framework leads him to the proposition that middle-class mothers are recruited by the psy complex to collaborate with it in the moulding of children, whereas the childcare practices of working-class mothers are the object of intense surveillance, disapproval and attempts at modification. Undoubtedly, as regards the main social contexts of this book – the home and the school – we have to take account of the proposition that in both contexts care and control are inextricably interlinked. For children this may mean that for most of their daily lives they feel themselves under the control of adults whose agenda is far wider and deeper than that of providing a caring environment, or even a socializing environment narrowly conceived. In later chapters, we explore parental and school staff understandings of their care and control functions (Chapter 4), children's understanding of the negotiability of the social order – how far they can work with adults in order to establish a satisfactory daily life (Chapter 5), and the functions they ascribe to constructing their own domains, composed of their own peer relationships, in time and space which is not (or not so overtly) controlled by adults (Chapter 6).

However, it is important not to accept uncritically the concept of women as socially dominated agents in relationship to their children, but to explore in detail how care and control works out in the daily experience of women and children and the interactions between them. If one introduces the idea of children as participating agents rather than just as objects of socialization, that may alter the picture. Though as noted earlier (p. 2), the women's movement has taken some time to explore positive characteristics of their relationships with their children, these explorations have led to deeper understanding of both women's and children's structural position. Women's experiential knowledge of personal relationships and how this informs their moral judgements has been explored to show how women's moral character has been devalued, together with the work they do for and with their children (e.g. Rose 1986; Smith 1988).

Recent investigation by women of the experience of living with their children has led to an interesting development: the notion of the possibility of alliances between women and their children. Brown and Gilligan (1992: 220–32) float such a possibility at the end of their analysis of the muting and distorting of girls' voices as they move towards and through adolescence. They propose mothers as mediators between daughters and the harsh powerful pressures of (US) society to conform to gendered expectations of how girls and young women will speak, behave and relate to others. This vision has to be considered within its culturally specific context: girls attending a private school in the US Midwest. The specifics of both sexism and of well-to-do mother–daughter relationships in the USA will give a particular character to such alliances. The topic of mother–child alliances will be further discussed in Chapter 7 (pp. 152–5).

Emily Martin's work on *The Woman in the Body* (1989) provides further pointers to the focus of women's work for children. She proposes (1989: 197) a challenge to male-dominated theoretical and social structures. Thus she argues that as embodied women (people taking their bodies with them) move into the public worlds and across the public and the private, they challenge the very notion of the theoretical and social separation of the public (rational, detached) and private (emotional, bodily). So too, it will be argued in this book (see especially Chapter 5), do children move as embodied persons, intimately concerned for their interacting bodies, minds and spirit, across these two domains, in their daily lives at home and school. A major function of mothers' work for their children is to raise the status of their children's embodiment at school, to point to linkages between children's emotional, physical and mental well-being, and to ask that children be cared for at school. For though school staff stress their own caring function, and claim to work for the whole child, in practice the formal agenda to which they have to work emphasizes control and a cognitive focus. The evidence is that school staff recognize mothers' right and responsibility to oversee their children's health and welfare during the school day (Mayall 1994a, ch. 7). Teachers, whilst implementing state policies, do collaborate across the public and the private domains, with mothers, to maintain and restore children's health. Between them, mothers and teachers work out compromises, more or less successfully, for the welfare of children within a child-hostile regime.

Thus common cause between women and children can be proposed as a strategy wherein women seek informal alliances with each other and with children aimed at promoting child welfare; this sort of activity is, as it were, an underground movement of people who have to face male domination in their contacts with the formal health, education and welfare services. Women do band together to help children, through acting as advocates, organizing groups, sharing information about sources of help, and providing space and time for children to spend time with each other; but both women and children are powerless to alter the services profoundly in their own favour. The tensions between operating in the informal world of women and in the more formal world of services are familiar to women in seeking a reasonable deal for their children.

Resources for child health

In considering the quality of children's daily lives, physical and social resources are crucial: the availability and quality of services and financial support for children. Serious attention to resourcing child health has never been high on the political agenda in the UK, through health, welfare or education services. The tone of grudging acceptance of the need to provide for children's health at school referred to earlier (pp. 24–9) can be traced in current policies. Debates on the causation of child mortality and ill-health have always been about poverty versus the carelessness and ignorance of mothers (Davin 1978); an opposition which has commonly found policy makers and health professionals lining up on the side of victim-blaming. State intrusion into private lives, individual versus state responsibility, and the specific issue of the division of responsibility between the state and the family for the care of children have been running controversial themes in the development of health, education and welfare services. A recent example, which perhaps unwittingly echoed the wording as well as the thinking of these early debates, appeared in *The Independent* (22 June 1994); under the heading: 'Fecklessness, not poverty, is the trouble with parents' where Susan Elkin argues that parents need education in 'parenting skills' [*sic*]. Of course, no one knows which of these skills lead to which outcomes.

The Black Report (issued in 1980, revised by Townsend and Davidson 1982), by contrast, settled for poverty as a major determinant of poor outcomes for children; it argued strongly for state action: for 'a total and not merely service-oriented approach to the problems of health' and for redistribution of resources within the health and associated services. Among their findings, of particular concern were social class inequalities in health and in access to health. They placed action to give children a better start in life at the forefront of their proposals for policy initiatives. Recommendations as regards mothers and children included improvements in direct services: free milk for children; better ante-natal and child health services and school health services; and adequate numbers of daycare places, providing both care and education. Also seen as vital were provisions through other services: increases in child benefit and maternity benefit; an infant care allowance; school meals as a right; measures to increase the supply and quality of public housing; co-ordination of services; and the establishment of a Health Development Council to play a key advisory and planning role in relation to a collaborative national policy to reduce inequalities in health.

Governmental rejection of the proposals as financially unrealistic (Townsend and Davidson 1982: 17) led to many calls for reconsideration. But seven years on, Margaret Whitehead's review of later evidence showed that 'serious social inequalities in health have persisted into the 1980s' (Whitehead 1987: 1). We know that the scale of child poverty has increased between the late 1970s and the 1990s (Bradshaw 1990; Wilkinson 1994). Currently, government figures indicate that 32 per cent of children live below official poverty levels nowadays (Department of Social Security 1994). A number of policies have served to increase child poverty and deprivation. The freezing of child benefit levels and tightening of regulations in the social security system have been important contributors (Bradshaw 1990: ch. 6). The withdrawal of right to benefit for 16- and 17-year-olds has led to hardship (Children's Rights Development Unit (CRDU) 1994: 78) and coupled with the financial difficulties faced by local authorities to look after the housing and employment needs of young people as they leave care, has led to homelessness on a large scale among young people (Parton 1991: 170–1). Services and benefits for children and for adults living with children have suffered under the Conservative administration (from 1979). Community child health services are being reduced in terms of staff and services; among health visitors, staffing levels and numbers of students are being reduced, according to a recent Health Visitors' Association study (Health Visitors' Association 1994). In the absence of firm guidelines from the Department of Health, the amount and character of provision by the SHS varies widely in primary schools across England (SSRU 1994); children's access to this important source of health care and advice thus varies.

In the education field two policy moves are particularly important in diverting resources away from children. As noted earlier, LEAs are no longer obliged to provide school meals for all children and to provide meals at a particular price and quality. The only statutory requirement left is to provide free meals for children entitled to them (Sharp 1993). In the years since 1980, government spending on school meals is reported to have halved and a Department of Health survey has indicated dismay at the poor nutrition of school-age children (*Guardian*, 4 September 1992).

Secondly, the level of financial resources available to provide a basically adequate education for all children is seriously inadequate and declining. In 1990 the National Confederation of Parent–Teacher Associations (1991) carried out a survey covering about 8 per cent of all children in primary and secondary schools, asking parents and teachers jointly to fill in a questionnaire. Among the findings, those relating to parental contributions are especially disturbing. In 96 per cent of primary schools the home–school association had been asked for funds to purchase equipment, books or classroom teaching materials between 1988 and 1990 (compared with 82 per cent in 1985). Requests to primary school parents increased threefold over 1985. Home–school associations spent £8.53 per pupil in primary and £4.81 per pupil in secondary schools – a 50 per cent increase in the primary sector and a 74 per cent increase in the secondary sector compared to 1985 (against an increase in inflation of 30 per cent over the five-year period) (National Confederation of Parent–Teacher Associations 1991).

The report notes 'Thus home–school associations are supporting the state educational system to the extent of 27% of capitation in primary schools and 7% in secondary schools.' Such subsidy – which only relatively well-off parents can be expected to provide – will undoubtedly increase inequalities in access to well-funded schooling (a topic not studied in this report).

More recently the government's own figures indicate that class sizes are inexorably rising; nearly a third of primary schoolchildren are now in classes of over 30 children (*Guardian* 21 December 1994: 6). Under these circumstances, classrooms will be less comfortable places for children and teachers will find it increasingly difficult to provide care as well as control. In 1995, reports that the government's reduced grants to local authorities are likely to impact most heavily in the education service, have led to (justified) predictions that teachers be sacked and, again, class sizes will rise (Travers 1995; Mayall *et al*. in press).

Many policies which fail to take account of children have detrimental effects on their health. For instance, traffic policies are certainly killing children through accidents and may be harming their health through pollution.' Road accidents are the main cause of accidental death to school-age children; in 1991 they caused 61 per cent of accidental deaths among children aged 5 to 16 (Department of Transport 1992). Children as pedestrians are especially likely to be injured or killed; and twice as many accidents happen on the way home as on the way to school (Royal Society for the Prevention of Accidents 1993). While preference is given to traffic, while schools lack after-school facilities and while play areas remain unsafe we may expect these accidents to continue. The obvious limitations to children's mobility caused by traffic dangers have been documented in a report showing that the age at which children go unaccompanied by an adult to school has risen markedly: in 1971 80 per cent of children aged 7–8 were allowed to go to school alone, but by 1990 the figure had fallen to 9 per cent (Hillman *et al*. 1991).

Daycare provision is an area where national policies strikingly favour private over state provision, and have ensured that, even compared to the 1970s, access to daycare is determined more sharply by social class and income. Children's well-being in the pre-school years and their readiness for primary school experience is thus stratified. The short history of a recent débâcle is as follows. The Children Act 1989 recommended clear, enforceable guidelines for daycare (minders and groups) and these were issued in 1991 (Department of Health 1991). Local authorities welcomed these as a vehicle for raising standards through the legally enforceable regulations. But in 1993 (partly at the request of organizations representing private provision) they were watered down. Tim Yeo, Parliamentary Secretary at the Department of Health, said that the guidelines were being used by 'over-zealous and rigid local authorities to exert a strangle-hold on day care services' and they should adopt a 'flexible and understanding approach; they must balance the need to set standards with the desirability of expanding services' (Department of Health Press Release H93/475: 11 January 1993). Local authorities now found that they were unable to raise standards, to drive out the worst cases and to increase equal opportunity for mothers and children. The situation now is that more mothers than ever return to work in their child's first year of life, and for women with a child under the age of 10 years, there has been an increase in employment rates of 8 per cent between 1985 and 1988. But there has been little increase in state provision (Moss 1990), and mothers are thrown on to the expanding private market, with its varying standards (premises, equipment, staff, availability, continuity, accountability) and the consequent bias towards better care for the children of well-to-do mothers. A voucher scheme (1995) for pre-school places seems likely to favour well-off parents, who can top it up, and to produce more low quality provision for poorer families.

A further twist of the knife on daycare is provided by the related problems faced by lone mothers. It is notable (Moss 1990) that whilst the UK has the highest proportion of one-parent households in the EU (12 per cent for households with a child aged 0–9), the employment rate for lone mothers is substantially lower than for mothers in two-parent households, for those with a child aged 0–4 and those with children aged 5–9. Since the differences are largely due to lower levels of part-time employment among lone mothers, it must be the case that the absence of affordable or free daycare affects lone mothers' decisions. They cannot afford to work part-time, given the costs of daycare. The increased poverty among lone parents and children is indicated by DSS figures (1994), which indicate that in 1991/2 74 per cent lived below average income compared to 28 per cent in 1979.

Study of the allocation of welfare resources indicates that in many countries, children are discriminated against as a social group at macro level (in terms of service and income transfers) and also as individuals at micro level – within families (Wintersberger 1994). His work comparing the largely non-earning age-groups at the two ends of the life-span shows that income transfers tend to favour the old as compared to the young.

The UK evidence on the extent of inequalities in health status by social class, and on the reduction in services and financial support for children and their parents, indicates more than political unwillingness to intervene at the level of policy and practice to decrease inequalities. It is children who have borne much of the brunt of social policies in the 1980s (Bradshaw 1990: 51). By placing increasing reliance on households to bear the costs of child-rearing, government policies increase class inequalities in access to health and welfare. This shift represents an increase in state intervention in family life (Ennew 1994: 10). In complement we have the rhetoric of family values and parental responsibilities. It may be said that the moral panic over child abuse during the last few years both owes its development to the actualities of parental brutality towards children, in some cases under conditions of acute social and financial stress, and is used to individualize and criminalize problems which, to some extent are of the government's own making (Parton 1985).

This sketch of some areas where resources for child health are implicated indicates some basic factors leading to poor resourcing for child health. There is long-standing suspicion of the view that poverty may be the essential nettle to grasp; political will to commit public resources has been and is rejected in the name of private responsibility – allocated to mothers. Those who formulate and implement policies such as traffic and transport policies neglect the interests of children in favour of the dominant social group – well-to-do men;

this favouritism is irresponsible towards the majority: children, women and other minority social groups, such as the disabled and the old. Ideological preference for private over public provision has dominated official thinking on daycare for a century, and has affected the economic welfare of generations of children and their mothers. In the light of this analysis children and their mothers may be regarded as having considerable common ground.

Final points

The daily lives of children and their mothers are powerfully affected by the policies and practices outlined in this chapter. Both social groups are required to carry out important individual and socially useful tasks in the face of social policies of which few are positively enabling, many are indifferent and some are overtly hostile to them. The definition of what constitutes child health work by a range of professionals leads to identification of bodies of knowledge and skills which only professionals have; mothers in turn find that their own knowledge is described as inferior 'lay' knowledge. Children's own knowledge and opinions – as we shall explore in later chapters – tend to be downgraded in their contacts with health professionals; and tend to be regarded with particular suspicion in school. The public domain of childcare penetrates the private domain and if mothers and children are to resist professional knowledge and activity they must negotiate the status of their knowledge. Children in particular find themselves the objects of health care, rather than the subjects. They are the objects of large-scale interests: those of market-led purchasers and providers in the NHS, of health professionals, of epidemiologists of the normal, of the psy complex across the home, pre-school and school. Children's daily lives in the UK take place in social contexts where resources – services and finance – are only grudgingly accorded. Making daily life pleasant and productive for children does not seem to form part of government policy.

Children and their mothers have some common causes and some grounds in common. But there are also respects in which they need conceptualizing as social groups whose interests differ. Notably their relationships to dominant power structures differ. Whilst mothers and other working women may be regarded as agents of the state, children are positioned as the objects of women's attention. The extent to which children and women collaborate and conflict within these social constraints is one theme of this book. Clearly, it will be important to consider here how age and gender intersect as factors affecting women's and children's relationships.

This chapter has introduced a number of topics which will be taken up and considered more fully in the next chapter: models of childhood; the contributions of psychological and sociological insights and models to our understanding of childhood; and what we can learn from research studies on these topics.

three

Constructions of childhood

The research enterprise on children and childhood over the last 25 years has included some striking challenges to received wisdom within both psychology and sociology. What constitutes a proper discourse on children and childhood has been contested ground. This chapter outlines discussions and debates within and about developmental psychology before going on to discuss the 'new' sociology of childhood and how its frameworks and concerns lock into the topics of this book.

The book is grounded in a sociological approach to children's lives and to childhood itself. But it addresses issues relating to children's daily lives, which are as heavily influenced today as for the last hundred years or so, by the dominant discipline of child psychology. In particular, health, welfare and education professionals, as fieldworkers in the 'psy complex' (Donzelot 1980), continue to rely heavily on developmental psychology in their educative work with children and mothers. Developmentalism structures the organization and delivery of services, and has also been influential in underpinning sociological theories about children and childhood. Sociology has traditionally neglected children as a social group, and has subsumed children within the family and education system as projects for the work of adults. That sociology has thus not problematized children and childhood results from its uncritical reliance on developmental psychology and its complement: socialization. So it is necessary here to discuss these influential strands of child psychology, child development theory and socialization theory, and the critiques mounted about them in recent years. It will also be useful to point to ways in which psychology and sociology have some points of convergence in their more recent approaches to childhood, and to indicate some features of the broad sociological approach taken in this book.

Psychology and childhood

The positivist and universalist proposition that out there is 'the' child, to be identified, codified and described has long been both a tenet of developmental psychology and a topic for debate. As a tenet, the proposition can be seen as grounded in the attempt initiated in the early nineteenth century to constitute psychology as a science, using scientific methods to arrive at proofs (e.g. Hearnshaw 1964; Rose 1985). Many of the influential early actors in the child-study movement, such as Darwin, were natural scientists by training. Traditional positivist and universalist understandings of the enterprise of child study seem to have held sway and acquired increasing influence during most of the twentieth century, but critical movements began to gather force during the 1960s and 1970s. A landmark was Arlene Skolnick's review (1975) of theories of child development and of the relevance of social context. She points to the prevailing reliance in psychological thinking at the time on the concept of development unfolding from within, and the complementary neglect of social forces. Paradoxically, developmental psychology has been both individualist and universalist: individualist in its focus on the child set apart from social context; and universalist in aiming to uncover truths applying to all children. The individualization of children's development, within a positivist and universalist framework is a theme that will crop up throughout this book. Individualization is not only current among some academics, it is also convenient for policy makers: it allows them to focus on the individual case with its specific characteristics and dysfunctions – victim-blaming, rather than face up to the cost of providing appropriate social frameworks within which all children are enabled to develop healthily.

Within the psychological establishment, the study of cultural context and difference provided a way into broadening experts' visions of factors affecting children's childhoods. In search of information on cultural difference, the 1970s saw eminent men setting off to the USSR (Bronfenbrenner 1971) and China (Kessen 1975) to study cultural differences in child-rearing. The contribution of Kessen is particularly important; he edited a selection of varying philosophical treatises on childhood (1965), and provided an influential paper on 'The American child and other cultural inventions' in 1979, later revised and discussed at a Houston Symposium in 1981 (Kessen 1983). The argument developed through this body of work was that both children and child psychology are cultural inventions, defined by larger forces; thus in the case of US culture, the forces cited are: a commitment to (positivist) science and technology, the critical importance of maternal input, and, most centrally, a belief in the idea of the individual and self-contained child. Notable too were the contributions of Bronfenbrenner (1979), who encouraged psychologists to move away from a focus on the isolated individual, with its complementary method of testing individual children in laboratory conditions (in strange settings, doing strange things with strange people). Instead he proposed 'ecological validity'; children should be studied within their natural environment;

and account should be taken of a range of social contexts, schematized as widening concentric circles surrounding the child: outwards from parents, family, through to social institutions such as schools, and on to social policies and macro-level politics. However, these contexts were proposed essentially as background variables within a positivist frame, rather than as components of an agency-structure interaction.

Indeed, under the influence of such comparative work and of social constructionist theories, it has been argued that the root ideas of psychology are based not in fact but in ideology, and that it might be more relevant and useful to think in terms of visions of infancy (Bradley 1989), constructed according to the interests of the observer. McCullers (1969) explores the notion, prevalent among nineteenth-century biologists, of parallels between the development of human societies and the development of each individual, where the individual, through the years to adulthood retraces or recapitulates the progress of human societies towards its current civilized state. He points out that this notion can be traced not only, very evidently, in the works of G. Stanley Hall (for instance, in his influential work on adolescence, first published in 1904), but as one important strand in the thinking of many influential psychologists, whose own background was in biology: Freud, Jung, Werner, Vygotsky and Piaget. This argument is fully developed by John Morss (1990): through his examination of the historical foundations of developmental psychology, he finds that the discipline is founded in and constituted by two kinds of assumptions – biological and philosophical. The discipline is based on biological assumptions – the evolutionist thinking of the nineteenth century which offers the vision of developmental ascent from biological beginnings to social maturity. In this model, change over time in the child is progressive – towards the maturity of adulthood. The philosophical assumption of the sensory origin of experience proposes that 'information is received by the child in the form of sensations tied to specific sense modalities' (Morss 1990: 229). These two interlinked notions have thus served to emphasize physical factors in child development. Further, the universalism of traditional child psychological thinking is tied into these biological assumptions; social events that are observed to take place in a given context – for instance, certain mother-to-child practices – are interpreted as natural, and proposed as universally applicable. Like those in the social constructionist tradition, who argue strongly for the inherently social character of children's development, Morss moves to the conclusion that developmental psychology is built on 'rotten' foundations. He regards the theorizing of social foundations in the construction and reconstruction of human development, under the banner of contemporary Marxist thinking, as the most promising way forward.

Morss's critique of developmental psychology is complemented by that of the Stainton Rogers team (1992) who site their analysis in the idea of narratives; psychology itself must be regarded as a set of stories, whose angle, or argument, suits that of the teller. As they note (p. 38), psychology drew on natural science and specifically chemistry to posit socialisation as a melding process of nature and nurture (in a process analogous to chemical processes of the fusion of elements); but since the chemical analogy is a metaphor for what takes place in childhood, rather than a model of a process, psychology is left stranded – unable to explain process.

These critiques within and towards psychology have focused on developmentalism and socialization: interlinked concepts, indeed components of the same package. Socialization theory justifies its model of adult–child relationships in part through reliance on the notion of developmental stages, where the work of mothers and other socialisers (notably teachers) is required to ensure children's safe passage through these stages. The establishment in the minds of psychologists of the concept of developmental stages, tied to age and maturation, with Piaget widely credited as the principal twentieth-century influence, has such wide and deep currency that it is difficult to think of children without using his scheme. In particular, education theory in the UK has been dominated by his cognitive approach to children (Gipps 1992).

It is a paradox of the construction of psychological knowledge that the biological and the cognitive are seen as linked and are universalized. For we have a discipline which can be seen as rooted in biological 'truths', where children's development unfolds along pre-determined lines; but the agency of adults is also required to socialize children, and adults, especially mothers, are held to account for deviant or dysfunctional development. Further, when it comes to the socialization of children, at home but especially at school, cognitive development, also along pre-determined lines, through a series of stages, is regarded as both critical and problematic. Piaget's work on cognitive development has formed the basis of teacher training, and has concentrated the attention of educationalists on the development of children's thought processes: their logical abilities; their concepts of causality; and their understanding of the conservation of number and mass (Gipps 1992). And here is another paradox; for, within psychologists' and educationalists' thought, what children know and how they use knowledge to consider moral and practical issues in their daily lives has been of less interest than what cognitive stage they have reached. At its extreme, this vision leads teachers to assign higher value to steering children through stages than to giving them access to knowledge. Indeed an important reason why the UK government has clashed so profoundly with teachers in the 1980s is that whilst the government wants children to know things, many teachers think children should be occupied acquiring the cognitive tools for thinking and learning.

The net effect of Piagetian frameworks has been to devalue what children know, and thence their competence. The education service, at both policy and school levels, has been notably unwilling to take account of children's knowledge as a basis for participation in discussing issues of concern to them in their daily lives at school (CRDU 1994: Report 7). Some of the most interesting studies of children as socially competent persons, building on and deploying their knowledge, have taken place, not in the area of formal education, but in health service contexts. These studies have been concerned with children's health-related knowledge. This research has emphasized the importance of experience (rather than age or developmental stage) in determining what children know and the character of that knowledge: its depth and range. Thus, Myra Bluebond-Langner (1991) has found that children's knowledge and understanding of their sib's cystic fibrosis and its implications for family life depends on the length and quality of their experience of the condition and its stages, and not on their age. Most powerfully, too, she found (1978) that it was experience that led to knowledge among dying children; they acquired knowledge of their prognosis through observation of social arrangements and conversations during their hospital stays. Similarly, Priscilla Alderson (1993) found that children's understanding of their own serious health condition, of treatments and management, was not age-/stage-related, but condition-related. In the field of educational studies at primary school level, it has been social relationships – playtime and friendships, rather than the formal curriculum, that has attracted study of children's knowledge and knowledge-based activity (Sluckin 1981; Davies 1982; Pollard 1985). Studies within the formal curriculum have generally focused on achievement of the basic tools for thinking: reading, writing, calculation.

A further feature of the power of the concept of stages is its implicit assumption, as already noted, that there is a finished and finite stage – adulthood, where people have reached mature cognitive ability. This notion devalues what people learn throughout their lives and how they learn: and it also over-emphasizes the importance of childhood stages, and the need to study them. Cognitive, emotional and social development through adulthood is not a common research topic. Arlene Skolnick (1975) challenges the concept of process and progress through the long years up to adulthood. She discerns in many developmental theories a point of change, somewhere between the ages of 5 and 7 years, and suggests that it might be more appropriate to think in terms of two major stages of development: infancy and post-infancy, during which time 'the child comes into possession of essentially adult-like mental capacities'. This suggestion would have implications for understandings of adolescence and adulthood, which might then be seen, not as turning points, but as part of the continuum of life beyond infancy. Skolnick refers to Baldwin (who wrote an overview of child development theories in 1967); he argues for two main types of psychological functioning: a primary process – primitive, direct, impulsive and non-cognitive; and a secondary process – more controlled, thoughtful and logical. As she points out, his identification of these two main stages in development fits with established social customs; in many societies it is around the ages of 5–7 years that children assume adult responsibilities, start formal school (in the USA and Europe), receive first communion in the Catholic Church, and in the past became legally responsible for crime.

Within psychological thinking, therefore, children's competence is a problematic and disputed topic. I argue in this book that parental and teacher views on this topic differ. The social expectations and norms inherent in adult dealings with children will be taken up in Chapter 4, where children's acquisition of knowledge and their work are considered.

Psychology, sociology and childhood

Children's competence has been explored through sociological approaches. In the 1970s, the sociologist Denzin used the insights provided by symbolic interactionism to point to flaws in the concept of developmental stages as the critical basis for thinking about children's daily lives and activities. He argued that the psychologists who propose developmental sequences share a common quality: 'they fail to see the human being in active interactionist terms. They pay little attention to the fact that humans are symbol-manipulating organisms and as such are capable of engaging in mindful, self-conscious activity' (Denzin 1977: 20). Denzin argues that the theories of learning proposed by such influential figures as Watson, Freud, Hull, Skinner, Piaget, Bruner, Gesell, Spock, and the behaviourists have been systematically translated into theories of education in which 'the' child is viewed as passive, to be controlled, taught, tested, '. . . these theories of learning, then, complement and support the broader position that children are incompetent social beings' (1977: 20).

It is probably relevant that some of the most acute among male theorists have been those, who, like mothers, engage daily with children in natural contexts. Or to put it another way, it may be significant that mothers' concepts accord with those of professional observers who have personal day-to-day interactions and relationships with children. Thus Denzin (1977) not only observed the fact that his own children were interactive learners; he acquired experiential knowledge that they engaged in play as work; he found through interaction with his children that they were not objects of socialization, but people who had some control over ways in which conversations and actions resulting from them developed, and this control included power over adult's actions. Quoting mainly incidents and conversations between his own children and himself, he shows how children set or modify the agenda, require responses, get what they want, teach their parents how to behave. If anything, in day-to-day transactions, he shows his children are too competent for adult comfort.

Until recently sociology could be accused of over-complacent reliance on the tenets of psychology. Two main points will be considered here: the first concerns cognition and the second socialization. Sociology has taken up and used as a point of anchorage the topic of cognition, a central topic for psychology. Just as psychology has been largely concerned with cognitive development, so sociology has been concerned with rational man [*sic*] as a social actor. Sociology could ignore children, since within psychology they were pre-defined as cognitively incompetent. Turner (1992: 73–91) traces the dominance of interest in cognitive bases for action, through consideration of such influential figures as Weber, Parsons, Berger, Giddens and Bourdieu. He notes their struggles with the idea of the embodied actor and his [*sic*] lived experience as a basis for action; and concludes that in their theories the body is a 'residual category'. With other writers (e.g. Hochschild 1979, 1983; Scheper-Hughes and Lock 1987; Shilling 1993), Turner has been influential in reconsidering the lived body: the emotional and physical understandings that contribute to social interactions and are themselves modified by these. The idea of the lived body is immensely important when we are considering children, whose bodies and emotions are important to those who care for them and to themselves as they negotiate social positions in such central arenas as the home and group settings. Bodies and emotions as fit topics for sociological enquiry regarding children are taken up more fully in Chapter 5.

The second point concerns socialization theory. Childhood has in general not been a topic for sociological theorizing. It is as if childhood was not the appropriate province of sociology, which concerned itself with important matters such as men's work in the public domain. Childhood was the province of psychology, and its unexplored, uncontested theories could be relied on by sociologists as a basis for defining children as objects of socialization in the family and in the education system. The mother, whose natural place was the private domain of the home, had the task of teaching her young children basic social morality; socialization for older children took place within the education system and aimed at the production of the young adult as a useful and acceptable citizen. This classical Durkheimian position is of course gendered, since girls do not become full citizens, but merely serve to reproduce the next generation and to carry out essential but simple work within the family. 'For it is the family that can distinctively and effectively evoke and organise those homely sentiments basic to morality and – even more generally – those germane to the simplest personal relationships' (Durkheim 1961: 19). Within this model, children are essentially passive. And moral teaching rests not on women's cognitive strength but on uncontested, received tradition, which they pass on to their children.

Within the regimes promoted through the psy complex (health visiting, social work, teaching), women's socialization work and children's part in it are still largely unproblematized (Brook and Davis 1985). As suggested above, sociological theorists first used the insights of interactionism to criticize the socialization thesis promoted by Parsons; they argued it was limited in its construction of the child as passive (Morgan 1975: 41). Morgan's commentary on R.D. Laing's work on parental (damaging) one-way influences on children – defining their identity and transmitting values to children – also draws on interactionism (pp. 125–8). But though Morgan noted children's participation in interactive encounters, his critique did not move on at that point in time to rethink the positioning of children and childhood in the family.

In general, sociological interest in the family as a social system and in relationships between the family and the wider societal institutions has been concerned with relationships between the adults and with adult understandings, especially of tensions between adult family responsibilities and work –

that is, paid work outside the home (e.g. Rapoport, *et al.* 1982; Bernardes 1988; Wilson and Pahl 1988). Children have not only been a minor consideration (in both senses), but have also been unproblematized; that is, children's child-hoods as lived out in families have not generally been systematically studied. As understood and promulgated in these works, socialization, though tinged with interactionism, assumes acceptance by the child of values and norms already in place (e.g. Bernardes 1985). Interest in parenting has not been matched by study of 'childing'; indeed my ugly coinage here results from the fact that there is no word to include children's intergenerational activities and relationships in complement to those understood within the term 'parenting'. This theoretical vacuum at the heart of the nuclear family extends to the work of some feminist commentators in the 1970s. *Re-thinking the Family*, a US collection of feminist papers edited by Thorne and Yalom (1982) is concerned largely with rethinking women and parenthood. Indeed for many feminists the parenting of children has been regarded as constituting a root cause of women's oppression (see Oakley 1994 for discussion). And this view has been held not just by academic feminists but by mothers themselves: Boulton (1983) found that middle-class mothers of under-5s viewed motherhood as a more or less onerous job and felt career frustration; only the working-class mothers viewed children as companions, whose contribution to the enjoy-ment of daily life they valued. We have to move on to some of the later work of Gilligan and her colleagues (Brown and Gilligan 1992) for the possibility of alliances between women and children to be floated as a theoretical way to face the oppression of women and of children within paternal control. It is indicative of the history and legacy of strong divisions between specialities that conferences have recently been organized with the specific purpose of dragging family and childhood specialists together and making them talk with each other. In a recent seminar David Morgan (1994) discussed possible linkages and working partnerships between the sociology of the family and the sociology of childhood; he stressed the impacts of children on the family: in shaping and modifying both the family and the individual parents, just as the family and the parents shape and modify children and childhood.

The capturing by psychology of childhood as a field of study, and its neglect by other disciplines is noted too by Jean La Fontaine (1986) through her consideration of the history of anthropology. Under the influence of Durkheim and Radcliffe-Brown, social anthropology assigned to psychology the study of the individual and argued that the proper study of anthropology was social groups, roles and relationships in relation to social structures. La Fontaine notes that in the last 20 years or so it is through the study of the household, and in particular through study of the economics of the household, that children have become a focus for anthropological study, since in many societies they contribute very obviously to its economic welfare. Indeed, this theme has been taken up within the sociology of childhood, in considerations of industrialized Western societies (Qvortrup 1991; Oldman 1994). In recent years the activities and discourse of children have become a focus of UK anthropological observational work which has studied the construction and reconstruction of self, identity, social groups, through interaction and discourse (Haudrup Christensen 1993; James 1993).

Paradoxically it is the detail of observations within psychological investigations that provide some of the fullest and strongest evidence of children's agency; yet the implications of children's agency have not been fully followed through. Observers have long been aware of children's own contributions to their own socialization and to remaking the adults with whom they live as parents. For instance, Danziger (1971: 62) noted long ago that even the young infant has at his [sic] disposal two powerful means of controlling his caretakers – the cry and the smile, through which he engages as a social being with those around him. For it is not only parents who have the power of reward and punishment, so does the young child. 'After he has been on the scene for a little while, his parents are not the people they were before – their socialisation has begun' (p. 62). As constituent members of a social system, parents and child thus form a system in which both control and socialize the other. However, this model still assumes a functionalist framework and a superior role for the adult as socialization agent in response to children's developmental stages (for further discussion see Chapter 4).

It has been within the context of understandings promoted through the development of interactionist frameworks that the critical movement has acquired momentum. Some of the most acute comments have been made about children's own participation in the construction of their own identities, of their relationships with others, and of social worlds within families, schools and in children's own domains apart from adult-dominated systems and institutions. However, it is noticeable that even texts which mount a sustained critique of developmental psychology have often maintained a positivist stance and research methods that fit with it. For instance, Siegal (1991) carried out a comprehensive review of Piaget's work, and quotes the many studies that have shown his findings and inferences from them to be faulty. In general, the reruns of Piaget's tests have led to the finding that children's cognitive abilities are greater than those he limited them to (e.g. Donaldson 1978; Tizard and Hughes 1984; Hughes 1986). Siegal derives from his review two major points: not only the artificial character of the tests, but especially the way psychologists have talked with children have led to the sort of answers they give. For instance, if adults ask a silly question children may nevertheless, politely, give an answer, and if an adult persists, children may provide an answer they hope will satisfy the adult. Yet Siegal then describes his own work, which has retained the same basic method: the laboratory test environment, where the children are asked questions (albeit in a relatively child-friendly manner) after seeing an experiment or series of actions. An instance he gives is a test where the adult shows a glass of white milk, pours the milk into a blue transparent container and then asks 3-year-olds whether the milk is blue ('a reality question') and whether it looks white or blue ('an appearance question'). From the point of view of an ethnographer or sociologist such methods ignore the impact of the strange social context, the power imbalances between child and adult which may affect the answer, and the possibility that children in the course of ordinary activities in familiar settings will demonstrate understanding of differences between appearance and reality.

This sort of abstraction of children's actions and discourse from ordinary social contexts is likely to lead to distorted findings. Even more seriously, the point can be made that such methods and the individualistic orientation of the work have served to exclude for serious consideration the interplay of human lives and learning with social forces. The individual is all. Children's learning is decontextualized from social contexts (Burman 1994: 174–6). As Jacobsen puts it:

> Psychology . . . [has] dealt to a large degree with individuals abstracted from their social and historical contexts. When people's interplay with society was abstracted . . . psychology came to give a false ideological picture of real human lives. Furthermore articles and textbooks in psychology . . . [have been] criticised for depicting human beings predominantly as passive objects to be manipulated, not as active willing subjects able to co-determine their own fates.
>
> (Jacobsen 1985: 66)

In the last few years, the rethinking of children – upgrading them to the status of persons – owes a good deal to the critical movement in psychology, where key texts have been the two books edited by Richards (1974) and Richards and Light (1986). In particular Harré (1986, 1993) and Ingleby (1986) have drawn our attention to the importance of social constructionism as a basis for developing more appropriate and flexible theories for understanding childhood and complementary methodologies for acquiring empirical knowledge.

As Ingleby (1986) describes, proponents of social constructionism (under which he includes a number of schools including symbolic interactionism and post-structuralism) have argued that merely exploring social influences on individual development was not adequate to explain individual and societal interactions. It was necessary to transcend the dualism of individual and society. Social institutions, human thought and action must be approached in terms of meanings, negotiated and constructed through language, in interaction between people. So psychology should be concerned not with individuals but with what goes on in the space between them, that is, with the language and constructed meanings that structure action. Within post-structuralism emphasis moves further, in stressing the construction of agents themselves through interaction and the complementary creation of power relationships. Discourses do not distort reality, they create it.

Within this Foucauldian framework, the construction of ideas about childhood is a central example of how the creation of knowledge takes place. For instance, IQ testing, child-centred pedagogy and welfare provisions are practices that create a population of adults and children disciplined in certain ways. Professionals construct ideas of what a child should be; and they do this not just by direct teaching of mothers, but by enlisting mothers as agents in socializing work. Thus health visitors, pre-school staff and social workers do not take over the functions of the family; they intervene in private lives to regulate what goes on in the family. They teach mothers to aid and abet the models proposed by the psy complex. The pre-school child is defined in certain ways through the teaching of these professionals, acting as agents of the state. For instance the model pre-schooler is co-operative, friendly, alert and obedient. Mothers learn that they must school their child to be fit to engage with school social and academic norms when they reach the age of 5; the school entrant should be able to manage dressing, know her colours and numbers, be accustomed to behaving sociably as a member of a group. And the teaching directed at mothers continues once her child enters school; as Smith (1988) describes, mothers are taught to behave appropriately as the caregivers of the school-aged child in order to present that child at school each day as an acceptable schoolchild (see also Ribbens 1993).

Social constructionism has been important in helping us understand the mechanisms whereby human beings both individually and as social groups continuously negotiate and renegotiate identity and activity within local moral codes; and whereby those codes are constructed, reaffirmed and operationalized. For the purposes of considering children it is critical to give credit to the social positioning of children as a social group, *vis-à-vis* the social power of the adult groups with which they negotiate. Within consideration of children's negotiations with adults, due account and weight need to be given both to ways in which adult power is maintained and used, and to children's resilience and resistance. That the present cohort of children will be the next cohort of adults may give them an edge in their negotiations with adults: for though children present a threat to adult order, they also comprise its best hope. In other words, adult interest in controlling children is in some cases mitigated by respect for what they will be.

The inter-relationships between agency and structure and their relative power are not issues on which there is likely to be accepted positions, even provisionally. The debates in Giddens' work on structuration (1979) provide a means of considering social situations and interactions each on their own merits. The mutual construction and reconstruction of both agency and structure through the action of each on the other is attractive, notably in that (at any rate now, for the moment) it seems to fit the way things work as we experience and observe them. However, Giddens himself has not taken full account of power as an issue in structuring childhood. Thus he can say:

> The unfolding of childhood is not time elapsing just for the child: it is time elapsing for its parental figures and for all other members of society; the socialisation involved is not simply that of the child, but of the parents and others with whom the child is in contact, and whose conduct is influenced by the child just as the latter's is by theirs in the continuity of interaction.
> (1979: 139)

This account neglects power imbalances between the two social groups; nor does his textbook on sociology (revised 1993) take account of recent sociological developments and problematize the condition of childhood. In considering the social positioning of children, and their interactions individually and collectively with adults, considerable weight has to be given to intergenerational power imbalances: the specifics of children's relative powerlessness compared to the power of the adults with whom individually and collectively they interact.

Though developmentalism and functional models of socialization theory have suffered a beating in the last 20 years, they remain remarkably powerful. The alliances developed between medicine and psychology (Armstrong 1981; Rose 1985), and between education and psychology (Gipps 1992) have proved resistant to change. Health, welfare and education professionals not only 'do' psychology in their training, they also call on psychological experts to advise them both routinely and in cases of difficulty. Educational psychologists and child psychiatrists are brought in to advise on underachievement, in child abuse cases (Parton 1991), in legal cases (King and Piper 1990; Haugli 1993), and on truancy and school refusal (Carlen *et al.* 1992). A major problem arising out of the use of psychological expertise in such cases concerns the reification of knowledge; for whilst scientists, including psychologists, may offer their findings tentatively, or provisionally, policy makers and practitioners ask for clear factual information and guidelines. The implementation of policies and practices based on theories can reify these with a force that the adviser did not intend.

So it is appropriate to summarize here how children are understood within traditional developmental frameworks, and to point to some complementary features of the current social positioning of children.

Firstly, in complement to developmental understandings of the child as natural and universal, proceeding through biologically conditioned stages, the idea of the normal child has acquired high value. Normal children are the goal, judged according to physical, developmental and social criteria. Furthermore, theory and method combine to direct attention to the individual case, and to characteristics of that case. Culture becomes a constant. Psychological rather than social factors are likely to be drawn on as explanations for children's actions, their success or failure.

The individualizing of children, within the framework of the universal child, serves to draw adult attention away from the social forces that condition childhoods, and from the commonality of children's experience within childhoods controlled by adult social norms and frameworks. The subjection of children to the power of adults and their common interest in resisting adult power and in operating as a social group is sidelined.

By siting actions within a deterministic framework, developmental psychology has been influential in devaluing the purposeful character of action, and in so doing it has devalued children's agency. This process obscures the fact that growing up is not simply a matter of acquiring skills, but, as Ingleby

(1986: 300) puts it, 'the site of complex political tensions between children, parents and the state'. In assuming an ordered sequence, strongly related to age, developmentalism has been blind to the critical function of experience in people's learning throughout life. Children's contributions to discourse and thereby to the construction of their lives is devalued, since it is adults who lay claim to appropriate knowledge as a basis for deciding how children are to live their lives.

UK social policies operate in line with these theories. As non-persons proceeding through an ordered sequence of stages, children as objects of social interventions are divided by age and setting. The health, education and welfare complex works to achieve normalcy through observation, measurement and testing. Mothers are regarded as the principal agents of socialization until children are 'ready' to start first school, and mothers' attitudes and practices are the object of surveillance and education through the health and pre-school services and systems. Teachers at school are regarded as the principal experts for school-age children; and aim to continue the education of mothers. This division of labour draws on Durkheim's (1961) pronouncements about the socializing functions of the education system, which builds on the simple precepts mothers pass on to their pre-school children.

Within social policy, children are subsumed under the family and under women. For instance, children have few rights in their own name. Three examples out of many indicate the subjection of children. Children, unlike adults, are not protected from physical or mental violence: parents and other carers may carry out 'reasonable chastisement' of children. Parents not children are ascribed rights within education in the 1991 Parents' [sic] Charter, though the civil servants did their homework on the children's rights movement and made token reference to children's rights in the 1994 update. Under the 1991 Child Support Act, mothers' refusal to name the absent father can lead to reduction in benefit (CRDU 1994: 75).

The non-person status of children implies separation of the social and intellectual worlds of childhood from those of adults, a division compounded through the provision of child-oriented social institutions, such as nurseries, schools, play centres. The theory and the practice serve to strengthen each other. In theory and in practice children are largely excluded from adult social worlds and confined to institutions constructed for them.

Relying heavily on developmentalism, socialization theory has taken an essentially functionalist view. It has assumed the society as given; children are to be taught how to fit in. Essentially it is assumed within the education complex that adults have the relevant knowledge and that children are to acquire it from them. Education and welfare practices favour the adult task over the interactive children we actually live with. Socialization theory thus downplays the interactive contribution of children as agents in constructing the social order. Within the home and the school, the theory provides a basis for the authority of adults. In particular, though the world of education stresses starting from the child's knowledge and educational needs, children's contribution to learning, as agents building on their experiential knowledge, is likely to have low status compared to the official curriculum implemented by the school.

The sociology of childhood

I have suggested above that whilst the child as object of socialization, and the child in progress through ordered stages of development have received onslaughts from many quarters, the rethinking of childhood itself has lagged behind. Childhood has occupied a theoretical vacuum at the heart of debates about the family; and debates about women's and men's relationships with children have been largely limited to questions of the division of adult labour. It seems adults have been unwilling to question their formulations of 'the child' because that would entail questioning what they wish to take for granted: the worlds of adulthood, as constituted by and for adults.

Further, whilst the critiques of established child psychology theories have come from many quarters, over a considerable period of time, not only do these theories have very considerable resilience in policy and practice fields concerned with child health, welfare and education, but the construction of a more wide-ranging child psychology paradigm has also proved difficult. Concepts based on interactionism and social constructionism have begun to make headway in recent years (a topic to be considered more fully in Chapter 4). In the complementary field of sociology it has required both large-scale enterprises and the detail of individual studies to begin to establish a sociology of childhood.

Changing childhoods – theoretical response to social change

The critical movement in and towards child psychology, combined with the more general social constructionist developments within sociology, as outlined above, can be regarded as one kind of impetus for rethinking childhood within sociology. The comparative movement within psychology, where different childhoods were observed and linked conceptually to varying social conditions, has taken place not just across societies, but within them, and may have helped reconsideration of children's social position and of what social lives are appropriate for them. Another set of factors has probably been influential: the condition of childhood as a topic of concern. The international children's rights movement has comprised pressure to improve the legal status of children, to end physical punishment of children, to give them more of a say in matters that concern them; it has been supported through the 1989 UN Convention on Children's Rights, ratified by the UK government in 1991. In the UK, debate about violence to children, fuelled notably through a series of child abuse cases, provided one main impetus for the 1989 Children Act, which in turn has raised the consciousness of professionals who deal with children. UK concern about the child as victim has been complemented by concern about the child as threat: child abuse and juvenile crime have raised questions about childhood innocence and childhood knowledge; and, more broadly, about adult visions of childhood.

Though the rethinking of childhood has taken place concurrently in different countries, it is appropriate to begin with the nordic scene where the impetus for the most concerted effort so far has been located. In Scandinavia, large-scale changes have taken place since the 1950s in the social lives of young children. In response to state demand for full adult employment in the interests of economic growth, to pressure from women for equal treatment as parents, and (perhaps) to interest in maximizing the potential of a scarce, but uniquely valuable resource – children, Scandinavian countries, especially Sweden and Denmark, have put in place (since the early 1960s) a wide-reaching pro-gramme, including parental leave and childcare services, for both pre-school and school-age children (Melhuish and Moss 1990). Children's daily lives have changed dramatically in consequence of these initiatives. Most children now spend many hours a day in group care; their parents are away from them much of the day; and most families now live in cities and towns, rather than as formerly in smaller communities.

Apart from the USA, where the academic study of child development and childcare is a massive industry, Scandinavia must have one of the largest enterprises (given its population) devoted to the study of daycare and its impact on children's daily lives and development. More generally, and more sociologically, work has been conducted on the quality of children's lives under the changed conditions within which childhoods are lived. Rita Liljeström (1983) voiced some concerns early on, at the Houston symposium referred to earlier (p. 43). She interpreted the widespread provision of nurseries and after-school centres as leading to the institutionalization of children in concrete utopias, where impersonal buildings housed a series of technical and pedagogical solutions to a social problem: the supervision of children while the parents worked. She identified three principal problems with the emerging format of children's lives: children are deprived of initiating their own activities, but instead learn that staff organize these; the estab-lishment of staff with expertise is tending to undermine parents' faith in their own competence and empathy with their children; and professionalized care asserts moral neutrality, based on tolerance and scientific method, and is not rooted in community values. Children in daycare institutions, she alleges, will be unable to make sense of what they and the staff are doing, or why and with what goal they are doing these things. Liljeström maintains that these institutionalizing developments have been organized without consideration for maintaining two crucial values: links between childcare ideals and practices, and the sense of cohesion in local communities (*gemenskap* or *gemeinschaft*), within which traditionally children lived their daily lives with mothers and other local women.

Similarly, in a large-scale study across the five nordic countries – the BASUN project (Childhood, Society and Development Project) – attention has been focused on how children's daily lives, and most importantly their development, has been altered by institutionalization (Dencik 1989). Children at pre-school learn early on, it is alleged, to exercise self-control with respect to affective behaviour, and to be socially flexible; the home becomes the intimacy centre, a zone of stability, and a decoding centre for family members; but parental values become invalidated since children spend a major part of their day with other sets of adults.

The dramatic Scandinavian experiment in changing children's childhoods has promoted rethinking about inter-relationships between the triangle of parents, children and state. Traditional formulations have thought of children mainly in relation to parents, with the state as a back-up; but Scandinavian policy now has an altered focus: children are a shared responsibility of the state and parents. Under these circumstances, it is appropriate to think of children's own direct relationships to the state, its policies and goals. In addition, concern for social justice and the rights of individuals in these countries has led to a movement to regard children and parents as independent subjects with separate legal status. Thus the stage has been set for extracting children out from under the family, conceptually, and thinking about them, not only as individuals, but also, more widely, as a social group.

Childhood as a social phenomenon

Within sociology, the Childhood as a Social Phenomenon (CSP) project is the most important child-oriented enterprise so far, and can be seen as rooted in the above events and considerations. The project, begun in 1987, developed out of and progressed under the auspices of the European Centre in Vienna. The enterprise has been organized throughout by a small team, with Jens Qvortrup from Denmark generally acknowledged to be the leader. Participants from 16 industrialized countries embarked on a programme of work, to document and analyse the condition of childhood in their countries. Each participant team was asked to collect macro-level data for their country, on the following five main topics:

- the sociography of childhood: the demographics and statistics of childhood;
- the activities of children: at school, in leisure time, in paid employment, at home;
- distributive justice: the distribution of societal resources towards children, on what criteria, and the division of resources between the generations;
- the economics of childhood: the nature and distribution of costs, children's contributions;
- the legal status of children: relationships between the state, parents and children, issues of protection and autonomy.

Data on these topics has been issued in 16 country reports between 1990 and 1993 (Bardy *et al.* 1990–3), together with an Introduction by Jens Qvortrup (1991). Other publications include a collection of papers on the rights of children and the politics of childhood (Heiliö *et al.* 1993), and a compendium of the statistics of childhood (Jensen and Saporiti 1992). In addition, experts from a range of fields were asked to contribute comments in the form of papers at a conference in 1992 (Qvortrup 1993). Some of the participants in the project also wrote general papers focusing on themes arising out of the data and discussions (Qvortrup *et al.* 1994).

Clearly this has been a large enterprise, generating reams of data and many analyses. Equally, the findings of the whole enterprise cannot be summarized here. Themes specific to the issues discussed in this book will be taken up as appropriate. Some of the main issues and themes within the new paradigm of childhood are noted here.

- The sociological standpoint adopted – taking children as a social group and childhood as social phenomenon – has served to draw attention to the proposition that children's interests as a group are specific, and should not be considered solely within family or adult interests. Like other social groups, but specifically, children's lives and childhoods are affected by socio-economic factors. These include the allocation of resources, the legal position of children and the social status of children and childhood. Notably, adult understandings of what children are and how childhood should be lived are important determinants of children's childhoods.
- Childhood is to be regarded, not as a preparatory stage, but as a component of the structure of society. Children act as participants – in interaction with other components, such as families and schools. Their activities are to be conceptualized as constructive and reconstructive, in interaction with and integration with adult activities. Their activities are also used instrumentally by adults.
- Children should be regarded not just as the objects of adult attention and the recipients of social and economic resources, but also as contributors to societal resources and production: through their unpaid work at home and school, and in paid employment. Children are thus to be conceptualized as embedded in the division of labour (rather than as beneficiaries or losers from it).
- The social condition of childhood in many countries seems to be character-ized by protection and exclusion – by adults, from adult social worlds. An important theme here concerns common confusion of the natural (biologi-cal) vulnerabilities and dependencies of childhood, with those which are socially constructed.
- Sociological thought has remained adultist; children have not been regarded as appropriate topics for theorization. Though feminism has taken account of mothering, it has not rethought childhood, but has relied on notions of children's needs, in accordance with developmental theory. An important task, therefore, is to rethink sociological theory in the light of the admission of children as a social group.
- In complement to adult theoretical perspectives on childhood, most of the

arrangements and institutions provided 'for' children are, in essence, provided to serve adult interests. The rethinking of sociological theory to include children as a social group should serve as a basis for rethinking policies directed at the social positioning of children and childhood.
• Children's legal position has encapsulated adult views of children. Children's rights have been subsumed under those of their parents. They may be seen as a minority group, with concomitant oppressions governing their lives.

These propositions have exposed to view some features of modern childhood which offer uncomfortable messages to adults. For instance, children may not appreciate unreservedly the social arrangements made for them. To put it another way, theorizing childhood allows us to understand and contextualize the resistances and rebellions of children: to school, to families. As indicated earlier (p. 12), it is theoretically important for adults to listen to children. For if adults wish to construct theoretical frameworks about children, this cannot be done adequately without paying attention to their experiences and views. Theory that does not resonate with experience is, at least in the long run, doomed. An example is the disjunction perceived by women between what men told them was their sociological position, and how they understood it, experientially, themselves; sociological theory has had to be recast to take account of women's experience and their theorizing based on it.

Taking account seriously of children's experiences and views would present a challenge to the adult social order, which would be far-reaching in its effects. For instance, segregation and exclusion would need reconsideration: the segregation of children within certain social institutions (such as the school) and their exclusion from others (such as theatres, pubs) and from social occasions such as parties, funerals. The re-ordering of the social and physical environment (currently framed to favour male adults) in favour of the welfare of all the rest of us, but most particularly for children, is overdue. Children's participation in the division of labour, including both paid and unpaid work, certainly needs rethinking. The ordering of adult time and adult space in the public and private domains needs reconsidering in the light of children's interests.

Sociology of childhood, the contributions of individuals

The research world has seen a good deal of action in rethinking childhood in recent years, and whatever is said in this book will undoubtedly be overtaken by further research. In the UK, the scene has been characterized mainly by individual effort, rather than by concerted programmes of conceptual and empirical work. Yet in the most recent years (since 1991), some undergraduate and graduate courses have been established on childhood, within both sociology and anthropology, using and developing the paradigm outlined above. An ESRC programme of research on 'Children 6–16' will begin late in 1996.

Some of the important influences on rethinking childhood have been mentioned earlier: the collections of papers by Richards (1974) and Richards and Light (1986). Chris Jenks (1982) edited a book of papers on childhood, and his Introduction outlines many of the points that have since been taken up. He notes that the social propensity to naturalize childhood involves using childhood as a device to endorse models of society based on socialization theory, with the child as that which is yet to be, a 'structured becoming'. His analysis of Parsonian functionalism and of Piaget's theories lays the ground for future work in this area. Allison James and Alan Prout (1990b) have played an important part in theorizing childhood as a social construct. In particular, they drew attention to anthropological work on age as a principle of differentiation and stratification. Their paper develops themes relating to the time of childhood and time in childhood, and the centrality of time as a concept structuring how children are required to 'spend time' at different ages. The topics they raise will be further discussed in Chapter 6.

Some of the main topics addressed by researchers from the 1980s onwards concern children's ideas about the social worlds they live in, how they acquire and negotiate identities, their health beliefs, and their activities, including their work. Researchers have pointed to the need to study children not as a strange tribe but as a social group with interests in the larger society they belong to. Carolyn Steedman (1982) studied girls' ideas about what families are and might be. The collections of papers edited by James and Prout (1990b) and Mayall (1994b) include many that describe the impact on childhoods of adult social policies and interests. Study of topics such as child abuse (Kitzinger 1990) and street children (Glauser 1990), allowed for exploration of concepts of childhood and of children's oppression.

Anne Solberg's (1990) investigation of children's participation in the division of labour raised issues of dependency and autonomy in the lives of children. Her paper is complemented by further studies; Virginia Morrow (1994) explored the work, paid and unpaid, carried out by secondary schoolchildren (aged 11–16), in the context of ideas about childhood as a period of dependency and about the complementary notion that children cannot or should not take responsibility. Similarly, Marianne Gullestad (1988) documents the work of children in caring for younger children. There is a growing literature on children's caring work, in parallel with the 'discovery' that they do it (Aldridge and Becker 1993; see also Chapter 4, this book).

There has been increasing interest in children's own health knowledge and perspectives on health, health care and services. This interest seems to derive from current interest in 'lay' knowledge as a component of the health care system and more specifically from the large governmental investment in health education as a means of improving the nation's health (Wilkinson 1988; Farquhar 1989; Backett and Alexander 1991; Bendelow and Oakley 1993). The work has both arisen out of and given new life to belief in children as moral agents, as participants in health care rather than as objects of it (e.g. Prout 1986). Attention has also been drawn to the subduing or muting of children's voices in paediatric consultations (Silverman 1987; Aronsson and Rundström 1988; see also Chapters 4 and 5, this book).

Important studies have been carried out on children's negotiation towards gendered identity. Barrie Thorne (1993) and Allison James (1993) have both considered the case of children in school, especially through the development of their friendships. Indeed children's activities outside the formal curricula offered by adults have increasingly been a focus for attention. Though children's play has long been a province of the psychological gaze with the aim of studying the learning potential of play – in and out of the classroom (e.g. Moyles 1994), there is a tradition of observing play with other aims. The Opies' famous work in documenting games and songs (Opie and Opie 1959, 1969) has had the great merit of forefronting children's creative, as well as reproductive activity. In more sociological vein, some pioneer work has been carried out on what children do out of the jurisdiction of adults: their construction of their own domains (Moore 1986); and their reconstruction of the adult-oriented social environments to suit their own interests (Ward 1988, 1990). Ward's work in particular points to intersections between adult social environments and children's creative resistances to them.

The sociology of childhood and this book

This book is based on the ideas adumbrated here on the sociology of childhood. The attempt in the succeeding chapters is to use these ideas, in intersection with those in other branches of sociology, both as a means of understanding data, and to explore in more detail some themes within the sociology of childhood. Thus Chapter 4 will consider the social environments within which children live their daily lives, the power they have to negotiate and their contributions to the social order. Chapter 5 will explore how the sociology of the body is both useful for thinking about children's daily lives and is itself modified by the incorporation (!) of children. Chapter 6 will be concerned with issues of time in the lives of children, and with power issues in relation to time; it will discuss children's social positioning as a social group in relationship to and interaction with adult social groups, as represented both at home and at school.

The emerging paradigm of the sociology of childhood provides useful bases on which to discuss the main topics and themes of this book. First of all, in pursuing the proposition that children may be regarded as a social group, it helps us to lift children conceptually out of the family and to consider what they have in common as a group. The psychological individualization of children gives way to sociological consideration of how, as a group, their lives are affected by large-scale socio-economic factors (as discussed in Chapter 2), and how, if at all, they are able to negotiate within these structures. The introduction of the idea of power as a force structuring the relationships of adults with and to children helps us explore the extent to which children find their voices subdued in their lives at home and school and, more generally, in society.

Data collected with children will be used to consider their participation in the social construction of their lives and identities in two main settings: the home and the school. It will be argued that the models of childhood and the specific character of the power relationships vary between these two settings; these variations will be explored to show how they structure children's participation. Children's contributions to the social fabric will be an important theme of this book. It will be proposed that at home they contribute through their activities in self-care, in constructing family relationships, through participation in household maintenance and through more conventional forms of work. The work they do at school will be discussed in relationship to its devaluation in the education system. Theoretical problems raised by traditional concentration on parenting and teaching (from a top–down perspective), rather than on interactive relationships between adults and children, will be an important topic, and will be explored through children's own accounts of their relationships with mothers and with teachers. The theme of protection and exclusion as characterizing adult approaches to children and to childhood will be pursued, particularly in relationship to children's social lives in and around the home. Children's own understandings of the restrictions they encounter on their mobility and social lives, and also the high value they put on participation in the social order will be important considerations.

four

Home and school as children's social environments

Introduction

This chapter moves from consideration of theoretical structures proposed for understanding childhood, to an exploration of the ideas of the main adult players with whom children interact during their daily lives. Their own experiences will be at the forefront in Chapters 5 and 6. In this chapter, the aim is to focus on characteristics of the social environments of children's daily lives, and in particular on how adults think about children's knowledge and participation in two social worlds: the home and the school. The approach taken here is that children participate in social interactions from their earliest days; that they contribute to and construct these social worlds, in association and interaction with others; in turn their identity develops through these interactions, which teach them how they are constructed and understood. I argue that children's negotiating strategies and abilities to arrive at a comfortable, health-maintenance way of life varies between these two contexts. The knowledge and moral frameworks enacted by the main adults there – mothers and teachers respectively – serve as modifying forces in structuring children's activities, and in determining their negotiating power.

The interactive approach complements that of psychologists who have explored how and why children acquire social and moral understanding. Bradley reviews the evidence from studies since the early 1970s on babies' interactions and documents the growth of the view that 'the child is deemed to be born peculiarly well-adapted for understanding other people and it is only Piaget's preoccupation with the logic of the physical world that has blinded him to this obvious insight' (1989: 123). Indeed Bradley's account of babies' early abilities and pre-dispositions is laced with comments on the obviousness of the findings of recent studies; it is as if Piaget is currently being identified as a blip in human knowledge about babies and young children. On Comenius' comment in 1623 that babies 'know what a wrinkled and what an unwrinkled brow means' Bradley notes that this was a well-worn observation of 'common-sense' philosophy. He quotes Darwin (1877): 'An infant understands to a certain extent, and as I believe at a very early period, the meaning or feeling of those who tend him, by the expression of their features.' Bradley's survey leads him to conclude that the sociability and interpretive skills of babies can be and has been observed very early in their lives.

Evidence of young children's abilities has been sought in studies carried out, not in experimental, unnatural situations, but in children's homes with their family. Barbara Tizard and Martin Hughes recorded the conversations of 4-year-old girls with their mothers, and Judy Dunn the conversations and non-verbal interactions between under-3s and their sibs and parents. In both cases one important aim was to reconsider existing theory; and the studies showed that learning of various kinds takes place earlier than psychologists had thought. Tizard and Hughes (1984) argue that children's competence as thinkers, and in particular their capacity for logical thought and for seeing things from the perspectives of others, starts much earlier than Piaget proposed. Their 4-year-olds demonstrated capacities he identified only in 7-year-olds. Dunn (1988) takes these explorations even further down the age-range and shows that under-2s indicate they understand other people's feelings and goals, and social rules, and by their third year they have insight into other people's minds.

These studies have been important in alerting psychologists and other professionals concerned with young children to children's capacities. It is a measure of the strength of Piaget and Kohlberg's influence in defining ages and stages for cognitive and moral development that it has been necessary in recent years for psychology to demonstrate babies and young children's social nature and their considerable abilities. Throughout Dunn's book she expresses astonishment that children can do what she finds they can (1988: e.g. 17, 20, 21) and she acknowledges that this surprise derives from the power of the Piagetian tradition and from experimental testing results. Yet for the non-psychologist reader the conversations and activities quoted in these two important books are instantly recognizable and unexceptional. Anyone who lives alongside young children could cap these conversations with examples of their own, and would take it as obvious from children's behaviour that they are innately social. In other words, it is currently common sense that children are social, moral persons.

Recent work on children shows a convergence between psychology and sociology, at least as to the sources of theoretical approaches. Judy Dunn acknowledges the relevance of G.H. Mead's arguments on the development of a self. For Mead, as she notes, the growth of self-awareness is linked to a child's understanding of others and to a grasp of how others respond to and perceive her (1988: 79). As Mead himself puts it:

The individual enters as such into his own experience only as an object, not as a subject; and he can enter as an object only on the basis of social relations and interactions, only by means of his experiential transactions with the individuals in an organised social environment . . . Apart from his social interactions with other individuals, he would not relate the private or 'subjective' contents of his experience to himself and he could not become aware of himself as such, that is, as an individual, a person, merely by means or in terms of these contexts of his experience.

(Mead, on The Self, in Strauss 1964: 244–5)

The approach taken in this book is in complement to the important psychological studies briefly referred to here. But it is distinctive and more sociological. The psychological approach is essentially positivist – so for instance, Judy Dunn is concerned to arrive at definitive accounts of children's motivation to help each other (1988: e.g. 103), as if there were a truth out there to be identified. Though the insights of symbolic interactionism have centrally influenced the methods she used to collect data, and the interpretation of data, the further implication – that people's identity, relationships, moral understandings are constructed and reconstructed through interactions and discourse – is not pursued. Nor does she take account of the researcher's interactive relationship with the researched people and with the data.

The psychological approach is, ultimately, concerned with the promise children show: how children develop towards adulthood, rather than with the here and now. From a sociological point of view, we *are* concerned with the here and now, with children participating and contributing now within social groups, such as the family. It is proposed that children not only learn from, but also contribute to the social environment of the home and the school. It is argued that children's knowledge and their social positioning is negotiated and renegotiated through their interactions. The central focus is on children's social positioning as it is negotiated and structured. The argument being advanced is presented *as* an argument, a point of view, advanced in the belief that, just as children interact with their sibs and their parents, so, as onlookers, we interact with the data. We can only suggest an interpretation, based on how we construct what we observe and on how the data in turn and continuously serves to modify our perceptions. In this respect, the sociological enterprise takes Mead's propositions to apply both to the people and social worlds observed, and to the observer's understandings of these.

Children and the division of labour

In Chapter 2 I noted that whilst the founding fathers of sociology and their male descendants regarded the private domain as theoretically uninteresting, being the site of women's natural work in support of the public sphere, it was women who took up the task of problematizing the home, and their work in the private and public domains. Children, however, remained unproblemat-ized: as objects of socialization, subsumed within the home and the school. Within the new sociology of childhood, the social positioning of children has been reconsidered. Important strands in the argument were developed by Jens Qvortrup (1985, 1987). He argues that just as children traditionally took part in productive work as soon as they were physically able, so nowadays they contribute to the division of labour through their work at school, their domestic work and, in some cases, paid work. The work of children, which in non-industrial societies was a component of the productive work of adults in households, has now become specialized. Specifically, children have become schoolchildren. As such, they have a specific position in the social division of labour, working to acquire the knowledge and skills demanded of them in the adult world. As a group which takes part in socially necessary activities, children can be regarded objectively as a class, although they lack conscious-ness of their social position, essentially of their dependency and of the oppressive character of their relationships with adults. Children therefore have the objective but not the subjective characteristics of a class.

These arguments are explored by David Oldman (1994), who claims that children may best be regarded as a class whose position is in economic opposition to that of adults – who exploit their activities. He develops this argument through consideration of 'childwork': the work adults do to and on children (in homes, pre-schools and schools). Care and education institutions are provided in the interests of adults rather than of children – they provide work for adults, and they require children to work towards adult ends.

Both Qvortrup and Oldman use and extend the concepts refined in traditional sociology. Central to their arguments are classic definitions of work, as activity that contributes to social production and economic strength. They reconsider the concepts to include children in the division of labour; and this reconsideration is important in extracting children from their asocial posi-tioning as objects of socialisation, and in identifying their social position as a class. Further, this conceptual work has the great merit of explaining children's inferior position on rights issues. Where children are defined as a class carrying out specialized activities under the direction and control of adults, the subsuming of children's interests under those of adults can be both explained and justified.

However, the presentation of children as active contributors to social production in the public domain leaves us with the problem of how to think about children as people within households and across the private and public divide. It is useful to compare this enterprise with that of women, who have found it necessary to reconsider definitions of work, taking account of women's activities in both the public and private domains, and thence the relationships of the private to the public domains. Similarly it is relevant to widen consideration of 'work', taking account of children.

The argument proposed here is that children contribute both to productive and to reproductive work. These contributions are carried out in the contexts of intricate and changing relationships with women, who act both as controllers and as enablers of children. The proposition is that we may think in terms of somewhat uneasy and continually renegotiated alliances between women and children. Indeed, exploration of these issues is important not only in the interests of reconsidering children, but in order to rethink women in relationship to their own and other people's children. Early feminism, resting on socialization theory, tended to see children as objects of women's work, and a cause of their oppression; yet it is clear from common-sense experience that women's relationships with children have a more central place in their lives than this formulation suggests, not only in providing purpose and content but also as a critical determinant in developing the specifics of women's knowledge and moral character, based on attention to affective and contextual considerations.

The main outlines of these propositions are set out here, to be considered in detail through this and the next two chapters.

The social order of the home

I argue here that children contribute to the maintenance of the social order of households, through at least three activities: self-care; activities that help maintain the home as health-maintenance setting; and the construction and reconstruction of family relationships, within the immediate and extended family. The gender order ensures that the critical relationship for young children is generally with their mother – who takes the major share of childcare. I suggest that whilst women teach and control children, they also enable children to contribute. Children act in alliance with women. Women and children make and remake the home. Home is where moral issues are debated and moral codes established, including those relating to health. These codes provide not a basis or support for more important education activities carried out in schools, but the central beliefs children carry with them to school, and against which they judge (and often find wanting) school-based codes and precepts.

Children's activities and their identities are forged and reconstructed in the light of their interactions with others, and especially parents. It is crucial therefore to take account of the strength, resilience and negotiability of parental, and in particular maternal, understandings of children. The first point to make concerns the unique character of the development of these understandings. Whilst people bring ideas about children and about parenting to day one of parenthood, the experience of being a parent and of doing parenthood, as everyone knows, constitutes one of the most dramatic knowledge-acquisition processes that people go through. Adults learn from the experience of caring for and interacting with their children. Cultural norms and individual experience interact in unique ways. Of specific importance here is the cultural understanding and teaching by their baby that here they are involved with a person; being a parent therefore involves not objectifying the child, but subjectifying her – a position which children themselves demand.

Adult understandings of gender structure children's experiences of being parented. Evidence from mothers' and fathers' behaviour and talk to under-2s indicates that they make gendered distinctions between their girl and boy children (McGuire 1991). The research literature also indicates that children of nursery school age have taken on the idea of gender-appropriate behaviour, but, interestingly, have understood that the acceptability of certain gendered behaviours varies across social contexts (Dunn 1988: 172–3). Mothers are faced with difficult and to some extent contradictory tasks: preparing their sons for a gendered social world, heavily enforced, as at school; and making clear (if they so wish) that such stereotypes do not hold for the home. Though it seems likely that mothers do rear their boys to face the public world, evidence is lacking on this point (Henshall and McGuire 1986; see also Statham 1986).

Crucial to the moral order of the home, and to mothers' impact on their children, is the character of the knowledge women bring to mothering and further acquire experientially during their lives with their children. Carol Gilligan has reconsidered the character of women's moral knowledge in the light of Kohlberg's celebrated six stages of moral development. In his model, women do not generally get beyond stage four, where a person is 'still' context-bound, taking account of relationships. Stages 5 and 6, are those where a person uses abstract context-free moral reasoning to arrive at moral decisions and choices. Needless to say, the enquiries that led to this formulation were carried out by men, on boys and men, and led to a formulation in favour of men (Gilligan 1993: 18–21). Gilligan asks for higher valuation of women's moral thinking: their 'orientation towards relationships and interdependence' as bases for contextualized judgements (p. 22). Belenky and colleagues (1986) take up these themes in their exploration of women's ways of knowing, of the character of morality grounded in relationships, in context, in careful consideration of the detail of a problematic situation. But gendered power relations impose on female consciousness: they found (as do Brown and Gilligan 1992) that many girls and women described themselves as powerless in the face of male supremacy to speak in their own voice, and effectively lost their voice in social contexts dominated by men. Girls approaching adolescence were particularly vulnerable to cultural messages about what they should be and how they should behave; they lose their own voices under these pressures. These propositions, though rooted in another culture (the United States), possibly expounded using extreme cases to make the point, and open to the charge that they stereotype women and men as polar opposites (Epstein 1990), nevertheless provide an important way into thinking about the interactions of women and children, both at home and at school. The affective component of learning, and the affective component of knowledge, in particular moral knowledge, is a neglected but surely important topic.

Walkerdine and Lucey (1989), using the transcripts from the Tizard and Hughes study of 4-year-olds talking with their mothers, argue that adequate interpretation of these conversations requires consideration of the intersections of class and gender. They argue that in working-class households mothers socialize their daughters into acceptance of their class and gender position; for girls in middle-class households the oppression takes another form: they are taught, falsely, that they are autonomous, but that story conceals their oppression and serves to distort their understanding and powers of resistance. Further, one may argue, gender compounds with social class disadvantage: working-class mothers, compared to middle-class mothers, will be less able to help their children face the world. Yet their girls learn from their mothers that the work women carry out at home is real, important work; whereas their boys can find little evidence that they have valuable work to do at home or in the public domain, with its high rates of male unemployment.

The character of women's moral thinking is critical to the development of children's learning at home, and how this learning differs according to gender. The home is not just the first but the most fruitful early ground for children's learning, in part because the affect is so strong (Tizard and Hughes 1984: 249–52). The topics they discuss with their mothers are of direct concern to them, rooted in daily life, often stretching back into the past and on to the future. The discussions are rooted too in children's deep-seated affection for their mothers, which keeps the child physically close to the mother, involved through observation and participation in her mother's activities – which, again, provide a source of conversation and knowledge. On the mothers' side, their affection for their children means, apart from anything else, a willingness (at least some of the time) to engage in conversation, to answer questions. Mothers' intense daily continuous interaction with their children means they have unique knowledge of what their children are thinking about, what references they are making, what are their concerns, worries and hopes. Learning from mothers therefore takes place in the context of emotional commitment on both sides, which provides impetus and groundwork (cf. Dunn 1988: *passim*). The fact that mothers are constantly having to make moral decisions and adjudications in daily life at home provides evidence for children of the contextual nature of those moral judgements.

But the significance of what children learn at home from their mothers will differ for girls and boys. For girls, what they learn at home about making decisions and judgements holds now and in the future; it is all of a piece morally. Yet they will find their knowledge devalued in the public world. Boys have to learn that the morality learned at their mother's knee is not gender-appropriate; they must learn abstract (stages 5 and 6) moral thinking; their mothers' codes will not hold in the market-place.

Children in the division of labour at home

The stratification of children by age and stage runs deep. Thus it is commonly assumed that there is a period in the teenage years – called adolescence – when people are in the process of becoming adult; part of that process is taking on the tasks of adulthood – including health care. Adults' emphasis on the crucial character of changes during adolescence towards responsible action serves both to obscure the activity of children in their early years and to stress parental socialization activity.

In this section, I draw on the study Marie-Claude Foster and I carried out focusing on under-2s – the children were 21 months old when we first talked with their parents (see page 9). Interview data we collected from mothers and fathers suggest three main contributions by children to the social order of the home: the assumption of self-care tasks; the carrying out of jobs that help maintain the home as a healthy social organism; and the construction and reconstruction of family relationships within the immediate and more extended family.

The drive towards independence as to bodily care is a common theme in mothers' talk about their young children. As mothers note, for the child one way of cutting down on maternal control is to take over some jobs oneself. From the mother's point of view, daily life becomes less onerous when hands-on caring tasks are reduced, and the experience of watching the child acquire skills and independence also serves to shift mothers' conceptualization of her: the young child is less of a dependent person and the object of care, but becomes through action a person who asserts her own knowledge and wishes.

> *Mother*: Things like dressing, he tries, he pulls things off, he loves to do that. Now I get his jumper off except for one arm and he pulls it off and he feels very pleased with himself. He tries to put his shoes and socks on. He tries to put his mittens on. He's learning a little bit about himself as well, because when he – I've only just noticed this in the last few days – when he wants to urinate he starts to hold himself and he goes 'Oh!' But he's learning a bit about his own body now, as well. I'm sure there's lots more I can't think of.

Mothers and fathers in this study commonly reported on children's assertiveness. They made their wishes known, mainly through action and through the manipulation of their parents, and thereby demonstrated their understanding of what they need and wish for.

> *Father*: He'll go and stand by the door when he want to go out. Tug you by the hand and show you his coat.

> *Mother*: If he wants orange juice he'll get the cup and the juice. If he want biscuits he go and get them and then come back to the fridge and tell you . . . if he wants his milk, and you're sitting down he'll pull you to the fridge, pull your chair. You get to know the signs really!

> *Mother*: At the swings, she leads the way – takes you to the sandpit and drags you in, heads off for the slide and climbs the steps.

Within the limits of their physical and emotional dependence on their parents, these young children indicated that they had views on what suited them, balancing up rest and activity, nutrition, warmth, to suit themselves.

Mothers also reported that their children wanted to engage with the daily round of family activities. They observed what was going on and tried to do it too. As they acquired each new skill, their range of activities increased further: a child who can hold a knife will try to cut with it; children who can crawl start dusting; once they are on their feet they participate in fetching and carrying, as they watch adults do these things. Thus a child watching a car being unpacked and shopping being carried into the house, will pick up an object to carry in. In the Under-Twos study, children were reported as taking part in jobs about the house: dusting, stirring the cake-mix, doing the washing up.

> *Mother*: He always has, he takes the dustpan and sweeps down the stairs. But it used to be — just going through the motions. He was copying. Now he does it for real. It's not exactly perfect. But he's taking part, doing it.

Before they could speak, children indicated how the day should be spent. They thus contributed to decisions about what constituted a good day; how family members should spend their time. Though their concern may have been to suit themselves, they were reconstructing the day for the adults, who found themselves being manoeuvred out of the house: towards the playground or round to a friend's; playing ball, showing books, visiting a particular shop. Similarly, 'as every mother knows', children have forceful views on food and drink; will refuse what they do not like and demand, indicating without words until they learn them, what they do want. Again, their contribution is in ordering the events of the day; promoting and provoking activities that fit with their wishes; and in so doing reordering the home.

At a more general level, parents (in line with psychologists) report that children teach parents about how children grow and develop; and about appropriate parental behaviour to meet the growing child's interests.

> *Father*: It gives a lot of happiness watching a child growing, just — you know a bit about how you grow yourself . . . She's changed in the last six months . . . Now if you go out she says 'Bye'. If you say 'Shut up', she says 'Shut up'. You play music, she dances and she says 'Bravo' and claps. If she wants tea, she carries the cup just like that. We communicate better now, she with us, us with her.

Parents of the under-2s indicated a range of ways in which their children participated in constructing family relationships. For a start, changes in the daily routine brought about by the presence of a child led to changes in family customs, and the building of affective strengths.

> *Father*: Our eating pattern has changed completely. I mean we have breakfast — that's a big change in our lives — neither of us ever had

any breakfast before. I used to rush out straight from bed . . . It's changed our eating habit pattern, and it's made the whole family more sociable . . . I think this breakfast together is fantastic. We all sit round. And it's good.

Incorporating children in activities, or doing them because there is a child, led to improved social life for everyone:

Mother: Sundays the three of us spend it together. We do more things [now] and last weekend we went to the Royal Academy to see an exhibition and we took Timothy and we had lunch out at a restaurant . . . I mean he seems to appreciate things and you know he looks at pictures when we go out and he points to them. And he listens to a bit of music.

Most important, children were described by their parents as affectionate people, who take part in constructing relationships with others, and in so doing redefine family relationships.

Mother: He's always loving the baby [three months]. Kissing, hugging her. Trying to give her toys. And if the baby's crying, I tell him to give her her bottle and he'll give it to her.

A mother said in response to the question: what do you enjoy about him?:

What is enjoyable? Oh, when he starts laughing, and comes in [to bed] and goes on you, and kissing you and giving you a hug, when you get up in the mornings. He starts smiling, alright, and when you smile back at him he just roll over and come over you, kissing you.

Children were described by mothers as company, as people with whom a more equal relationship is developing now that they are older.

[compared to when she was younger] I don't think I look after her as much. She is more independent of me now and we're more like chums. It's on a different level. I can't really describe it but it's on a different level. More of – we have our arguments, it's mother and daughter, but it's a different sort of mother and daughter because we have this sort of rapport that we have together. [*Has she changed?*] No, she's always been like it, but she's a lot more forward now than she was. [Mother goes on to say that child is taking over jobs, not just copying, but doing useful things.] I can say to her, 'Can you get me something from over there?' and she'll go and get it for me.

Companionship was valued in the context of the growing ability of the child to take part in social events.

Mother: Now she's like a little person to me [compared to babyhood] . . . the things they do are nice and make you laugh . . . are quite funny . . . If you go out you can just go in somewhere and have something to eat together [instead of having to take babyfood with you].

The constructive character of children's affectionate behaviour, in inter-action with the adults who are in close relationships with them, stretch beyond the immediate family at home, to the wider family.

Mother: With my own mum, before he was born, we each had our own life. Now it's more like a joint effort – watching him grow, being proud of him, both of us. Having him, it's made the whole family closer. She's a gran now, and we talk together about him, make plans, work through problems. I ask her advice now. I never did that before.

And a father, who has been explaining that the extended family lives abroad, speaks of the importance of their first child to the whole family.

Father: It has tied our family together, and brings happiness to us as well. Yes, we . . . I mean we talk as man and wife, sometimes, but you know that something is missing at the same time. So the child is here and it makes quite a difference . . . [*How has it changed your life?*] In the family way, because now we have something to do, that fills our time; the child is here and the atmosphere is different.

These parents, like others whose important relatives lived far away, talked about the value of keeping contact. However tight their budgets, telephoning relatives to talk about the children was important. This was not only to ask advice of experienced mothers and sisters, it also served to strengthen the bonds between family members. The mother, elsewhere in the interview, stressed how lonely she had been, isolated in this country, but that now her child provided company and a focus for her life.

In summary, parental accounts of life with under-2s forcibly suggest that children regard themselves and are regarded as people with contributions to make to the social order of the home. Their learning takes place in the context of events and considerations that matter to both children and their parents, and in the context of deep affection and commitment. And the home provides a social environment in which the detail of children's daily lives is a matter for negotiation, where children are recognized as having rights within the overall moral order.

The perceived competences and contributions of children before they are 2 years old provide the bases for their participation in the division of labour at 5. Linguistic competence by that age, and their experience of social living, provide a complex environment for children's participation. Mothers report that they can do most of the ordinary self-care activities (dressing, etc.); how much depends on other factors: their busyness, motivation and demands on parental time. Similarly, 5-year-olds can and do help around the home, but may find other activities engage them more. As family members they are skilled in negotiation, firmly established as members of the family. How these points work out will be taken up in more detail in the next chapter.

The social order of the school

The primary school presents the 5-year-old with a specific moral order, which differs from that of the home. Three main topics will be considered here. They concern relationships between the moral order of the school and the messages delivered to children; how the knowledge that women may bring to teaching is negotiated in the face of agendas in place in the education and school system; and the use (and abuse) of children's knowledge in school.

The moral order of the school

The moral order of the school as a type of institution comprises both the social order intrinsic to the historical vision of the role of the school, and the formal order required to implement the curriculum. Each particular school will implement too the social order arising from its own traditions and staffing. Though the school as an institution is heavily influenced by psychological theory, its role in society was put firmly in the sociological camp by Durkheim. Faced with what he regarded as a breakdown in political and moral unity consequent on the fall of the monarchy in France, he proposed the school as the social institution that would teach children the social and moral codes of the wider society and 'incline' them towards the collective social life appropriate for citizens. The school was better than the family for this task, since whilst the family's functions were those of 'emotional release and the sharing of affections', the school offered intellectual activity, taking place in a collective environment (Durkheim 1961: 230–6). This functionalist view resonates through commentators' accounts of the role of the school (e.g. Blyth 1965), and through teachers' accounts of their work. For though functionalism may be old-fashioned among theorists, it remains the common-sense model on which people operate in their day-to-day work.

Formally the moral order of the school comprises the teaching and learning of the curriculum and the social customs deemed necessary to ensure that this is done. These may include such demands as: obeying the teacher, fitting in with timetables, behaving in a reasonably orderly and quiet way, not interfering with other children's work. Underlying the formal, overt curriculum there is a vast array of informal agendas, including the moral ethos and social customs of the school (e.g. Jackson 1987; Cullingford 1991). It is the task of the newcomer to learn these and to learn fast, if life at school is to be tolerable (Waksler 1991a); children learn the intricacies of school-appropriate social behaviour through formal instruction and through their interpretive competence in correctly interpreting signals and events (Mackay 1991). Here the reception class teacher at Greenstreet (see pp. 10–11) explains how she has to teach the children school norms:

> very early on there are lots of sessions on the carpet, explaining how we do things, and I might notice that a few of the newer ones obviously haven't grasped that they ask to go to the toilet and so on. So I'll sit again and talk about that . . . I suppose that's what my job's about: making them look after themselves. I think socially, or – yes, I do expect them to look after themselves. And you help to direct them into situations or move them away from a group into another group where you think they'll work better. Or – you know, you are aware of what's going on, but much of the time – not much of the time, some of the time – I leave them to try and resolve situations for themselves, and you know they are supposed to be independent. They know where things are in the classroom, they get things for themselves; they have to find things, put them back, get their own milk out and get the straws out of the packet and then throw them away when they've had their milk.
>
> (Mayall 1994a)

Most discussion about the moral order of the school aims to consider its relationships to children's academic achievements. There are plenty of contradictions for children here: such as the conflict between the demand for individual achievement versus the emphasis on group conformity; and the conflict between schools' valuation of timetables, versus the person's desire to use time as appropriate for the activity she is engaged in. But when we turn to matters of health maintenance we find possibly an even more complex and contradictory scene.

As part of primary classroom teaching, whether through formal health education sessions or, as is more common, through cross-curricular methods, children are given health-maintenance instruction. This will include sessions on what constitutes health-promotive behaviour, and on how children should take responsibility for self-care: for ensuring that they eat well, pace the day, and take exercise. Yet the school probably does not provide an enabling environment for children to maintain their health. In very few primary schools do staff cook the meals or control what is provided; in few do children have any say in what food is provided (SSRU 1994). Schools do not, on the whole, enable children to brush their teeth, nor do they provide places where children can rest. Exercise takes place only when school says it may, and commonly in overcrowded and hostile playground environments.

Thus at Greenstreet, two major confused messages were presented to the children. Independence as a value acquired a school-related definition. The moral order of the school encouraged independence, but becoming independent meant learning conformity to school norms. The independence learned at home did not have currency at school. The reception class teacher quoted above clearly indicates this shift in meaning. And overt messages about good health behaviours conflicted with socially endorsed restriction: children could not enact them. (See Chapter 5 for children's experiences of the regime.) Indeed the very notion of independent health-related activity based on knowledge, choice and decision conflicts with the demand schools make for conformity.

Educational agendas and teacher knowledge

Teacher knowledge bears uneasy relationships with educational agendas. State diktats on educational ideologies, goals and practices have always been topics for discussion and dispute among those nearer the chalk-face (e.g. Blyth 1965; Finch 1984). But innovations in UK national educational policy in the 1980s have provided particularly forcible reminders that ministers think teachers are paid to do a job for the state; the iron hand has been starkly bared. Among these innovations the establishment of a National Curriculum and of testing have been among the most significant, together with governmental emphasis on schools' accountability to parents – which, though a chimera, since parental choice is largely inoperable, has rhetorical value. There is now a clear disjunction between teacher and governmental ideologies. The particular vision of primary education within which primary school teachers have worked – of child-centred policy and practice – was one which was both consistent and acceptable to them: school policy and practice was one with the teaching in developmental psychology they received as trainees (cf. Walkerdine 1984, 1985). As suggested earlier, these developmental theories still hold sway in the hearts and minds of teachers and of their teachers, but governmental views propose a more instrumental vision, focused on the needs of the state rather than on the needs of children (as teachers would define them). In practice, teachers are being required to implement a centrally designed curriculum, and to test children's achievements within it.

It is critical here to consider the joint issues of how child-centredness actually has been operationalized, and how women's knowledge intersects with the formal directives on education. The theory behind teacher enthusiasm for the child-centred curriculum came in for devastating critiques in the years following its endorsement in the Plowden Report (Department of Education and Science 1967) from both educationalists and politicians (see Conner with Lofthouse 1990). The extreme version of it, that children needed only to be given the opportunities for exploratory learning, in terms of equipment and space, with the teacher hovering above, was roundly denounced as ignoring the essential ingredient of learning: interactive discourse. Peters (1969: 16) argued that the Plowden Report 'ignores the inescapably social character of thought and language, of processes of transmission, and of motivation'. Indeed, these criticisms seem to have been widely accepted; interactionism no doubt played a part; and it is said that a minority of primary schools implemented Plowden whole-heartedly: estimates vary from one-third, to one-quarter, to less than 10 per cent, depending on the criteria used and the timing of the estimate (Maclure 1984: 144).

Judging by the teachers whom I have observed in action and discussed their work with, their implementation of child-centredness included endorsement of an interactive approach to learning. They used discussion sessions with individual children to help them through reading, writing and maths tasks. However, in the infant classroom they also provided tables and centres with activities laid out (painting, sand, bricks, water, puzzles, board games, home corner) in recognition of learning through experience and exploration. The teachers did not interfere with children's engagement with these activities, although they controlled when and for how long children could work at them. However, though teachers cite the concept of readiness as evidence of a child-centred approach, definitions of readiness are based not on the individual child but on the age of class groups and the year group (of the school) they are in. What children experience will depend on adult understandings of child-centredness, readiness and developmental stage. These understandings inform the design and layout of the classroom, the delivery of the curriculum, the length of sessions. This theme will be taken up in Chapter 5, but one example makes the point. At Greenstreet, when 'infants' suddenly became 'juniors', they found that the morning was 20 minutes longer, and that play was no longer a recognized part of classroom activities. Their class teacher was surprised when children commented on these points. She had not thought to question the regime. Its suitability for individual children was not an issue.

It is indeed a paradox of the moral order of the primary school, that the rhetoric of child-centredness serves to set in place a rigid adult-controlled social system, based on age and stages. The point was made long ago by Sharp and Green (1975); they were criticized on the grounds that their argument was based on theory rather than on observation of what actually took place (Hargreaves 1978; and see King 1989). But their argument is supported in the work of Valerie Walkerdine (e.g. 1984), which includes some observational work. It certainly squares with the scenes I observed at Greenstreet (see Chapter 5).

In particular it is relevant to note here the importance of the concept of children's 'needs' in the discourse of teachers. What is provided is justified in terms of what children need, although, as has convincingly been argued (Woodhead 1990), such needs are largely cultural constructs, and, of course, devised by adults. The implementation of a regime responsive to child need is through such aspects as the organization of the school day (e.g. length of sessions), the provisions available to the children (e.g. sand), and the pedagogy (e.g. the balance between individual work with the teacher and exploratory self-directed activity). Teachers are themselves components of the structures set up in response to the ideology of children's needs. In this respect they are similarly placed to women working in other branches of the psy complex, such as health visitors and social workers.

Primary school teachers, as women, operate uneasily on two conflicting understandings: of how women should behave and of how teachers should behave in the education system. As I have argued, women at home bring to their relationships with their own children contextualized morality, attention to the individual case; and children's learning is promoted by the emotional bonds they have to the adult and to the topics under consideration. Contextualized morality, Burgess and Carter (1992) argue, holds for the perspectives of first-year trainee teachers: they put high value on personal caring relationships with the children. Indeed the students they interviewed explicitly compared the teacher with the mother: a hurt child should be picked up and cuddled 'just like I would do with one of my own'. For these first-year students, teaching was about bringing out the best in each child or, as one put it, 'being a mother figure'. Other students explicitly linked this mothering role with the classroom as family and class teacher as mother. This vision of the teacher as mother-figure has been traced by Carolyn Steedman (1988), who argued with reference to the early development of pedagogy that the primary school teacher, historically, was to be 'the mother made conscious', combining the educative skills of the middle-class mother with the natural affectionate behaviour of the best of working-class mothers.

However, whilst this vision may be traceable historically in the writings about women teachers, nowadays we have to bring into play the processes of professionalization and their impact on women's knowledge and behaviour. The value of caring for children that young women may bring to their years as student teachers is required to give way to the demands of professionalization. Thus, trainee teachers encountered during my Greenstreet project reported that their school tutors told them not to develop personal relationships with children; instead they must develop an even-handed, distant and equable stance; physical contact must be minimal. King (1989) compared infant and junior teachers observed with their classes: infant-class teachers exuded professional pleasantness, affection and equanimity, and in junior class teachers the professional manner was brisk and business-like. The key word here is 'professional'. Paradoxically, given trainees' initial motivation, becoming a teacher involves acquiring distance from the children. Teachers themselves give a number of reasons for this process. Keeping order and getting the work done require dealing with the children as a class; favouritism is a danger to be avoided. Most importantly, among the teachers I interviewed, the job of the teacher is defined and limited; teaching comes before care. For them, there was a split between the two functions, which for the mother at home are inseparable, the one requiring the other.

In my studies of primary schools, I have found a clear division of labour as to the care of children. Though teachers monitor child well-being, and though they do, observably, care about the children, and do give practical and physical care, it is usually the non-teaching staff who are allocated hands-on care within the informal division of labour: classroom helpers, playground supervisors and the secretary. Staff divide up caring labour broadly according to its two components: caring about (the emotional commitment) and caring for (the activities involved) (Graham 1983). Even the non-teaching staff, however, are faced with conflict between maintaining the social order of the school and caring work. As one playground supervisor said, her job is to control the children's activities and prevent anti-social behaviour, but her interpretation of children's violence in terms of emotional neglect meant that she would much rather pick them up and give them a cuddle.

In practical terms it seems likely that the division of labour understood and practised between the teacher and the non-teaching staff has been reinforced through a number of initiatives: the introduction into classrooms over the last few years of assistants (paid and unpaid women); the emphasis integral to the National Curriculum on teacher's specific knowledge and skill; the increased emphasis coming from governmental directives on delivering a testable product (child achievement); the increase in paperwork – which, simply, takes up a lot of teacher time; and the increase in class sizes. All these factors may contribute to teachers' view that their job is specific and limited to a narrowly defined educative function. The army of non-teaching staff (assistants, supervisors, the secretary) in practice do most of the hands-on care.

There is then a point of tension between the women's ways of knowing and the knowledge they acquire during the process of professionalization. If it is the case that young women entering the world of teaching start with a moral understanding based on contextualizing judgements and actions, and on caring attention to each child, if indeed they do start out wanting to put individual children's knowledge at the centre of their work, then their progress through experience in training, and on the job, is that of adjusting their sights to a social and moral world controlled by larger forces, and one which demands they adopt 'professional' attitudes. These include internalizing the tenets of developmental psychology, which in turn lead teachers to be sure that they know children's needs, and are indeed responding to them by implementing the social norms of the school. Non-teaching staff care for ill children, and do first-aid treatment for children who have accidents, but they too have to work within the control system of the school.

The process whereby women's knowledge becomes subsumed under the knowledge and agendas institutionalized under the public social order is familiar. The same story is told for nurses: student nurses quickly learn that the caring work they thought they were trained and employed to do, becomes defined in ways that then serve to distort and transform it: towards technical decisions, distance, efficiency. This process has been examined for hospital nurses by Ingela Josefson (1988), who provides a dramatic example of a case where a nurse – in the event justifiedly – rejected a young doctor's diagnosis in favour of her own experiential knowledge, which allowed her to recognize the importance of a set of symptoms she observed, but which were not recognized as significant in textbook knowledge. The case of health visitors is also instructive. They are trained nurses with an extra year's training for community work. Their work is not hands-on with children, but educative and supportive work with mothers of young children. Interviews with them indicated that they placed higher value on their book-learning knowledge of child development than they did on their experiential knowledge of child-rearing. They had adopted the public knowledge appropriate for their work as agents of a state surveillance system (Mayall and Foster 1989: 58).

Teachers, school and the evaluation of children's knowledge

The analysis so far suggests that teachers are encouraged to think of the school as a model environment designed for children, with teachers as the holders of the relevant knowledge to provide what children need. In addition, teachers are taught to keep at an emotional and physical distance from the children in their charge. This teacher knowledge and practice provides a general framework within which children's own knowledge is likely to have low status.

It has been observed that though children's knowledge acquired in the pre-school years is regarded (notably in the Plowden Report) as a determinant of the character of school learning, this knowledge – which they continue to acquire outside school – is not regarded as a component of learning at school (Blyth 1980). What children bring from home is suspect in the eyes of many policy makers and teachers, for whom the family, its moral and social teaching, are pathologized. Maternal behaviour and its effects on children's knowledge are widely regarded as a problem, as data from the Greenstreet study (Mayall 1994a: ch. 7) and from others (e.g. Manicom 1984) show.

By and large, the curriculum of the school is designed and implemented without regard for the knowledge children bring to it (e.g. King 1989; Saunders 1989). This stance has been boosted by the introduction of the National Curriculum, which explicitly denies children's knowledge and experience as a determinant of the agenda. The National Curriculum also imposes on the teacher through the sheer weight of the tasks to be accomplished; there will not be time in the day to introduce and develop topics through the knowledge, ideas and suggestions of the children. Indeed a nationally designed curriculum can be regarded as essentially antithetic to the notion of responsiveness at individual level. This has been one of the principal points made by the opposition to it – which is a measure of the strength of child-centred ideology that persists in schools. At Greenstreet children's own contributions were relegated to Sharing Time – once or twice a week when individual children brought items of information or experience to recount to the class.

The inherent conflict between school agendas and children's agendas comes into the open in respect of health maintenance. Children, like other people, have unique knowledge of how to maintain their body and spirit in working order, and this knowledge and the immediate wishes intrinsic to it, is very likely to conflict with the demands of group living and standardized days at school. These conflicts are explored in Chapter 6: how far can children negotiate a reasonably comfortable, health-maintaining daily life within this regime, where staff are accustomed to denying their knowledge and to implementing the formal agenda? Nevertheless, traditions in the education system also include respect for the concept of caring for the whole child (Finch

1984: 77–8): provision of state education has been seen as entailing taking responsibility for the welfare of children, and indeed has been seen as necessary if the central educative functions are to be efficiently carried out. And within that tradition, teachers' concern for children's welfare, however compromised by directives and customs emphasizing professional distancing, will form part of the understandings that inform interactions with the children in their charge.

Children in the division of labour at school

Viewed through the perspectives of sociologists of childhood, children may be regarded as contributors to the division of labour. Through their specialized work of learning at school, in acquiring the knowledge and skills needed for taking up socially accepted activities as adults, they are engaging in both productive and reproductive work. They are also providing work for adults, the childwork analysed by Oldman (1994). This vision turns on its head the vision of teachers, who are more likely to talk in terms of their own hard work to get the necessary knowledge into the heads of the children. For teachers, children are projects for adult work. Children's subjective experience at school therefore can include both contrasting elements: their understanding that they are working; and their understanding that their work is undervalued. Perhaps most critically, children indicate their understanding that their agency is underplayed.

If we now return specifically to the work children do at home – self-care, home maintenance, and affective relational work – we can briefly outline what are likely to be teacher perspectives on children's work at school. Children, as the data will show, have some difficulty in caring for themselves at school. Teachers receive their bids for autonomy with suspicion; and this comprises rejection both of the physical and emotional content of discomfort and of children's rights to participate in discussion about the school's social order. Children asking to get a drink of water, or claiming to be ill, are likely to be faced with suspicion and adjudication of their bid to care for their health.

As to the maintenance and promotion of the school as a healthy environment, school staff do not regard these as appropriate functions for children. As has been noted, they come to a ready-made establishment, provided for them, in their best interests. Few children have any say in how they spend the day, on what division of work, rest and play suits them, on how to rethink playtime to maximize health maintenance and minimize threats to well-being. Though some schools are taking a lead in improving children's democratic rights, by incorporating their views, perhaps the biggest stumbling block is the adult view that the school is a child-centred establishment and that children are not responsible (Cowie 1994). Giving away control is hard for adults trained to believe that children are socialization projects. And as pressure to deliver government targets mounts, teachers are likely to find even less time to work with children's wishes.

Children's engagement with the construction of affective relationships is a further topic to be considered in the next chapter. Friendships and alliances with other children are a major source of interest and concern for children, as several research studies show (e.g. Sluckin 1981; Davies 1982; James 1993). Children's relationships with their teacher are structured through the demand that teachers keep their distance, in tension with the affection and concern teachers feel for the children and children's need to turn, in times of trouble, to someone for help.

Children's social positioning at home and at school

This chapter has considered some features of the home and the school as children's social environments. The aim has been to provide indications of ways in which the adults in each setting think about children, with an emphasis on the knowledge of women, who are the main players. Also of concern have been the more reified features of the two environments: the understandings that are jelled in the structures of the environments. These topics have been considered to indicate some of the main features of the social environment in interaction with which children and adults act and negotiate with each other.

Some general points emerge out of the discussions about children's social positioning at home and at school. Firstly, there are broad differences in adults' understandings of what children are and of appropriate child–adult relationships. Judging by parents' accounts, they see their children as interactive persons from the earliest days, and they see 2-year-olds as constructive agents within the family. Relationships between parents and their children include adult exercise of power, both, perhaps, as a component of adult views of appropriate child–adult relationships and also in the interests of socializing children appropriately. But it is also in mothers' interests to enable children to take over self-care jobs, and to encourage them to help in home maintenance. Affective relations between parents and their children may often be fraught with conflict and battles, but they are based on deep commitment. Thus parent–children relationships have (at the least) a dual character: caring and control. At school, teachers' accounts indicate that they regard the children as characterized within the developmental model, and as the objects of their socializing and curriculum work. Children's self-care work is subjected to the demands of the formal curriculum and school social customs; they play little part in school health maintenance. The organization of the formal and informal curriculum lays out a clear hierarchy with teachers in control over children's activities. Children's own ability to negotiate an acceptable social position and way of life is conditioned by the relatively highly reified models of children and of adult behaviours.

The second broad point concerns the contextualization of children's knowledge and learning. The topics and events which form the basis for children's learning at home constitute part of their experience, and thus have meaning for them in the context of their own lives and relationships. Children's learning at home takes place in the context of mothers' uniquely detailed understanding of their children's knowledge and concerns. At school, however, the central topics (the three Rs) about which children are to learn are abstracted from ordinary daily experience; and the teacher lacks knowledge of the bases for the child's learning. The layout and equipment of the infant classroom are designed to promote exploratory learning, particularly cognitive learning; but the grounding of these explorations in children's social experience and in interactional relationships and discourse is lacking.

Thirdly, and particularly with regard to health: the home presents to the children a coherent moral context; broadly, the proposed moral codes square with the practices. At school, formal education agendas and messages contrast with the regime in place.

These differing moral contexts have implications for the meanings of children's independence. In both settings, independence is construed within the social norms that construct daily life. But whilst at home becoming independent comprises congruence with the social norms; at school it means incongruence, for the formal health messages conflict with the school's social order.

Fourthly, the two social environments provide differing understandings and implementations as to body–mind links. In both contexts adults talk about caring for the whole child, but mothers acquire their learning experientially: they learn there are links between their child's physical, emotional and intellectual health status, wishes and perceived needs, for neglect of one will compromise the others. At school, though concern for the whole child is part of professional understandings, the division of labour separates out responsibility for the intellectual enterprise from physical care; and in classrooms the intellectual takes precedence.

This chapter has proposed that incorporating children into division of labour theory has some promise. It is not only according to classic definitions of work – as contributing to production – that children may be seen as participants. Children also act as agents in reproduction: the production of themselves as people engaged in self-care, and as people contributing to the home as a health-maintenance, affectively supportive environment. Through these activities they take part in the construction of self and the environment.

The discussion here of the home and the school serves as a context for considering in the next two chapters children's own understandings of these social environments and their negotiations with them. Consideration of children's positioning *vis-à-vis* social agencies must put particular emphasis on intergenerational power imbalances. Clearly children largely live out their days within social customs and environments which are either designed with adult interests in mind or, if ostensibly designed for children, are so designed according to adult beliefs and knowledge. This puts children as a social group in a uniquely disadvantaged negotiating position compared to other social groups. In the next chapter, children's own experiences of social environments at home and school are the main topic, described in order to consider agency-structure inter-relationships and interactions. Intercut with these considerations is an attempt to consider body–mind inter-relationships.

five

Children's lived bodies in everyday life

Introduction

The previous chapter described features of the social contexts within which children act. This one will take up the tale to consider those actions, and in so doing will draw together some of the topics discussed earlier.

In Chapter 3 I noted that just as psychology has been concerned with cognition and promoted its value as a discrete phenomenon, so has sociology accepted and perpetuated this focus; the two disciplines have indeed disciplined ways of thinking about thought. The emphasis on cognition, and the complementary splitting of mind and body, have served not only to perpetuate body–mind dualisms in the mind of theoreticians and practitioners, but also to exclude children from consideration as a social group, on the grounds (apart from other grounds) that their cognitive development is in process rather than achieved. Here the concept of cognition is at issue. Important work has been carried out by feminists to challenge these traditions through consideration of women's social positioning. Two strands in this work will be taken up here, in order to consider how they help understanding of children's social positioning. The first is linkages between male social constructions of women and understandings of the significance of their bodies. The second is how women see inter-relationships between bodies and minds.

Many writers have pointed to the ways in which malestream thought has interlocked constructions of women's bodies with those of their social positioning. Women's capacity for reproduction and the physical characteristics of the reproduction system have been grounds for assigning women to the bodily and emotional; and for limiting women to the private sphere (e.g. Rich 1977; Gilligan 1993). Ann Oakley has documented the history of men's taking over of women's reproduction in order to show how physical and social domination have been achieved (1984). Sara Ruddick summarizes the catalogue of subjection:

> Reason is associated with mind, objectivity, detachment, culture, impersonal concern, public order and agreement. The body in turn is associated with subjectivity, passion, nature, particular affections, domestic confinement, parochial prejudice, and irresolvable difference. A rational person is one for whom the capacities and values associated with reason control and order the properly subordinated capacities represented by the body.
>
> (Ruddick 1990: 194)

The feminist reconsideration of dominant social constructions of women's 'natural role' and 'natural (inferior) capacities' has required challenging these, and, most importantly, rethinking knowledge. As Hilary Rose (1986: 161) says: 'Human knowledge, whether of the arts or sciences, comes from practice, from working on and changing the world. As people work on nature and transform it, they gain knowledge of how nature – including their own nature – is organised and may be explained.' Women's experiences of childbirth and childcare can and should be reconsidered in terms of experiential understanding of body–mind links. These experiences, the care of their own and their baby's body, and the work of child-rearing provide a complex of inter-related activities. In considering these it becomes misleading to talk about the relative contributions of the mind, body and emotion, and essential to recognize that women's understanding challenges the traditional format of discrete concepts. Learning based on experience and reconstructed through the activities of caring about and caring for produces a fusion: experiential embodied knowledge and activity.

Women's exploration of their knowledge has provided a context for challenging the social order in general. Emily Martin (1989) argues that study of women's experiences and daily lives requires challenging received conceptual distinctions between the public and the private. Women move between home and paid work taking with them and managing their physical and emotional lives in the social world of the workplace constructed by men without reference to these. Thus the idea of the public domain (rational, non-bodily, impersonal and detached) is challenged by women who bring what is designated as private (emotional, bodily, personal, involved) into the public. She shows too how women, armed with their experiential knowledge, challenge dominant assumptions: the private domain is of value, not as the emotional reproductive back-up to the rational productive public domain, but as a source of knowledge valuable in promoting a healthy social order.

An important dimension of female experience of their bodies is explored by Iris Young (1980), who points to the socially determined constriction of girls and women to narrower spaces – both physical and social – within which they may act. She draws on observation of how girls and boys use their bodies both in ordinary day-to-day movements and in sport, and argues that 'a space surrounds them [women] in imagination which we are not free to move beyond; the space available to our movement is a constricted space' (Young 1980: 143). Further, she argues, women live their bodies as object, in the sense that a patriarchal society defines them as object, as 'a mere body'. Young is contrasting female with male experience and behaviour; and the school playground graphically illustrates how girls' activity – how they deploy their bodies and how much playground space they use – differs from boys' activity. One may also extrapolate from Iris Young's analysis to consider child–adult relationships: how children's bodies are constricted and defined to suit the adult-controlled social worlds, both at home and at school.

The incorporation of children into sociology should reinforce the centrality of embodied experience in everyday life, since children's learning is a basis for life-long knowledge. Children learn that their social value depends partly on the evaluation of their embodied activity. Broadly, at both home and school children are required to submit their bodies to adult control and restriction, but home offers emotional and moral approval of bodily achievement as an end in itself, whereas school sees bodily control as a means to an end. Children's body work at home – working to take control of bodily functions – provides them with knowledge of how bodily behaviour links into the social order. In the first two years of life, children find that their achievements in skills such as walking, eating with fingers, spoons and cups, excreting in socially acceptable times and places receive social approval. Their own intimate knowledge of links between their bodies, feeling and minds is constructed and reconstructed through parental recognition, that is, their perception of their social value is embodied perception. Older children bring their bodies with them into the public world of school, and endeavour to maintain some control over them in a social context which both devalues and regulates the body. But, once they get to school, children find little scope for the enactment and development of their bodily achievements, nor do they meet delighted adult recognition of them. As will be suggested, children, like women, have little power to change the cognitive emphases of the school's social order. Their subjection to its order is paradoxical, since it is only through building on their knowledge that schools are likely to be effective teachers.

Feminist work on the body, and on inter-relations between bodies and minds, outlined here has, in short, opened up for debate political as well as sociological issues: the conduct of social affairs in the workplace; the contributions of women, children and men there; and the social construction of the public–private divide. Yet the feminist contribution has not been of central concern in recent male work on the sociology of the body. The last ten years have seen a number of theoretical discussions by male sociologists. The literature reviews and reconsideration of social theory carried out by Turner (1992) and Shilling (1993) do pay tribute to feminist work as one major strand, but do not recognize its central theoretical and political import. Perhaps the deliberations of Turner and Shilling about bodies in relation to cognition are structured by their cognitive approach. Social constructionism, as constructed within these ivory tower debates, has found it difficult to find a place for the physical body. Women, who are used to living with their bodies, have less difficulty in living with a theoretical framework in which bodies are both constructed through social relationships and social power, and themselves participate in the construction of social relationships (see Howson 1994). However, both these writers have put the body firmly on the sociological map – as Turner says, the initial point that human bodies have to be regulated, coerced, trained, modified in the interests of changing nature into culture requires a theory of body–mind relations and interactions (1992: 15). Both Turner and Shilling argue for recognition of embodied living and for the potential of the body – how it is elaborated by culture and developed in personal relations.

One of the central themes discussed in current work on the sociology of the body is the issue: in what sense can we say that people have bodies. One proposition here is that people are conscious of their bodies only when they go wrong; 'As long as we are healthy, nothing strikes us about our bodies. However, when our well-being is disturbed, one notices one's body' (Buyten-dijk, in Leder 1990). This proposition has been used to account for the absence of the body in sociological theory, where the person has been understood less as an embodied self and more as a rational (or non-physical) agent. But this proposition runs counter to the perception of most people, for whom the lived body in health (as well as in deviations from it) is critical to their experience and knowledge. In daily life, the task of managing one's body in social worlds constructed for young healthy male adulthood makes the body ever present to those who deviate from that norm. Both young and old people recognize and experience the natural changes attendant on, respectively, growing up and growing old (Hockey and James 1993). Acquiring a will of one's own, secondary sexual characteristics, grey hair and changes in eyesight are important experiences but not in themselves problematic, though they may be defined as such – the terrible 2s, the Sturm und Drang of adolescence, the decline and fall of middle age. Again we may fruitfully compare women with children, and consider the relationships between them in the light of their experiences of their bodies. As Emily Martin (1989) documents, women's bodily changes, through the month, through pregnancy and childbirth, through the menopause are present to them in the private and public domains: as embodied living, experienced bodily and emotionally across a gamut of feelings from positive and welcomed to negative and rejected. And women's day-to-day people work forces them to recognize the bodily, and interlinkages between bodily and emotional well-being.

In particular, children are conscious both positively and negatively of their bodies, in daily encounters during their early years. Their bodies are present to them through the behaviour of adults. Not only are they routinely and affectionately handled by adults (dressing, toileting, hugs, lifting), but they are also encouraged to think about their bodies, as mothers urge them to eat, take them through the processes of toilet-training, praise their physical achievements. Establishing the normalcy of one's child includes discussion between mothers, above the listening ears of their children, on the minutiae of growth and development. And adults comment on children's rapid growth, size and beauty. More negatively, children's bodies are subject to regulation: not to hit out at others, to confine excretion to certain places and times, to accept confinement in buggies and car-seats. Increasing age brings bodily responsibilities: not to hit your younger sib, to sit still at meal-times, to hold hands across the road. Children themselves, as Allison James (1993: ch. 4) describes, consider their physical growth as a marker of status – when I'm big, I'm going to big school. She also notes how children (aged 4 years) show their ancient scars, not so much, she argues, to get adult sympathy, but as part of their thinking about their embodied social identities, developed over time, through bodily encounters.

Women's relationships with their children are constructed and reconstructed through the care of children's bodily and emotional well-being. Typically mothers can describe in detail changes they observe in their young children, and will consider what balance of physical and emotional factors may account for these changes. Thus in the *Keeping Children Healthy* study (Mayall 1986), we asked mothers what recent changes in their child they had noticed. The range of changes identified by mothers included the following: changes in appearance (eyes, skin, hair), in appetite and energy, in breathing patterns, temperature, mood, desire for physical contact, crying; the emergence of aches and pains (in head, ears, stomach, arms or legs), vomiting, diarrhoea, runny nose, cough, spots and rashes, swelling or inflammation, cuts, bruises. We then asked what, if anything they had done about any changes they had observed, what they thought caused changes and whether they were a sign of anything; also whether they were worried by change, talked to anyone about it and/or sought help. Here are some examples of the notes we made on mothers' accounts about some of the minor events (mothers also reported more serious ones).

> Change in appetite – it happens about once in every three months or so. He often goes through that. He goes off his food sometimes for three days. It was last week. He drinks plenty of milk so I put a rusk in his bottle, but when I gave him his food he turned his nose up at it. He only ate a biscuit, tinned soup, milk and rusk. He's too lazy to eat. [*Why do you think it happened?*] He was a bit irritable – it might have been because I began putting him on the pot. And he wasn't sleeping very well. He'd get up four or five times in the night for a couple of nights. He does that quite frequently. He wasn't ill. He was playing as usual. Perfectly alright. [*Were you worried?*] No, because if he doesn't want to eat you can't force him. I told my husband, I told my mother and father because they had him one evening – and I said, don't force him to eat, just put a rusk in his bottle.
>
> (Mother of boy aged 23 months)

At the end of last week [seven days ago] she was a bit ratty and really tired, you could see the cold coming on. No, she's over it now. She did lose her appetite for a day or two. So I just offered her less [food]. It lasted about two days. She had a cough and a runny nose. She was a bit heavy round her eyes – and she's got big eyes and when she's got a cold you can always tell, because they, the lids are heavy as if she's just going to fall asleep.

(Mother of girl aged 35 months)

Both of them had a drink of orange juice and they both brought it straight back up. They were out in the garden. It was because it was so hot and they were so hot and bothered. It only happened once, about four weeks ago. I was a bit worried. I brought them in and cooled them down a bit, gave them a good wash – in a warm bath, and put a T-shirt on them and let them play in here [living room]. They cooled off and calmed down. I just talked to my neighbour opposite [about it] – because I take them in there sometimes, and she said it must be the heat.

(Mother of boy and girl aged 25 months)

It was August, my friend's wedding. She went to the wedding, to the reception in a flat, 30 people in a flat this size, and no other children. She screamed and bawled a bit. She didn't like all those people making all that noise. Yes, I was worried: I don't like her crying, so we left quite early. I just stayed with her more, held her, kept on trying to give her bits of cake to make her happier. It went on for two hours, lots of people said, 'What's the matter – is she teething?' It was difficult, because people kept trying to take her [pick her up] and that started her off again and made her worse.

(Mother of girl aged 18 months)

These four examples, typical of many, indicate mothers' knowledge of the range of their child's normal behaviours and moods. They show how mothers assume that the physical, social and the emotional are interlinked. Interpretation may include both physical and social factors: thus a child going off his food may be reacting to toilet-training. The examples indicate knowledge of minor adjustments that will restore well-being or alleviate distress. They also show how mothers manipulate children's bodies and emotions as a linked enterprise to restore their children's well-being.

Children at home – constructing and reconstructing bodies and minds

Children's control over their health maintenance is the topic under discussion here. This implies consideration of how, and how effectively, they manage their bodies, their minds and their emotions to preserve a sense of well-being. Children's social positioning, how they interact with, negotiate with and resist adult approaches and practices will be considered, taking in turn children's daily experiences at home and school, in the context of the points outlined in the previous chapter. To recap: four main points were made about factors affecting children's experiences in the two settings. Firstly, child–adult relationships are structured by the specifics of adult understandings of children; and parents and teachers differ here. Secondly, experiential learning at home contrasts with abstracted learning at school. Thirdly, the degree of 'fit' between moral precepts and practices differs in the two settings. Finally, the home and school provide differing understandings and implementations of body–emotion links.

Here data from 5- and 9-year-olds is explored to consider their understandings of their social position at home. I would argue (with Freund 1990) that contentment with one's embodied self is mediated through emotional feedback on one's performance. During the first three years or so, children's newly acquired competence, in one area after another – grasping, using tools and toys, feeding, walking, excretion – attracts praise for their bodily skills from parents – who are glad to recognize that their child is doing well, and glad to relinquish some basic babycare tasks. Children's increasing linguistic ability also calls forth praise, and allows them fuller understanding of and participation in the enthusiasm with which adults greet their accomplishments. Yet children's own work and their acquisition of knowledge is devalued through the psy complex; and so too is mothers' and fathers' delighted experience of their children's achievements. The emphasis by health and welfare professionals is on mothers' responsibilities for socialization work.

Self-care

Broadly, at 5, Greenstreet children's accounts indicate that they had both the relevant knowledge of and competence to carry out self-care activities under the overall care of their mothers, while at 9 they were fully competent, although in most cases their mothers supervised them. Two 5-year-olds speak first, about their early morning activities. Both 5- and 9-year-olds assumed that they controlled self-care, in the sense that they had the means and the encouragement to do it.

> *John*: I got up and I had Ready Brek. You can put sugar on it to make it tasty. You mix it with milk. I got dressed, and I got my bag and my apple and brought it to school.

A second example:

> *Dan*: I wash me first.
> *I*: Yourself? [sceptical adult]
> *Dan*: Yes, my face, my hands. I get dressed. I put my shoes on, on my own. I get ready for school, I get my book. I remember it, to bring it back.
> *I*: Do you have breakfast?
> *Dan*: Yes, I have my breakfast. Toast, banana, Piedmont.

I: What's that?

Dan: It's apple juice, it's sparkling. Then we go to school with my daddy or my mummy. I cross the street by the lollipop lady.

These boys had just started in the reception class, and their accounts of what they did at home indicated pleasure, pride and confidence in their achievements there. One of these is to slot together the worlds of home and school: remembering to take back the book borrowed overnight and put an apple in your school-bag.

This next boy was a year older, in the same class. He was more matter of fact; his account suggests an established pattern, that he did not even think about, but accomplished as a matter of routine.

Chris: Well, I get up and put on my, always my dressing gown and my slippers. And I have breakfast: cornflakes and milk and sugar. Then I wash and clean my teeth. Then I get dressed and go to school.

As a context for understanding Greenstreet children's experiences of school, I asked them to talk about and draw pictures of what kept them healthy. Of the 21 reception class children who took part, 15 mentioned food and 9 dental care; 8 mentioned taking exercise. These numbers are higher proportionately than in the large-scale Southampton study (Williams *et al.* 1989); presumably because I used more than one method, in less formal circumstances, than in that study. In the following conversation two 5-year-olds discuss their part in health care.

I: Do you do things to keep healthy?

Sandra: Not really.

Rita: Not really.

Sandra: Not really at school.

I: Or at home?

Sandra: Well, we do at home.

I: What do you do at home?

Sandra: Well, allergies of milk, so . . .

I: Are you allergic to milk?

Sandra: Yeah. So you know I have to eat lots of vegetables, no milk, that all the time. It's really boring, but I am allowed chocolate.

I: So what do you have in your tea? Do you have tea? Or on your cereal? Do you have soya milk?

[Sandra explains how the seal on the soya milk container kept coming off into the milk, so now they don't have it.]

I: What other things do you do to keep yourselves healthy?

Rita: Well we don't do very much.

Sandra: Brush our teeth.

Rita: Yeah, we brush our teeth and we, we, I drink lots of milk to keep my teeth nice and white.

I: They're very white.

Rita: That's because I drink lots of milk.

Sandra: I had my new milk-free cornflakes today, that means without milk. And I had juice in it and it was lovely.

Rita: I'm allowed to have anything.

I: So whose job is it to keep you healthy, do you think?

Rita: Mum and Dad.

Sandra: Mum and Dad.

Rita: And yourself.

Sandra: And yourself.

I: How about your teacher, do you think your teacher cares whether you are healthy or not?

Sandra: Not really.

Rita: Not really.

I: Do you think your teacher knows when you're not well and stuff?

Sandra: Yeah, we have to tell her.

Noticeably, these two girls see the home as the site of health care, and mothers rather than teachers as the relevant adults. Sandra's milk allergy had probably led to her specific experiential knowledge and familiarity with conversations about food. Diet and dental care emerge as front-runners in health care practices. Responsibility for care was split between parents and children.

The following account (by an 8-year-old) takes up the discussion of the character of the moral code as implemented at home, compared to school. Children's control over the day's activities was seen as higher at home; in particular, the opportunities and freedom to take exercise were greater. On the other hand, home could be boring.

Erica: You can lay in; watch telly all day. You can go swimming, and you can't do that at school unless you go to swimming lessons. You can play with your friends at home, like you can go out in the garden whenever you want. You don't have to, because you, cos there's certain rules at school, there's more rules at school than there is at home, and out on the playground, isn't there?

I: Are there bad things about home?

Erica: Yeah, sometimes I get bored, sometimes I get bored at home. That's about it.

Nine-year-olds were very familiar with the language of health care. Asked to note down what kept them healthy, most mentioned food (22 of 25) and exercise (22); nine mentioned hygiene – including dental care. It thus seems that both age groups had taken aboard adult messages about health maintenance – at least at the level of responding to adult questions. As will be seen later, for children at school issues of food and physical activity (including play) were uppermost in their minds as problematic areas, where school imposed restrictions.

The question whether they should take responsibility for their health was a debating issue, with some emerging gendered aspects.

I: Whose job is it to keep you healthy?
Bob: Mum's.
Harry: Your mum has to keep telling you to do your teeth and washing your hands, because you never like –
I: She has to?
Harry: Yes, because you might not want to.
Enid: I do my teeth because I want to, because I don't want to have fillings.
Bob: I do, without her telling me.
Harry: My mum always has to tell me.
Richard: Same with mine.
Bob: And they tell you to wash your hands. You have to be told, when you get your hands dirty.

In this conversation, all four children note that they are people who want to do or not do certain things. The boys emphasize their wish not to take sole responsibility, while the girl stands for doing so. However, the issue of how far to take responsibility for one's own body is a matter for debate, as the following top-speed conversation shows.

I: Whose job is it to keep you healthy?
Anita: Our mum.
Pat: Our dad.
Tim: It's mainly our job.
David: Mainly.
Tim: Because we're the ones . . .
David: . . . we're the ones that have to take care of ourselves. Like, when we live by ourselves we will.
Tim: So we should, like, do that. We're keeping ourselves healthy by doing things ourselves. It's my body, so it's my job.
Anita: It's us mainly. We do it. Sometimes! Like your mum and dad, they might nag you, take your vitamins, or whatever, eat your greens. But we're the ones who do it. Our mums and dads do encourage us to eat things, take vitamins, so that's partly. But us, mainly.

These two excerpts suggest strongly that these children assume it is appropriate for them to do things, with or without reminders. As one mother said, her son was not acting entirely independently, since he knew she expected him to do certain things, and she would check if she thought he was 'idling'. Whilst defining their parents as having a role to play in staking out the rules and reminding you of them, the children are saying that responsibility for acting is shifting to them.

Contributions to home maintenance

Both mothers and children referred to contributions children made to the social order of the home. With under-2s, mothers' accounts suggest that children were taking the initiative in engaging in the work of home maintenance (Mayall and Foster 1989: 25). With 5-year-olds, most mothers report asking children to help in order to accustom them to the idea of responsible participation. Children, however, suggest that at 5 they regarded the contribution they made as real, in response to the moral code of the home. In this respect one can see a development over the years of childhood, as described in other studies, for instance, Fortes' study of Tale children (1970). For those children by the age of 9, as for the children studied here, jobs were for real in the eyes of mothers too.

The interactive character of the establishment and reconstruction of the social order is indicated at the conversational level in the following extracts from an interview with a mother, with her 5-year-old son, Bill, contributing:

Mother: He's much more mature now, more responsible, dresses himself in the morning.

Bill: My teeth.

Mother: Sometimes brushing your teeth. And he's willing to take his share. For instance, we were out shopping and size for size he did, he carried some bags. He started saying, 'I'm only little', but in the end he did, and he was running home at the end, so he could carry them.

I: What do you think are the most important ways of keeping him healthy?

Mother: He did have trouble going to the loo. I found when he was with his Dad [who lives elsewhere] he wasn't eating fibre. So now he has bananas.

Bill: I do eat bananas . . .

Mother: I wish he'd eat more green veg. He won't eat anything hot.

Bill: I will eat cucumber.

Mother: Yes you do eat cucumber. Yes, you do eat cucumber and tomatoes. But he won't eat any hot vegetables. I know it's not sensible [i.e. of mother to think that], but I think he should.

Bill: I do eat eggs and cheese!

I: Do you have any rules?

Mother: Oh, dear, it's mainly don't hurt each other . . . I don't like it if they keep punching each other.

Bill: Not break the furniture up!

Mother: Yes! What else, Bill?

Bill: No chocolate –

Mother: – unless they've eaten something decent beforehand.

Bill: No smashing the windows!

And so on. This 5-year-old and his mother suggest a shared understanding both of what is expected, and of how behaviour is negotiable within the overall limits set by the mother.

Children commonly described negotiation and the flexibility of the moral order as attributes of home. These two 5-year-old girls discuss the relative merits of home and school with an emphasis on how adult control varies between the two. At school you have to do things. At home there is more negotiating power.

I:	What do you like best about being at home?
Sandra:	Um, not, not, nothing much.
I:	Nothing much? Do you prefer being at school?
Sandra:	Yeah, I prefer being at school. Do you, Rita?
Rita:	Well, not really.
Sandra:	I do because it's fun. It's not all fun, because sometimes we do boring work.
Rita:	Sometimes we have to do really boring things and . . .
Sandra:	[shouting] . . . and sometimes we have to do really hard things that we can't even do!
Rita:	And sometimes when we don't want to do something, the teachers won't let us not do it.
I:	So you have to do things at school?
Rita:	Yeah. Sometimes we don't have to.
I:	Do you have to do things at home?
Sandra:	No, not really.
Rita:	Well, my mum tells me to put my stuff away. I don't really.
Sandra:	I don't really, either.

It was noticeable that among those 5-year-olds who had younger sibs, numbers of jobs and levels of responsibility taken were higher, according to mothers, than where the child had no sibs. This was true of both girls and boys.

I:	Does she look after herself more, or less, nowadays?
Mother:	Yes, and also, being an older sister, she does a lot for the little one [aged 3] too. Like helps her with her shoes; putting her clothes on the right way. Everything: she gets food and drinks for her from the fridge; she takes her to the toilet, gets the toilet paper for her. All that sort of thing.
I:	And she does all that for herself too?
Mother:	Oh, yes. She's not very good on laces, though. That's about the only thing.
I:	And do you think she should do more – or less, nowadays?
Mother:	No, I'm happy. She does a lot. Very much. It's more than a lot do, I get the impression. She remembers things. She reminds me of things I have to do, like, you've got to give me my dinner money. She's very good on things like that.

Similarly, a mother talked about her 5-year-old son's participation and helpfulness.

I: Does he look after himself more, or less, nowadays?

Mother: He gets dressed himself. He makes his own bed, and he makes [his two younger sibs'] beds. He wants to go across the road to the shop, because he wants to help with the shopping. But I've told him, we're waiting for a year till he's 6.

I: Have things changed recently?

Mother: He's found out that he's got more responsibility. In the playground – he knows what he can do and can't do, and what he can and can't take to school. He told me, I have to take indoor shoes to school – I have to take off my outdoor shoes when I get there. He tries to be teacher at home, he teaches the others [sibs] how to do things, and he acts the teacher, copying Miss X. He does housework, he washes up, makes beds, polishes, not very well. He'll tidy up my bedroom for me. He's great.

Children were thus engaging in household routines and taking aboard parental edicts about what was good and bad. In both the above quotations as in the second in this section, an important new responsibility children took on was linking the worlds of home and school. They knew the minutiae of school requirements: to return the book borrowed overnight, to make sure mothers provided dinner money on the right day, to remind mothers that indoor shoes should be provided and taken to school. Thus, though mothers do much of the liaison work with schools (see Chapter 6), children themselves play an important part, from their first school days.

Both 5- and 9-year-olds indicated their understanding that their mothers (in some cases their fathers) provided the moral order, with which they negotiated. Both groups identified parental control over personal care and home maintenance activities as structuring their daily lives, though the older children experienced parental control as stronger and more irksome. They also perceived that parents regulated the home and children in the interests of adult agendas.

Peter: Like my mum. She only lets me have an hour on the computer.

Ian: It's so boring. They reckon I've got better things to do – it's so boring!

I: Like what?

Ian: Cleaning my room, having a bath, or being out in the garden, or and play with my friends – even if they're out. Or being bored! I'd spend two hours, three hours [i.e. on the computer] –

Peter: – you can do tunes on it.

Ian: Any computer you can put games on it.

Peter: I'd play on it.

Ian: My dad gets as much time as he likes on his computer.

Peter: He's an adult!

Ian: Adults can do what they like.

Peter: They can go out. They say, 'Right now, you go and clear the table.' They just drink something and read the newspaper and do the crossword. They're allowed to drive. They can can drive to Switzerland if they like. They don't get bored! [laughter]

These 9-year-old boys were playing conversational games, amusing themselves (and the interviewer) by levelling attacks on adults. However, this dialogue resonates with other comments on parental power to limit and condition children's activities; and on children's lack of autonomy, compared to adults'.

At 9 children were clearly aware that the social order of the home needed maintenance through family members' contributions. They were willing to modify their own life-style, regulate their own body and emotion as part of family life: to take on some tasks, within the context of negotiation. So health care was understood as comprising more than personal care.

Constructing and maintaining the social order of the home, according to both the children and the mothers, is a matter of negotiation. Rules are made by the adults, but how and when they are implemented depends on consideration of relevant factors, including family history and habits, child characteristics, child age, the particular circumstances at the time, including the child's mood or recent experiences, and the desirability of keeping the peace. An interview with mother and daughter both contributing (like that recorded above with Bill) indicated something of how discussions and shared understanding help to determine the girl's behaviour at home.

Mother: She organizes her own clothes basically.

I: In what sort of way?

Mother: Well, she sometimes washes things.

Kate: Me? Wash my clothes? I never do!

Mother: Yes, you do. Occasionally, you wash them at the weekend.

Kate: Not often.

Mother: Basically what I mean is that she chooses what she's going to wear and sorts it out and manages to get into her clothes, which is reasonable; and occasionally she will wash some small things.

Kate: Occasionally.

I: Is there any other way she's looking after herself?

Mother: Yes, I supppose lately you've started making meals for everybody, haven't you? Saturday lunch you make.

Kate: And making sure I cut my nails. I've got a habit of biting them; I used to have them long but this year I've been biting them much more.

Mother: Yes, she's been very bad this year.

I: So Saturdays you make lunch?

Mother: Yes, most Saturdays she does it. That's perhaps your Saturday job. Occasionally it gets missed, that's because we're doing other things. Sometimes the system breaks down.

Kate: Actually it breaks down so much I've only done it – four –?

Mother: You've done it quite a lot, no, well you've done it lots of times.

Kate: Twice then.

[Later, the interviewer reverts to jobs]

I: Does she – do you – have any jobs around the house, apart from making lunch?

Mother: Not specifically, no. What she tends to do is that when things are in crisis she's very good at helping then. So when we are overwhelmed with work, she is really quite good.

Kate: And I always set the table, that's another one.

Mother: Oh, that's true, you always set the table.

As presented to the interviewer, this girl's self-care is more or less in her own hands as regards everyday actions. Her mother said as regards washing, brushing teeth: 'We don't have rules, she just does it.' She was also forcefully pro-active in deciding how she and her mother should spend the day.

Mother: Very often if I don't particularly feel like it and I say 'Shall we go swimming?' in a voice that suggests I'm not particularly keen to go, she'll be keen to go. She's probably much more sporty than I am, with exercise and fresh air. She probably, well, not instigates it, but is a mover in that more than I am.

During the interview, when we were talking about how she stays healthy, Kate said: 'That reminds me. I've forgotten my cod liver oil' – and went off to take it.

The data suggest that girls do more in company with their mothers than boys do. One example is the preparation of packed lunches, where girls more than boys reported doing this, with mothers' help. Gender was also an issue, especially among the children from poorer backgrounds, as to the weight of domestic responsibility: especially in their written accounts, girls, and especially the two ethnic minority girls, reported being required (rather than asked) to do housework, and noted that the boys in their families did little or none. This fits with other data, for instance the data analysed (not by social class) by Anne Solberg (1990): the time spent in housework was highest for women, then girls, boys and men, in descending order.

Children's contributions to relationships at home

The data from 5-year-olds does not permit of comment on how they saw relationships at home, although as suggested above, some children were described by their mothers as looking after younger sibs. Mothers' accounts of children's activities at home suggest (unsurprisingly) their affection for and pride in their children (see also Newson and Newson 1970; Tizard and Hughes 1984). By and large the children's own accounts suggest an undifferentiated account of mothers and of fathers – they did not discuss individual characters and relationships; but as noted earlier, the character of the control mothers exercised was the main specific point that emerged.

For the older children, there is fuller data. The association of girls with their mothers in carrying out household maintenance acts in complement to apparent differences in 9-year-old girls' and boys' relationships with their mothers. More of the girls' accounts suggested close relationships with their mothers than of the boys' accounts. This suggestion may be a function of boys' view that such relationships should not be spoken of. But it does fit with other data: Gunilla Halldén (1994) found that boys' stories about their future families contained fewer accounts than girls' did of mothers as the managers of the family and of relationships between children and parents.

However, gendered distinctions are not clear-cut in these studies. Several Greenstreet boys, in their writing (which was private, as the group conversations were not), described their family relationships. One wrote of their new baby, whom he helped to look after. Another, who had great difficulty with writing, nevertheless wrote an account of his mother's sadness – deriving from her work; and explained how he tried to comfort her. Like some of the girls, boys talked about doing things with mothers – such as cooking, going on expeditions, talking about the day's events.

Both boys and girls gave fewer detailed accounts of interactions with their fathers. In some cases fathers lived away from the family, in many they were out long hours. Fathers featured mostly as people with whom there were specific activities – going on an expedition; or as having specific single noteworthy characteristics: such as insisting on table manners, being good at mechanics, being irritable.

The children's accounts suggest that by the age of 9 they felt a sense of responsibility for other people, in that they knew their own behaviour impacted on that of others in the family, and others' behaviour affected them. They were thus constructing themselves as people who build relationships. This finding links with the points made by Judy Dunn (1984: ch. 4): children of 5 or 6 tend to use concrete terms ('He hits me when he gets mad') to describe their sibs, whereas older children will use more abstract terms – 'she's kind', 'she's mean' – and will comment on a wider range of aspects of the sib's personality. In the Greenstreet study 9-year-old children noted tensions between the competitive and hostile behaviour of both themselves and their sibs to each other, and also the pleasures of playing harmoniously together. Hostility and affection had to be negotiated and managed. As one boy wrote: 'I like my brother – sometimes we play rugby together, but sometimes I don't because he can be a pain. And then I don't like him because he can pull my hair really tight.'

The character of living at home was described by both girls and boys in terms of whether or not it provided opportunities for social interaction (school scored higher here: it provided the company of other children). But, as above, interactions with family were a source of both difficulty and pleasure, as Alison's written account shows.

> *Alison*: I like being at home because I mainly like to be with my family, and I also like it at home because it's cosy and I like reading in my room. I don't like being at home because my brother can be a pain sometimes, and every time the phone rings it's for my mum. She usually takes an hour or so, but otherwise I like it at home. My mother sometimes says I have to hoover the stairs which I absolutely hate. I like to be with my mum because she's friendly and I mainly like living with her. My dad can be a pain like my brother – he can be grumpy over nothing, which I hate. Living with my brother is OK, I suppose. But otherwise all that, I love to live with my family.

In very many of the children's accounts, both written and spoken, animals figured as members of the family. Boys' and girls' relationships with these animals were recorded as unproblematically positive; whilst people answer back, pets do not, and giving them affection was not complicated by social norms about maintaining distance and hiding emotions.

Children at school – constructing and reconstructing bodies and minds

In this section the order of events is as for life at home: how the children see self-care; contributions to school maintenance; and relationships. The issues of concern are children's sense of control, their desire to do things and achieve things, and how they understand adult ordering of the social environment.

Self-care

Data from 5-year-olds indicate that their self-care practices at home were not current at school. The social order of the school assumed that children's health maintenance was ordered through school practices and determined by the demands of the formal curriculum. Such important matters as getting a drink or going to the lavatory were not within their control, but conditioned by school agendas. Control over food consumption was a major issue (see pp. 123–8). This conversation between the interviewer, Sandra and her mother indicates Sandra's experience of social control at school.

> *I:* And what about if you want to go to the lavatory?
> *Sandra:* Well, you have to ask Miss X.
> *I:* And does she let you go?
> *Sandra:* Sometimes.
> *I:* Why does she sometimes not?

Mother: Do you think sometimes if you've just come back from play, or if you're just going to be going to play in a couple of minutes?

Sandra: No, if you've just come back from play and you want to get a drink or you need to go to the toilet, she says 'No, because you had all that time to get it in the playground.'

I: So can you go and get a drink when you want one?

Sandra: Well, you have to ask the teacher first and if she says, 'No', you can't. Then if she says 'Yes', you can.

I: Sometimes she says 'No'?

Sandra: Yeah, sometimes.

I: Do you know why that is?

Sandra: Because she wants you to get your work done. Because she thinks if you go while you're doing your work, sometimes you stay there for a long time and you don't want to finish your work, that's why you stay there.

I: Is that true?

Sandra: Sometimes, sometimes people don't finish their work, they stay at the drinking fountain and they come back when it's playtime.

Children's physical activity was limited through the implementation of school routines. The reception-class day included many occasions demanding strict physical conformity. The day began with the class sitting on the carpet with the teacher, again before morning break, dinner break and afternoon break and finally at the end of the day for last discussion of the day, the next day and story-time. Lining up was also a frequent ritual of the day – for each of the three breaks and for expeditions to assembly, the school library and gym.

The demand made by the school regime for control over the body and emotions was powerful. Sitting on the carpet had a precise character: crossed legs, folded arms, no touching of other children, eyes front (towards the teacher). Lining up was also a strictly defined social event: movement was to take place only on the word Go! Requisite behaviours included due but not undue speed towards the line, lining up in single file, not jostling or pushing in, keeping your arms to yourself, not shouting. Infringements were quickly identified and reprimanded. A boy's enthusiasm to get to the playground and a girl's slow movement both called up comment. As the teacher explained, it was not just that 20 or more children had to be regulated, in the interests of preventing chaos, but that half her job was to get the children used to the 'way we do things here' (see p. 75). A mother here asks her daughter, who has just started school, how she got on:

Ros: We had the telly on, but we had to keep still. We had to sit on the carpet, with our legs crossed.

Mother: What else did you do?

Ros: When we lined up we had to be one behind the other, and keep our arms by our sides [demonstrates].

Mother: What things did you like about it?

Ros: Being with my friend.

The mother went on to say that at home stillness was not a requisite of TV-watching: her children roamed about, lay on the sofa, as they chose. Another mother, empathizing with her children's day at school, commented on the physical and emotional stresses resulting from the joint effects of large numbers and school social practices:

Mother: Actually I think overcrowding – I think it's such a cram, 28 of them into that carpet area, it must be a disaster, they haven't got enough room to move. Body heat, it gets very hot, she opens the windows. Yes, I think definitely proximity, all those bodies wriggling, nobody means to do anything naughty, but if someone's elbow's in your back you are likely to sort of say, 'Oh, get off', you know. I mean I hate that feeling like being on a crowded tube, I hate it, don't you? I get claustrophobic very easily. And they spend a fair amount of time in the day sitting on the carpet and they have to sit up and cross their legs, and sit straight and not keep wriggling, and sit up nicely and then who gets chosen for which jobs they do.

Gill Barrett (1989), discussing the early roots of children's disaffection from school, quotes children's reflections on their first days at school, which suggest that children experienced the social order as heavily controlling and demanding of conformity:

I didn't like sitting on the floor. There were no carpets.
Sometimes you get tired of working. You need a rest and a drink.
I couldn't cross my legs. My legs were too little. Look – they can fit now.
I didn't like getting into line when I came to school. I wanted my mummy to hold my hand.
When I first came to school I painted and readed and doing my book – my colouring book and I do some colouring – like scribbling.
When I first started school I drawed a picture and it was horrible [long pause]. I forgot arms and legs.

(Barrett 1989: 7)

Margaret sums up what for many reception class children were the main pros and cons of school. Playtime and exercise, including imaginative play were the good points. Having to do things and being told off were the bad points:

I: What are the best things about school?
Margaret: One of them is having playtime, one of them is doing apparatus and one of them is drawing, and playing teachers.
I: Do you like playing teachers then?
Margaret: Yes.
I: Are there bad things?
Margaret: Having to always, just, being told off.
I: What are the best things about being at home?
Margaret: That I don't have to do anything I don't wanna and I don't have

to write anything I don't want to when I'm writing. I don't have to play anything I don't wanna.

During my days with the reception class, I quickly formed the impression through observation that the newest children felt very much on their own. It was up to them to make out, through learning the social norms quickly. An important aide was a companion, someone to play with and help defend you against other groups of children. This impression was substantiated by some of the children's comments. In the case of illness or accident, children did not always go direct and alone to an adult; a common sight was a child leading her companion to the teacher or helper, or reporting that her friend needed help. Thus it seemed that children were subject to a highly structured regime, and also felt responsible for their own health care and, to an extent, for that of others. This snatch of conversation is part of a longer one about life at school, and it seems that Debbie was referring to responsibility at school (although the interviewer thought there was a wider reference – to care at home).

I: Do you do anything that keeps you healthy?

Debbie: No.

I: So whose job is it to keep yourself healthy, to make sure you're well?

Debbie: Mine.

I: You think it's your job? You don't think it's Mummy or Daddy's or the school's? Do you think it's up to you to make sure you don't fall over?

Debbie: Yeah, cos I'm the one who's not running, or not, aren't I?

I: Yeah, so you only fall over when you're running when you shouldn't be. What about things like keeping you well so you haven't got a tummy ache, or your ear doesn't hurt or your head doesn't hurt, whose responsibility is that?

Debbie: Mine. It's been hurting, my right ear.

I: Did you tell your teacher?

Debbie: It was just during play, and first play.

I: And does it hurt when you're inside, in the classroom?

Debbie: Unless people shout.

I: Right, so it only hurts when people shout, but does it hurt when you're outside in the playground?

Debbie: Yeah, and people shout, and they're often screaming.

She then explained that she didn't tell her teacher, but waited until the end of school, to tell her mother. Debbie's older sister (aged 8) enlarged on separation from one's mother as an issue for school-age children.

I: So is it important to learn to be away from their mothers?

Erica: In a way, in some ways not. Because when you go to school, well, after a few weeks you're not with her for a whole day, are you, so that means you won't be wanting your mum all the time, will you?

I: No. So what do you do, if you're not with your mum?

Erica: If you get bullied, you just have to try and ignore them, or something like that, and just go away, or don't hit them back – just go and tell Miss.

I: So is that one way of coping?

Erica: Yeah.

I: Are there other ways of coping?

Erica: What do you mean – looking after yourself? Having your own lunch by yourself.

I: Yes.

Erica: Doing your own jobs, so you don't have to go, 'Mum, what's this?' You just do that yourself.

Some further points about health maintenance emerge from 9-year-olds' conversations and writing. After over four years at school, these children were indeed socialized into the social norms of the school. They did not complain about sitting on the carpet, lining up, getting a drink, going to the lavatory. They had grown accustomed to the regime and had learned how to manage it – notably by bringing packed lunches, and by judging when it was acceptable to chat and move about in class, or ask leave to go to the toilet. But they were vociferous on physical and psychological adult constraint.

Both girls and boys emphasized their enjoyment of enterprise and of achievement, and valued both mental and physical activities. School, particularly in its upper classes, did not offer enough opportunity for these. Children reported that school was highly controlling, work was repetitive (copying out 'in best', doing countless maths examples).

Sally: I find doing lots of sums very boring, because you know what to do and it's really easy, but then if you have to do a lot of them . . . Things like gym, drawing, painting, sometimes writing: they're interesting.

Phil: As long as you're doing something, it's not boring.

I: What's the best things about your lives?

Phil: Achieving something. I don't know, like on the computer, finishing a game . . . I think when you were younger, you were less bored, because you had so many things to learn. Maybe, so you were doing more, doing lots of things. And it was more play than work.

It was notable that children valued 'silent reading' (half an hour after dinner): the children chose their own book and got on at their own pace; thus they had some control over time use. Certainly they looked contented – they sat quietly and absorbed in their reading. Even here, though the teacher sometimes intervened:

June: My best part of the day is silent reading, because you feel like a
character in it. My best series is Sweet Valley – they are brilliant
books because they are true to life . . . It gets on my nerves when
Miss X just hints for us to read other books.

In children's accounts at both 5- and 9-years-old, two topics emerged as the
most important features of life at school: food and play – with the linked issues of
companionship and exercise. These two topics will be considered in Chapter 6,
where links between bodily and temporal issues are taken up. Here it is
important to note briefly how both nutrition and play are controlled in the
interests of school organization and adult interests.

As was indicated above (p. 101), children's control over self-care as regards
getting a drink was subject to teachers' understandings of their motives, in the
context of work requirements. Dinner-time is conditioned by organizational
considerations and by staff job remits. Ensuring that a whole school is fed in the
space of about an hour requires pushing children through the system.
Opportunities for choosing the food on offer, and for leisurely, pleasant food
consumption are constrained by time demands. Some children experience the
social occasion as unpleasant. In addition, dinner-time in many schools is
supervised not by teachers, but by non-teaching staff, whose job is to marshall
the large numbers. Commonly, as at Greenstreet, children sit in groups at tables
without an adult; this gives some freedom, for both positive and negative social
experiences. The abandonment of national standards for school meals (see
p. 27) has led to poorer menus, and evidence suggests that local cost
considerations have reduced the quantity of food available too (see Chapter 6).
All in all, children are likely to experience dinner-time as a low status occasion,
which is poorly valued by the adults who organize their day.

The value of play, for educationalists, is sited within developmental
discourses. Play is regarded as valuable – as a means of learning – for the infants,
but not for the juniors; the regime in the two stages of school life correspondingly
differs. The youngest Greenstreet children almost all made positive mention of
opportunities for play within class-time; the balance between play and work
seemed to work well for them. For the juniors, play was not so legitimated, and
children reported that the balance of play and work was experienced as
uncomfortable. Timetabled exercise – swimming, gym and playground games –
was not enough to redress the discomfort of hours of work in the classroom. On
the other hand, whilst the reception class children liked curricular exercise (gym
and games), playtime in the playground, though welcomed, carried challenges
and difficulties – they needed companions in order to protect themselves and to
make sense of school. The juniors, however, generally enjoyed playtime, even if
they were sometimes bored, because they had friends and established activities.
The physical character of the playground, however, is important in structuring
children's understanding of what matters to adults: bleak expanses of asphalt
and broken equipment symbolically represent adult devaluing of children's play
and physical well-being (Titman 1994).

Thus the school constructs ideas about what matters: children's cognitive achievement is valued above their physical welfare and above their social well-being. The school also delivers messages about what sort of body matters: it is a disciplined body, rather than an active one. Further, school suggests to children that what they hear in health education sessions does not matter, since the social environment of the school does not carry through the points on nutrition and exercise. There is a split in current practice between the moral messages of health education sessions and children's experience of the status of food and exercise at school.

Contributions to school maintenance

The quotations above indicate that, compared to the home, Greenstreet children found that the school offers little opportunity for children to contribute to the construction of the school as a social order. It will be a rare school where children contribute to planning and organizing the school day, and in particular to rethinking food and exercise – key topics for children's well-being. The social order was experienced as firmly in place; it was their task to conform to it.

Three main points emerge from children's own accounts. Firstly, they did not identify school as a health-maintenance environment. This was confirmed through direct questioning. Asked (in a whole-class brain-storming session) where their health maintenance took place, the 9-year-olds proposed the home; after further discussion they referred to sports centres and parks; then health service institutions; finally, when reminded where they were then sitting, they argued that, in case of illness, whilst school would administer first aid, staff would refer the child back to parents. As indicated in quotations in the above section, children regarded themselves as responsible for health mainten-ance at school.

Secondly, children regarded school as detrimental to health, particularly as regards food and exercise. It provided poor food and placed restrictions on eating and drinking and exercise. They perceived the detriment as both physical and emotional, and counter-productive: boredom and irritation affected their work.

Thirdly, children did not perceive the teacher as a health care worker. They found that sickness bids were often met with devaluation or dismissal, or with referral to the helpers, or to the secretary – who somewhat resented the assumption that she had health care skills and willingness. From the onlooker's point of view, the division of labour here makes the teacher as health educator a less than convincing figure.

Constructing relationships

Certain points arising from the children's accounts may be flagged here. It was essential to have friends; at 5 these provided protection and companionship;

they helped you to make sense of school. Bronwen Davies (1982: 70) puts it well. When children arrive at school they are thrown on their own resources:

> Making sense of this strange new world is a task they engage in with each other. The teachers may spell out the rules for classroom behaviour, but the sense to be made of it all is something adults cannot really provide. Friends are the source of meaning-making in this new situation. They are the source of meaning and therefore the source of identity. They can by their presence and shared meaning world, render the world a sensible and manageable place. Their particular mode of viewing the world with its accompanying language, taboos, rituals and sanctions which function to maintain this meaning world, are developed in interaction with each other.

At 9 friendships were firmer and more permanent. By this age, they were established along gendered lines and, at Greenstreet, also along class lines. For both girls and boys friendships extended beyond the school; children met at each other's flats and houses, ate meals together, went on expeditions, played games and went to sports centres.

For all the children one of the principal advantages of school was the pool of other children with whom to form friendships and engage in play. School provided space to play, almost certainly a larger space than they could find elsewhere locally, with adult sanction.

In this study, children were not asked targeted questions – for instance, for their views on their teacher. Instead they were asked to talk about their day, their likes and dislikes, what interested them. Under these circumstances, it is notable that the reception class children did not mention their teacher at all. They talked about food, play, friends and aspects of the formal curriculum. This point reinforces the earlier suggestion that children feel very much on their own when they start school; it is as if, lacking their mother, they do not seek a substitute adult. They look for support among their peers, rather than to their teacher. The older children, at 9, in both writing and conversation about their days at school, did refer to teachers as an important influence for better or worse on the quality of the day. In general, boys saw the teacher instrumentally – as offering good or bad teaching, and more or less control. Several of the girls talked in relationship terms, that they liked talking with her, or wished she would listen and talk with them. This point links with the observations of researchers such as Carol Gilligan (1993), who found that girls interpreted social issues in relationship terms.

Children identify mothers rather than school staff as their main caregivers and save up their hurts and problems for the end of the school day. But, in addition, the division of labour between teaching and non-teaching staff requires children to learn that teachers will not give unqualified recognition to their need for physical and emotional care. The research evidence suggests that when children are asked what qualities they like about teachers, they list kindness and warmth, but that only the youngest children are likely to find these qualities; older children rate their teachers more highly on qualities such as being interesting, wise, successful – and hard, but less highly on qualities such as kindness, fairness and warmth (see Tattum and Tattum 1992: 126–7).

Discussion

This chapter has addressed a neglected feature of school life: its character as health care environment. The sociology of education has generally neglected the body and focused on the cognitive functions of schooling (see also Shilling 1993: 21–2). Yet, as Shilling notes, it is obvious that schools discipline and shape the body. I suggest that the two enterprises: cognitive and bodily management and training are not discrete, but combine to constitute a powerful educational discourse. Children are required to subjugate their bodies: keeping still during maths lessons, not leaving the classroom for a drink. They are also asked to agree that bodies and minds are separate; that bodily comfort can be neglected in the interests of cognitive activity. Furthermore, though primary schools provide for curricular play and exercise as well as for playtime, children are again taught that these provisions have low status in the eyes of teachers, whose remit and expertise is within the academic curriculum.

Yet their experience indicates that cognitive, physical and emotional experiences are interactive: cognitive activity is adversely affected where they are uncomfortable and irritated by constraint. And children recognize that physical input to learning promotes both enjoyment and achievement – a point to be taken up in the next chapter.

Though sociologists' explorations of the social significance of the body have had very little to say about children as a social group, they have proposed useful frameworks for considering children's embodied agency in the social contexts they live in. Three main approaches are considered here: civilizing the body; regulating the body; and constructing the body.

Civilizing the body

The notion of the civilizing of the body through social agency owes its force to the work of Norbert Elias. Compared to the idea of socialization, which has deterministic, controlling and individualistic connotations, civilizing the body suggests a more positive, enabling and socially oriented enterprise. Using a historical survey, Elias (1978 (first published 1939): 140–1) argues that modern society (1930s), much more than earlier societies, demands a profound subjection of the instinctual life; children must rapidly acquire shame and revulsion, to meet the norms of adult behaviour. Mothers' tasks undoubtedly include teaching their children norms of social behaviour that are acceptable by current public social norms. Some of the most basic of these (establishing sleeping/waking rhythms, toilet-training, table manners, behaviour with other children and with adults) are socially assigned to mothers as tasks to be accomplished before children reach school. Pressure for mothers to meet the standards of behaviour is exerted by the wider society, through, as Foucault would put it, the activities of the disciplinary complex. Health visitors and pre-school staff see it as part of their function to instruct mothers on these points. Shilling (1993: 162) notes how this argument suggests a complementary distancing of adults from children. Children have to traverse a long heavily controlled journey before they are socially acceptable to adults.

Elias's framework is based on socialization theory and he assigns low status to children's agency: their collaboration and participation with adults, through learning and through assumption and acceptance of the social norms proposed. However, in his 1968 commentary on the 1939 book, Elias takes up issues to do with agency and structure, and argues for the interdependency of people, throughout life, in a 'figuration': 'a structure of mutually oriented and dependent people'. Using the dance as metaphor, he argues that it helps us see how to eliminate the separation of individual and society: 'one can speak of a dance, but no-one will imagine a dance as a structure outside the individual or as a mere abstraction' (Elias 1978: 260–2). But it has to be added here: if children participate in the dance, they are not equal participants: adults control the dance.

The civilizing process can be seen as entailing a division of labour, with processes directed – some at the bodily and emotional, and some at the cognitive. That is, as discussed in Chapter 4, mothers are socially assigned the tasks of training children, moulding their bodies and linked emotions, whilst schools assume the tasks of instructing children in the cognitive. The cognitive, assigned higher status through the male-ordered hierarchy of social institutions, is opposed to the bodily and emotional. Serious problems arise with this split, because the school is also proposed as the key socializing agency, preparing children, in the Durkheimian tradition, for adult social worlds. The school is thus defined as the principal agency for cognitive and social learning. But this proposition is deeply flawed. It fails to take account of the social character of children's learning on moral issues. As I have tried to indicate, children's learning of the moral order at home takes place experientially within a context of negotiation, based on shared concerns and mutual affection; and these bases do not operate at school. The interactions of agency and structure have specific characters according to social context, with more equal relationships between children and adults at home than at school. The evidence is that children do not take kindly to discrepancies between the spoken and the practice, nor to a social environment which they see is ordered primarily in adult interests.

Regulating the body

I distinguish here between civilizing and regulating the body. Civilizing aims at enabling the embodied person to participate in social worlds. Regulating involves controlling bodies and emotions in the interests of specific agendas: such as social, medical and educational agendas. Thus at home, a baby's first task is to accommodate to the social order; to eat and sleep in accordance with the 'tyranny of time' (Ennew 1994). At school, children's bodies and feelings are managed in the interests of delivering the curriculum. Through the health services, norms of bodily achievement are prescribed in the interests of monitoring the nation's health and assigning children to categories.

The evidence suggests that children experience school as highly regulatory. What and how they learn is circumscribed by social norms. They are required to accept physical discipline within prescribed group norms. Their emotions are directly subject to regulation: they should behave in certain ways; and indirectly through the control exercised over their cognition and physical activity. Home is experienced as exercising control too, but within more negotiable frameworks. The home is also a free zone (cf. Halldén 1993) where children as people are entitled to choice of activity.

The management and construction of emotions is of particular interest. Children are taught both at home and at school to link appropriate feelings to appropriate bodily behaviours. At home, competence in self-care and bodily management attracts social approval and consequent emotional and physical well-being. But both at home and at school, children are asked to regulate their bodies and manage their emotions, in the interests not of self-care, but of adult agendas and timetables. Whilst at home, these demands are mediated by emotional relationships and individual attention, the tension between satisfying school and self-maintenance takes place within more impersonal and group relationships. According to children, the result is sometimes emotional and physical ill-being at school. Adult teaching, control and care for children's emotions differs as between mothers and teachers, broadly along a continuum ranging from affectionate and intimate concern for the whole child to a more instrumental general concern, linked to implementing school agendas. The regulation of emotion is achieved also by children themselves in interaction with other children at home and at school. They learn with their sibs and at school how to manage their own feelings and to participate in the management of other children's emotions; at 5 they look after each other's physical and emotional needs by referring children for adult help; at 9 they discuss each other's health, and care for each other.

Constructing the body

Finally, the sociology of the body proposes useful ideas about the construction of people's bodies. Thus, in Bourdieu's terms (e.g. 1978; see discussion in Shilling 1993: ch. 6), homes and schools produce physical capital: they teach children's bodies to be socially valuable. As ever, adequate consideration of how these ideas operate as regards children require taking account of their particular social positioning: their social dependency and the complementary adult investment in children's minds and bodies. Clearly adults offer and impose certain ideas upon children's bodies. They gender them through discourse, behaviour and expectations; they construct them according to social-class norms; and assign status and age-related positioning through types of clothing and changes to appearance. The status and gender of children is inscribed on their bodies, through practices such as cutting boys' hair when they embark on social life outside the family and through school uniform, which marks entry into formal schooling.

Children's experiences as embodied persons differ widely according to the social estimation of them at home and school. In early childhood, they are accustomed to being valued for their bodies as part of their selves; on attending playgroup, nursery school and above all primary school, they find themselves alienated from their bodies, which are devalued as anti-social by the prevailing norms. Gender is important here: boys' understandings of the value of sporting prowess requires them both to subjugate that understanding at school, and to give it full rein outside school – not at home, where their bodies, like Ionesco's Amedée, burst the bounds of most flats and houses, but through football games in parks, estates and streets. Girls perhaps find more compatibility between the images of the body they are taught: athleticism and trim bodies promoted through the media are somewhat compatible with the body as proposed during life at school, supplemented by exercise at sports centres and on tennis courts. The UK education system presents a paradox: the state system which has operated on the basis of an ostensibly child-centred approach, in practice devalues children's bodies; whereas the private system, which is overtly instrumental, with schooling as a childhood means to an adult end of high social status, gives a larger share of school time to sports. True, these sports are often those which will give access to socially desirable clubs – such as tennis, cricket and squash; but in the meantime, children at private schools get a lot of exercise.

Children are very much the creatures of adult construction. As Emily Martin (1989) says, women take their bodies across the private and public domains, and thus challenge the ascribed character of each. So do children, but power relationships with adults limit their ability to make a place and space for their embodied selves. As a social group, children's daily experience at school is conditioned by the division of adult labour – which devalues the bodily. The paradox of the child-centred regime is that it is based on adult-centred notions of child development within psychological frameworks.

six

Adult time: children's time

Introduction

The previous chapter considered children's social positioning in the context of their embodied experiences of daily life at home and school. Data from children suggested strongly that maintenance of a reasonably comfortable bodily life (viewed through a broad health perspective) was more negotiable at home than at school. This chapter goes on to consider time in the daily lives of children: the intersections of adult and child interests and the experiences of children themselves.

Adult time can be seen as opposing and controlling child time; adults order and organize how children spend time, in adult interests. This argument applies across the time-span of childhood from the placing of babies with minders so that mothers can work, to the employment of teachers in institutions structured for their advantage rather than for the children's (Oldman 1994). Children, who lack the competences necessary to engage with a highly complex, differentiated labour world, are both protected and excluded from the increasingly child-hostile physical and social environment of modern industrialized countries (Engelbert 1994). Intrinsic to the subordination of children to the time of adults, are intergenerational power relations, for children are uniquely poorly placed to combat adult impositions (Ennew 1994). In her study of the current institutionalization of children in Sweden, Elisabet Näsman (1994) points to increases in adult control and diminution of children's choice, and she concludes that 'Children's principal way of gaining autonomy and status is growing up.'

These arguments, developed as part of consideration of large-scale data in the Childhood as a Social Phenomenon project, represent a counter-offensive to the notion that childhood is better provided for now in advanced industrialized countries than ever before. They can be seen as representative of adult concerns in countries which have purposefully altered the conditions of childhood, and, less purposefully, have swept children up in the changing social worlds of adulthood, marked by women in the labour force, special-ization within paid work and hostile environments.

In this chapter, study data are brought into play to consider how children think about their control over time. Two main points are discussed here in relationship to the large-scale arguments. Firstly, it is argued that children, as a social group like other social groups, do propose the value of time of their own – to use as they see fit; and that they do perceive possibilities for carving out such time, though gender and socio-economic considerations cross-cut this ability. Secondly, as a social group, children do not regard themselves as outside society: they think their activities are integrally entwined with those of other social groups. Indeed they perceive themselves as appropriately spending time participating in activities important within the social contexts of the home and the school.

Debate about children's use of time, and its construction and control by adults is framed in understandings of the merits and demerits of past times of childhood. An important historical legacy is the understanding that working-class children were exploited, working long hours for adult interests (e.g. Cunningham 1991), and that middle-class children led highly restricted lives in the rigid grip of social and moral conventions (e.g. Davin 1990). A counter-balancing theme proposes that children's playtime for both broad social classes in the good old days was creative time, free of adult control, spatially wide ranging. Thus Flora Thompson (1973) provides a picture of children playing on the village green, ranging the countryside, learning country lore, constructing and reproducing games; Richard Hoggart (1959) describes urban working-class children playing in the street, under the lamplight. The Opies (1959, 1969) catalogued children's songs and games in the school playground and in spaces and times beyond. The power of these accounts to structure our ideas of what childhood was, also serves to feed into our ideas of what childhood should be (for discussions see Ward 1988; 1990). The lost world of children's domains is a powerful image; and these visions remain part of a cultural heritage of thought, though the same writers and others have pointed to the darker side of the pictures they paint. Flora Thompson notes that children were turned out from under their mothers' feet, for the day – however cold – with very modest food rations; at 5 their journeys on foot to school were long and their experiences of school were harsh; their short childhoods were followed by propulsion into the harsh world of badly paid work (for boys as agricultural labourers and for girls as servants in wealthy houses). Hoggart's (male) vision has been countered by Carolyn Steedman's autobiographical account (1986) of a working-class childhood restricted by poverty and the class system. On the other hand, the alleged disappearance of games and songs into a lost golden age of child culture has been countered in Iona Opie's most recent book (1993), which documents these as they survive and are created in the playground of the 1980s.

One residue of these contrasting stories of past childhoods, in alliance with developmental visions, is an understanding that childhood is a special period of time, differentiated from the period of adulthood by the requirement that children be protected: granted the opportunity to grow, develop and learn, free from the responsibilities and constraints conditioning adulthood. This conceptual separation of childhood from adulthood carries with it many advantages, but also an important disadvantage: it denies children's social nature, their evident interest and competence in social participation. Yet whilst the notion of childhood's lost freedom may be somewhat misleading, it is a persuasive argument that children's freedom in time and space has in some important respects been curtailed. The construction of ever more hostile physical environments is a frequent topic of concern (Ward 1990): children cannot be allowed out, because parents fear for their physical safety in towns and countryside dominated by dangerous adults in vehicles and on foot. So children are escorted to school at older ages than they were 20 years ago (Hillman *et al.* 1991), and adults control and curricularize children's time, from babyhood onwards (e.g. Ennew 1994; Näsman 1994).

This chapter considers time as a factor structuring children's lives: adult timetables at home and at school, and across the two; adult understandings of how children should spend time; children's own understandings of how their time is structured and what constitutes good use of time. Children's and parents' accounts of children's activities at home and school strongly suggest that what they do is work in and for time present and time future, through their acquisition of knowledge relevant to their daily lives now and in the future. Time-use by children is a contested area, at both home and school: between the value of experiential living and learning now, and the value of preparing for the future. But as Dewey says, the two values are also intrinsically inter-linked:

> When preparation is made the controlling end, then the potentialities of the present are sacrificed to a suppositious future. When this happens the actual preparation for the future is missed or distorted. The ideal of using the present simply to get ready for the future contradicts itself . . . We only live at the time we live and not at some other time, and only by extracting at each present time the full meaning of each present experience are we prepared for doing the same thing in the future. This is the only preparation which in the long run amounts to anything.
>
> (Dewey 1956: 50–1)

Children and home time

How people spend time varies between social environments – time and space are interlocked. For children, these are framed by adult understandings and demands, which are specific to the social context. At home an important factor is mothers' ideas about childhood. It has been observed that mothers do not accept uncritically social demands for an unwavering, unremitting devotion to preparing their children for the social worlds of school and adult social conventions. Thus, in the Newsons' study of 4-year-olds, mothers described certain behaviours as unacceptable in the wider world, but permitted at home, at certain times of the day. In the morning the clock-bound demands of the day in prospect, on adults and children, made for 'hectic flurry'; and children might find themselves being dealt with, rather than attended to (Newson and Newson 1970: 257). But in the evening, rituals and comfort habits could be allowed, even encouraged; at bed-time, deference to children's own wishes could take precedence. 'Behind closed doors, with no expectation that the ritual will ever have to take place in the public eye, parents can and do meet their children a good deal more than half way' (1970: 332). The Newsons continued their study of this topic in relation to the children at age 7. 'Parents' (in fact they interviewed mothers) are described as upholding a dual role: as advocates of society's demands and as defenders of the child against those demands in the privacy of the family. They explain this duality in terms of mothers' understanding of the natural versus the social. Thus at home girls might be allowed aggressiveness and boys tearfulness, both which behaviours were socially unacceptable in the public world (Newson and Newson 1978: 441–3).

Gunilla Halldén (1993) has taken up these themes to reconsider mothers' belief systems. She points to two pervasive ideas in Western European societies: that time should be used (the devil makes work for idle hands) and that early experiences shape the child (the child is father of the man). These, she argues, are linked in the prescription that mothers' socialization work should be unremitting; the critical time of childhood at home must be used to the full, if children are to become adequate adults. She found, however, that mothers (in Sweden) operated a dual belief system: they accepted their socialization work, but also thought the home should offer space and time for the natural qualities of the individual child. The home was understood as a free zone for individuality. Her study, like the Newsons', shows that mothers permit within the confines of the home practices which would meet disapproval from the psycho-social monitors of child-rearing.

These studies form a useful basis for building on in the light of the visions of the child as participant actor discussed here. The Greenstreet mothers indicated that they regarded their children not so much as natural – in the sense of uncivilized or unsocialized – but as people, like other people, who made and remade the social conventions of the home, in interaction with their parents and sibs. Most importantly, children, as people, were seen as having rights – to create their own life, to make decisions and choices, within the limits of family norms and socio-economic possibilities. The children themselves regarded their participation in these activities as that of people with some, but limited, power.

Children's accounts of life at home indicate that their use of time comprises three main elements: free time, to do what you want; jobs (a minor component for most); and participation in household activities. Control over one's use of time is linked to control over space. In the Greenstreet study, children discussed the balance of adult control and child choice, both at home and school. At home, for children, as for women, a room of one's own is both physically and metaphorically valuable:

> *Tom (aged nine)*: I get quite annoyed when I'm at home. Mostly with my little brothers. I have my own room so I'm in that quite a lot. When I'm at home, which isn't that often, I'm normally on my own. When I come home from school, I normally just watch TV until supper which is at 6.00. When I'm in my room, I draw or listen to music or things like that.

Tom's freedom in a well-to-do household to decide on activity and to acquire cultural capital is in sharp contrast to the controls exercised over girls in poorer families, with gendered expectations of girls' domestic labour. Such girls live within double constraints: over their opportunity for space and time of their own; and over the use of their time. As Greenstreet girls indicated, a shared bedroom and the requirement to do domestic work, effectively meant that they had poor control over space and time.

I have suggested that the social order of the home rests to some extent on negotiated provisional demands and activities. An instance of how parents and children play with the concept of time arises in connection with the age at which children should do certain activities; the point at issue is social age versus chronological or biological age (James and Prout 1990b). According to mothers, their wish or demand for their children to do certain things (wash up, clear up, get themselves to bed) relates not only to the child's chronological age, but to the characteristics of the child, the social precursors of the activity in question, the current social circumstances, the mother's own experience, and her views on encouraging certain desirable activities and attributes. A good example is given by the mother of Jim (aged 9) and his sister (aged 13):

> Well, a landmark [this year] is that they take themselves to bed. They do all the getting into pyjamas and tooth-brushing themselves, without supervision. I was a bit doubtful about that because I suspect Jim may cut corners [on tooth-brushing] . . . But I used to get terribly irritable standing around while they got into their pyjamas. So I suppose it gradually became 'You get ready and then I'll come and read to you.' They've just got into the way of it. They quite like it, they do a fair bit of larking around. I suppose I got a bit bored with all that. I thought they could do it without me. It's, I see it as a bit of independence too.

This attention to the relevant factors underpinning change is characteristic of accounts of life at home. As noted in the next section, chronological age (and stage) have more uncontested sovereignty at school; attention to social age depends on teachers' individual willingness and time to respond to the child.

The Greenstreet children, like most people, commonly wished for more time to dispose of as they chose. Similarly, in an Australian national study of children in the primary school years, Goodnow and Burns (1985: 43–7) found that when asked 'If you could change one thing in the morning, what would it be?' Many children answered in terms of time: 30 per cent of 6- to 8-year-olds and 52 per cent of 9- to 11-year-olds. In many cases their answers also referred to choice and control: for instance, 'I wish they set the jobs but we could decide when to do them.' The largest group of comments on time referred to school starting time. If only school started later, it would give so much freedom to sleep, fix lunch, feed the cat.

Jobs at home – clearing up, making your bed – were discussed in Chapter 5. As Goodnow and Burns (1985: 50) point out, adults define certain jobs – relating to self-maintenance – as children's and these jobs acquire a moral quality early in childhood: other people should not be asked to do them. Children voice the complement to this point: they report tension between the adult ascription of responsibility to children for the tidiness of 'your' room, and child choice on time-use there. As one girl said, when she grew up she would make a point of having an untidy room. Brian explained that at school he feels heavily under the thumb of the class teacher, but 'at home you can do what you like, except sometimes you have to clean your room, but mostly you can'. Another boy, Ian, enlarges on this topic, in discussing what he finds irritating at home: 'Tidying your room. I know why they want you to do it, because things get broke, and you could hurt yourself. But basically it's like, your room, so you can do what you like with it.'

For the 9-year-olds, adult-controlled time-use competed with child-determined time-use. Jobs were an accepted part of being at home, particularly self-care jobs and some domestic work. But by this age many of them had friendships and lists of activities they valued: interacting with computers, reading, watching TV, playing alone or with friends. However, children's accounts indicate not only the wish to spend time in activity outside household concerns, based on their own agendas, but also pleasure in participation in family activities. Some indications have been given in the previous chapter of how children interact with parents and sibs; in this chapter some data is explored on how children take part in food preparation – a central household enterprise (pp. 123–8).

Children and school time

Here certain central adult-oriented organizational and curriculum features of school are critical in structuring children's experience of time.

Firstly, the length of the school day provides a working day for teachers, and a minding service for working mothers. At Greenstreet the school day was over six hours long for both infants and juniors. Some children also went to an after-school centre until 5.30 or 6.00. In the reception class, the younger children sometimes fell asleep or looked pale and tired towards 3.30. Recognizing this, the teacher balanced school time against child biological time: the end of the day was story-time. In one case, she recommended to a mother that she take her son out of school at lunch-time if she thought he would not last the day.

Secondly, school is organized according to children's biological age and children move up according to age (in some countries, such as the USA, attainment is the basis for promotion) (King 1989: 65). The corollary is that children's achievement, competence and social skills are judged according to adult criteria for that age-band (King 1989: 65, 80). Social judgement according to biological age competes with attention to the specifics of individual children.

Thirdly, children's time is organized according to the demands of the curriculum, which differs between the infant years and the juniors; play-as-learning gives way to the primacy of work. As Saunders (1989) puts it 'the child is gradually introduced into a culture which appears to reduce choices and opportunities for decision-making problem-solving and active involvement in the classroom'; instead pupils are required to engage in 'task-focused activities'. These organizational and curriculum practices are structured through developmental accounts, which focus on stages linked to ages, and on the years up to 6 or 7 as the age of symbolic play (Smith 1994). Primary teacher training is split in complement: with students focusing on either the 'early years' (nursery to top infants) or juniors.

Fourthly, and as discussed in Chapter 4, the principal interest of the education system is the time future of children, rather than the time present. Essentially school is preparation. From the children's point of view, childhood is being lived now, in bodily and mental terms, but their experience is that their present wishes must give place to school agendas based on concern for the future. In day-to-day dealings with the children, teachers have to balance the demands of children's time present and education's time future. Some of the implications of these organizational and curriculum points are exemplified in the following account by the teacher of the first-year juniors at Greenstreet.

Kathryn: Some of them do find it . . . stressful . . . when they get to the first juniors, they find it quite difficult because more is expected of them.

I: Yes, what sort of more is expected?

Kathryn: From, I mean just more, in that sort of working together and sort of more socially working together in groups. Also actual, more quantity. And they don't have as much time to play or, you know, sort of free choice. When they first come up they sort of say, 'Oh, can we play, can we play now?' and they were quite surprised when I said, 'Well, no, we do this. You can play occasionally, but . . .' [She goes on to explain that the morning is now 20 minutes longer than in the infants.] And they'd really, they'd be finished by 12.00. We couldn't really ask them to go on much longer than 12.00, and we'd sort of stop and have a story, for quite a while. And then gradually it, well sometimes we stop now and have a story, it depends.

These new juniors at Greenstreet experienced the morning as longer. Their teacher explained that she had not told them about this change, since most of them couldn't tell the time. School here was presented as given; the when and why of routine and custom was not made explicit. The teacher balanced the demands of the education system, based on age and stage, with the children's experience and feelings.

However, at Greenstreet, the reception class children did spend a lot of time being told school customs and norms. And it seemed from observation and their accounts that they were enthusiastic about school – they enjoyed the wide range of activities: both the formal learning and the opportunities for play in the classroom. Playtime was a challenge they were learning to tackle. The distribution of time seemed to suit them. The day was carefully structured with short (10–15 minute) sessions of writing, maths and reading with the teacher or one of the non-teaching staff; and in the spaces between children played with each other: at board games and puzzles, with bricks, sand, water, painting. They ran about in the classroom, talked and laughed; they invented and re-invented games. The day was punctuated with sessions on the carpet with the teacher telling stories, giving instructions, engaging in talk about the weather, describing future plans. These sessions, though physically constraining, offered them new information and ideas: the opportunity to learn how to interact with this novel social world.

In the juniors, expectations of children's social behaviour – as civilized members of a group – were increased. The balance of work and play shifted towards work, and the teacher had to consider how far and when to take account of children's welfare and to care for them in the context of curriculum demands. In addition to their comments, observation indicated that the 9-year-olds found the regime difficult to endure. Visibly they were impatient with the long periods spent having the next item on the agenda explained, with sitting on the carpet being told off for untidiness and unruliness, with waiting around (many studies show that most of children's time at school is spent waiting – Cullingford 1991: 117). They rushed out of the classroom at playtimes – because though (they said) playtime was sometimes boring, at least they could move about reasonably freely. They commented unfavourably on the change in regime in the junior years, especially as regards the shifting balance in favour of work over play. This was particularly true for boys, who wanted more exercise and disliked their present enforced sedentary days (pp. 131–2).

Girls were relatively more contented with the class regime; observation suggested that they had, more successfully than some boys, established ways of pacing the day by establishing satisfactory social rhythms (cf. Bellaby 1992). Girls' verbal skills have long been recognized as superior to boys' (Tizard *et al.* 1988: 7); and at Greenstreet they seemed happier than boys with the junior regime, where reading and writing were major components of the day, and where talking with each other filled the spaces in the formal curriculum. As Kate put it:

> With writing, what's good is you're thinking what to say, and you think, oh yes, what to say next . . . [later, after talking about the delights of physical activity] And I like chatting – I'm a chatterbox. I've got so many words inside. And it makes exercise for your jaws!

Angela's emphasis on verbal activity and learning, leads on to the suggestion that school offers poor opportunities for this nowadays, but Dan takes a more conformist view.

Angela: Reading. Arguing. It's good, because you can let out your problems, or just get mad at someone . . . [She notes that school was better when you were younger] You didn't think of being bored when you were younger, because you could always think of things to do. More to think about, more to take in. And you were learning more.

I: Whereas now, at school?

Angela: Because when you're at home you can do more things. You go to school because your mum and dad works and . . .

Dan: School might be boring, but I'd rather go to school than not because you don't learn anything at home. And at school you are learning new things, but things you have to do over and over you do need to do, otherwise you'd forget them

At 9, children clearly understood how school expectations and demands changed between the reception class and class 5. They balanced their awareness that they were being subjected to compulsory institutionalization which served adult interests, with their appreciation of what school had to offer them: learning and friendship. All the 12 girls (except 1) and most of the 16 boys (except 4) found some pleasure in school. But, alongside this, their sense of subjection to adult interests emerged in their talk and writing about their lives at school; schools are not just for teachers, they are also for parents.

> You have to go to school because your Mum and Dad go to work.

> You sit there and think, it's another half-hour before we can go home.

> School is boring. It lasts 6 whole hours and 30 whole minutes. From 10 to 9 till 3.30. When I walk in the school gate at 10 to 9 I feel tired. When I walk out of the gate at 3.30 I feel happy. I think the most important people in school are children. The best part of the day is when we go home.

In conversation about what they found interesting (and boring) whether at home or school, a theme that resounded through 9-year-olds' comments was the value of using time purposefully: doing things, as active participants. As Bob and Fred indicate (p. 13) building the Great Wall of China in the infants comprised active, fun achievement. Here Martin and Richard indicate the activities that give them satisfaction:

Martin: Messing about with blank tapes and recording things on them. I try and sing on them . . .

Richard: Like making things, but we're not allowed to do that at school. Making things out of wood. Cooking and science and experiments.

Martin: Yes, experiments, stuff like that.

I: Did you do some of that when you were younger?

Martin: Yes in the infants we did lots of woodwork. We used to melt wax in a spoon. And make fireworks – dribbling wax on to paper and it made like fireworks.

Richard: Put a candle into a bowl and let it go. Some people, if you put a candle in a bowl, it carries on burning. But at a certain point it stops burning.

I: Have you made things this year?

Martin: We've made books, haven't we. We've done paper-cut experiments.

I: If you compare being in the infants with now, is it different?

Martin: In the infants – it's harder now because you have to do pages and pages of writing. In the infants you just did half a page and that was your work. It's different now, you have to do much more.

I: Was it more interesting in the infants?

Martin: Well, you did a few lines and then it was playing.

Sarah and Bob similarly discuss what they enjoy doing. Sarah describes making a cake and goes on:

Sarah: Making big things, out of cardboard boxes, cars and dens and stuff like that.

Bob: Doing things on my computer – not just games, other things on the computer. Like I was doing this programme – you fill in things about your family: a family tree and your home, and what you don't like about your sister!

Sarah: Things like gym, PE, drawing, painting, sometimes writing. They're interesting.

Bob: As long as you're doing something, it's not boring.

Achievement here meant, not being taught, but active learning. Through the technological revolution school was offering opportunities to learn: on the computer. There was a gender difference: 11 of 16 boys, but only 2 of 12 girls mentioned the computer as something they enjoyed interacting with at home.

Gender bias in access to computers has been observed and deplored (Hoyles 1988); the picture may be changing before our eyes since later evidence shows that girls and women are using computers more (Grant 1994b). All the children spent time working on a computer at school. It seems that both girls through verbal interactivity and boys through computer interactivity did have some opportunities for creative learning.

In general, Greenstreet 9-year-olds described the early years at school rather than the later as offering opportunities for achievement. They recognized that the top junior years were the years of consolidating reading, writing and maths skills; children found practice, repetition, writing up 'in best' and teacher control tedious and irritating. Some, especially the boys, looked forward to the green fields of secondary school, where they would again learn and achieve, especially in 'science'. Alan's written account summarizes issues about children's experience of school: expectations of what school should offer, contrasts between the infants and the juniors, the delight in achievement.

> *Alan*: As I walk through the gates in the morning on the way to the classroom, I'm mostly not in a positive mood. On the way out, on the other hand, my mood is totally the opposite. I'm not really sure what I like about school. I like it with a good teacher and I absolutely hate it with a bad – a bad teacher is one that doesn't set work, or something of the sort. I think I like learning, but I like learning my own way on my own ideas, for that makes me feel like I've accomplished double. I think that I've liked the infants more, because I learned general stuff like reading, which I thoroughly enjoy now. And general numbers, which I like fooling around with. So far the infants have put some knowledge into me. The juniors have yet to have its spark.

Time and health maintenance

The above general points about the home and the school provide a context for this section. Here children's experiences in daily life are considered in relation to how time and particularly adult-oriented time structures their experience. Four topics of direct concern to children are explored: food, and in particular school meals; play, playtime and exercise; health maintenance; and the school health service.

Food

At home, the organization involved in assembling food for people is obviously a major enterprise for women, including thinking about meals and nutrition, balancing budgets, shopping, preparing, cooking, providing for varying needs and lifestyles and constructing the social occasion of food consumption. Women's work here occupies a good deal of time, carved out of time allocation for paid work, other aspects of home maintenance and childcare. The time constraints on mothers of producing food can mean that children play an active part in the work. And encouraging children to take part in preparing food and meals is part of education: learning the technical and social skills involved. The evidence from the Greenstreet and Bluelane studies is that children participate in the material and social production of food at home. It is an area where they think they have some limited control.

In the Greenstreet study, 19 9-year-olds completed food diaries for the day before – a school day – and these indicated that 11 children made their own breakfast; six of the 10 who took packed lunches to school prepared them; 13 found and prepared their own snacks as required; but adults prepared the evening meal. Twelve diaries for a non-school day showed that half the children took part in preparing a meal; both boys and girls took part in food preparation, with slightly higher proportions of girls involved.

In the Bluelane study, children in conversation and in food diaries again indicated they participated in preparing food at home: through both cooking and watching food being cooked; some were sent to buy take-away food. The children understood that preparing and consuming food was embedded in the social organization of the home, including adult timetables. In their stressed homes, where parents and older sibs worked long and varying shifts, or were unemployed or ill, the difficulties of assembling food for household members were evident to children. Most girls, but few boys, were involved in a range of aspects of food preparation at home: they watched food being chosen and bought, prepared and cooked, and they recognized the household division of labour for the various activities concerned, and the reasons for these divisions. For instance, parental work-shifts determined who prepared food, and at what times. Thus preparing and consuming food acquired importance through social relationships. Some children were learning to cook and to take some responsibility for preparing meals.

In both studies, therefore, the social order of the home encouraged children to learn about cooking and providing meals. Children had some control within the social events of food production: both the opportunity and the require-ment to participate ensured that children regarded themselves as active contributors. The centrality of activities surrounding food at home, in terms of time-allocation, and the range of activities involved, allowed for children's participation at some times and in some activities.

At school, low evaluation of nutrition within the education service together with the division of labour between adults determines what children eat and their social experience during school meal-times (cf. Morrison 1995). Cur-rently, healthy eating is less a priority for schools and caterers than financial viability (Coles and Turner 1992: 52). As the SSRU national survey showed, in 96 per cent of primary schools meals are provided by an outside caterer. Liaison between caterers and school staff varies, with 47 per cent reporting no liaison arrangements, 19 per cent holding policy discussions and 27 per cent ad hoc discussions and 5 per cent other types of liaison. In most schools (89 per cent) the children take no part in determining what is provided, nor in determining the social event of dinner-time (SSRU 1994: 29–33).

Teaching staff control children's experiences in the classroom, but non-teaching staff generally provide and oversee the school meal. Teachers have negotiated to disengage themselves from dinner-time duty, in favour of a well-earned break. Thus schools separate out the cognitive from the physical and social. Dinner-time – with its physical and social elements – is not part of the formal curriculum, but is in the hands of non-teaching staff, whose remit is supervision within a tight time-schedule. The division of labour here symbolizes the status of child welfare within education. As one Greenstreet father, very concerned about his daughter's nutritional status, said, there is a world of difference between primary school and day nursery:

> I don't know how much attention is given to what they eat at school. I ask them [the children], but they say they haven't eaten. It would be a benefit to the parents to know what they eat. At the [day] nursery, they paid a lot of attention to that. They gave them a good breakfast if they arrived early, and meals through the day. They knew what the children ate.

The difference is accounted for by the historical remit of day nurseries: to attend to physical welfare, and to compensate for inadequate care at home. Day nurseries are often accused of being insufficiently interested in the cognitive; at primary school the balance is tipped the other way.

Nursery schools and classes stand between the compensatory welfarist remit of day nurseries and the cognitive aims of primary school. As participant observer, I thought the Greenstreet nursery class teachers used the event of dinner-time as a caregiving, socializing and cognitive event. They each sat with a group of children, with the food set out on the table, and asked them to choose foods, encouraged healthy choices and held conversations with them, both about healthy food and about general topics. Children were required to conform to certain customs: sitting down at table, waiting to be served, using a fork and spoon, taking turns to talk with the adult, and finally taking their empty plate to the trolley. My observation was confirmed by the teacher who told me that her job – as at day nurseries – involved compensating for home conditions, caring for the children, and teaching them social and cognitive skills useful for the next stage of schooling. The nursery class teacher and reception class teacher worked together to make the two settings congruent and to ease the transition: practices in reception continued and developed those begun in the nursery class. The reception class teacher was the only one who sat with her class at dinner-time.

At Greenstreet food was cooked on the premises and served by the dinner ladies at a hatch. Children lined up, by class, starting with the youngest. All seven classes had to be served in about an hour. The menu always included a meat and vegetarian option, cooked vegetables, salad (on a separate table), pudding (usually cake-type) and fruit. Most children did not choose salad or fruit. The children sat in groups of six or eight; those who brought packed lunches sat at the furthest tables. The dinner ladies supervised the queue but did not sit with the children.

Five-year-old children's accounts point to food as one of the two major topics (with play and playtime) that concern them at school; their experiences included both negative and positive features. Some children reported enjoying the food itself, but only one commented favourably on the social occasion of dinner-time. Here are Rachel and Jane talking about what they like at school.

Rachel: Oranges I love, every day I'd have at school, and have apples.
Jane: All kinds of fruit.
I: You'd like that at school?
Rachel: Yes, of course.
Jane: I'd like to go into the kitchen and say 'I want loads of dinner.' Not yucky dinner like we sometimes have. But lovely dinner. Fish and chips and for pudding, fruit, every day.
I: Don't you get enough [i.e. fruit]?
Jane: You don't get enough. I always think – if you're a vegetarian you just get cabbage and chips. That's not very good. I eat fish.

School dinner as a social occasion was perceived as daunting by some children:

Heather: Some people eat really fast, they go [fast eating noise]. Too fast. So they can have some pudding. And they're dying to go to play. And they get stomach ache when they're playing. And some people crying and some people don't, at playtime. Cos they run around, and they can trip over.

As with other features of school, older children had learned to negotiate better experiences of dinner-time. Nine-year-olds reported 'luscious' or 'brill' packed lunches, which they prepared themselves. However, though they thus exercised some control over their food, the social event was controlled by adults. The following exchange took place between David (aged 5), Peter (aged 8), their mother and the interviewer.

I: Is that a nice time of day, having your packed lunch?
David: NO!
I: Why not?
David: Because the teacher at packed lunches, when you want a drink and you're thirsty, she says 'Wait till you've finished all your lunch.'

Later, he explained that this was a helper, rather than a teacher, who oversaw the packed lunch children. The mother added that the children were not allowed to take drinks to school to have with their lunch. Peter then said:

Peter: School dinner: it's a total rip-off, because by the time we get into the hall, it's cold and there is hardly anything left, and the

	puddings, I mean sometimes they're nice, but they always go before we get there.
Mother:	So do you not get pudding sometimes?
Peter:	Sometimes. Sometimes we just get custard, and I hate custard.
I:	Do you get enough to eat at school?
Peter:	Well, I don't think, well, there's probably enough there to be quite healthy, the food is healthy, there's usually enough, but it isn't very nice.
I:	So you don't eat it?
Peter:	No.
I:	And do you take any fruit to school?
Peter:	No, we don't. We have milk half way through the day.
Mother:	The reception class is allowed to take fruit in, but it stops there.
I:	So can you get a drink if you want one?
Peter:	No, well, there's the water fountain, but the one near our playground is broken.
I:	So, if you want a drink, you can't have one?
Peter:	Well, no. We're allowed a really small amount of water after our lunch – a cup.
Mother:	And if you're in the classroom and you need a drink, are you allowed to go and get one?
Peter:	No. You'd have to go and get it at break-time.

These exchanges indicate a combination of neglect and control by adults over what children consumed and the social occasion of dinner-time. On the one hand, there was no adult input to promote dinner-time as a pleasant social occasion; only one teacher made a point of sitting with her class. On the other hand, adults did intervene to prevent children satisfying their thirst and hunger when they saw fit.

At Bluelane, school dinners were provided and consumed under somwhat different conditions. The head teacher thought school meals were under threat: the LEA gave them low priority and Local Management of Schools might hasten their demise. Many children came from severely disadvantaged homes: 52 per cent of the children were entitled to free school meals. About equal proportions of children were from Asian, Afro-Caribbean and white indigenous backgrounds. Because pre-school provision was poor locally, some started school unable to speak English. The children's conversations provided glimpses of home life lived under stress: illness and injury; conflict between parents; work at unsocial hours and unemployment; violence within the home, and from local people; and above all poverty – which structured home life, including nutrition.

The provision of school dinner compounded the children's poverty rather than compensating for it. Though the school building was new (1980s), there was no kitchen and the dinners were prepared at another school, and brought by van in containers. The food was set out and served by the dinner ladies, who, in the space of an hour, had to serve about 100 children. Children were rushed through the queue and asked to finish eating quickly – to make way for others. Insufficient food was provided, with the most popular options running out early on. Much of the food was stodgy (pies, puddings, heavy quiches, pizzas). There was little fruit and salad provided. Because of time pressures, children could not make their choices known, and in some cases language difference and uncertainty compounded their problems. In many cases children failed to get the food they wanted. The Asian children in particular were badly served: though there was always a vegetarian option, some of the food was unfamiliar or offended against dietary customs. Some children ate very little and threw away a good deal. Though children preferred to bring packed lunches, some explained that family poverty required them to have the free meal. The poor provision in this case resulted from LEA lack of commitment and poor resourcing (and ultimately from governmental policies – see p. 27). Though the head teacher kept a log book on the meals, and discussed menus with the caterers, she was finding it difficult to secure improvements.

The data from the survey and from the two schools indicates how the school meal is constructed through adults' timetables, which themselves are structured through definitions of their job remit. Teachers in schools are concerned with teaching in classrooms, not with the educational aspects of nutrition. The dinner ladies' remit is serving and control, rather than nutrition; their observed wish to help children eat well was constrained by time. The meal is therefore a low-status component of the day; children experience it as a social occasion structured by time-constraints and by adult control over what, when and how they eat. Children's own control over the experience is greater where they bring packed lunches. Paradoxically those parents who can afford to pay for the meal find it cheaper to provide packed lunches, which may be nutritionally better. Children from poor families may get poor nutrition via the school meal.

Play, playtime and exercise

Time for play is important in children's accounts generally and in children's definitions of play, adults have no part. Clem Adelman (1989) concludes from consideration of a number of observational and interview studies that 'children regard play as activities in which they define the boundaries, initiate and conclude'; where adults are involved, children define the activity as work and the distinction lies in 'the moral relationships between the children at play and between the children and an adult's work' (see also Denzin 1977: 142–5). In a study of Swedish 6-year-olds, Kärrby (1990) found they defined play as pretending and fantasy, with a theme, and following rules; not activities organized by adults. Thus children's definitions of play are congruent with the more elaborated ones of theorists. Huizinga (1976) defines play as an activity outside the demands of ordinary life, with its own limited course and meaning, its own order created and maintained by the players, and its own character kept secret from outsiders.

Play is one of the main socially legitimated activities for children's time at home. But for many children, play requires companions. Otherwise it is reduced to board games, puzzles and the like. As one Greenstreet girl said: 'My mum says, go and play, but I've played everything and I'm bored with it.' Some children talked of playing with siblings, but age-related tensions tended to interfere. Lacking their peers at home children at both 5 and 9 complained of boredom. Watching television was the fall-back position. A frequent complaint was that adults refused permission to play out with others or to visit others; such permission would involve adults in supervision. Time for play at home was thus constrained through the social organization of time and space in the family.

Within the school curriculum, play has a place in the infant years, but not in the juniors, in accordance with Piaget, who observed that play was characteristic of the 2–6-year-olds, and found it educationally functional (Smith 1994). Educationalists have harnessed play as a means to educational ends (e.g. Matterson 1969; Moyles 1994), though their interventions destroy play as defined by children and theorists. Playtime at school, like meal-times, is structured by a combination of adult control and neglect. The children have to go out at specified times into the space allotted to them. But children themselves have to construct playtime as a social occasion. The daunting experience of being with large numbers of active children for a fixed period of time in a small space, leads the youngest children to stress the need for companions, as protection and defence. In the following exchanges with Greenstreet 5-year-olds, the opening interviewer gambit was to ask what they liked and disliked about school. Of the 21 children who talked with me (in pairs), 16 referred positively to play in the classroom (sand, bricks, Wendy house) or gym, and 17 referred to playtime, with 11 positive and 8 negative comments (some gave both positive and negative).

I: What do you like about school?
Ann: Playing games, drawing, looking at books. Playing in the home corner. And I like playing Mickey Mouse in the home corner and horsey games outside and turtles. And I like having [an] orange at first play – it's in my coat pocket actually and I like going home when it's home time and I like dinner.
I: The food, or being there?
Ann: Being there.

An older boy, who had more school experience, said:

Doran: Playing in the class and playing out.
I: What do you do?
Doran: All sorts of games. I like PE – cos it's all quiet and people don't push you off. Some people do get pushed off.

Playtime was also the occasion for violence, bullying and accidents.

Richard: I don't like playtime.
I: What do you do there?
Richard: Play games or fighting. I don't like that. People fight with me, I didn't do nothing.

Michael: I don't like playing games if it's with people who hate me.
Jerry: I play with them even though they're not my friends. People hate me, but I still play with them.

Ian: I don't like going out to play sometimes, because you get cold
            . . .
Oliver: . . . and not playing with anybody. Because it's not very nice. And I don't like looking around for people and them knocking me over.

The helpers explained to me that their job was supervision; to keep a general eye out to make sure no one got hurt. Sometimes children would come and stand with them or say 'No one will play with me.' Then they might try to integrate them with a group. But they could not initiate games, for this would divert their attention from supervision.

Playtime is currently arousing considerable adult interest, partly because of concern about bullying, but also in the context of whole-school health policies. Peter Blatchford and Sonia Sharp (1994) report on a range of initiatives in improving children's experience at playtime. An important ingredient of these initiatives is children's involvement in discussions, planning and implementation (see also Titman 1994).

Time for exercise is structured at school by the extent of adult enthusiasm and by current theories of the purposes of exercise. Primary school teachers, mostly women, may be apathetic about physical exercise and feel poorly equipped to teach physical education (Williams 1980). According to Greenstreet children and their teachers, exercise had low status. As the head said, her own lack of enthusiasm was influential (cf. Pollard 1982: 32; Acker 1990). The school had banned football at playtime, but had not instituted more positive policies or practices. Teachers noted that children who attended the after-school centre had better opportunities for exercise and formal games, compared to others.

Within the formal curriculum, children's bodies feature through the provision of physical education (PE) sessions. At the start of state education, PE was regarded (along with nutrition and health inspections) as necessary; its goal was therapeutic: restoring and maintaining children's physical fitness. Through the twentieth century the balance has swung between the aim of therapy and the aim of training for life – inculcating physical activity habits. But throughout the period PE teachers have struggled for more time allocation. In the 1930s, a daily 20-minute exercise slot was proposed; 50 years later, PE, as one of seven 'foundation' subjects, is battling for time against the three 'core' subjects in the National Curriculum (Bray 1991). Currently, the increasing influence of governors, coupled with pressures on parents to demand emphasis on the core curriculum, may lead to decreasing time-allocation for physical exercise (Sparkes 1992), (see also pp. 25–8).

The uneasy positioning of physical activity in the school curriculum also reflects a battle to conceptualize it as central to health education. The history of PE in the UK indicates an early concern to link physical activity with health education (Bray 1991) and it seems that in Australian schools sports sessions are currently seen as the principal vehicle for health education (Kirk and Tinning 1994). In British educational theory and practice, the cognitive is commonly separated from the physical.

Like the younger children, the Greenstreet 9-year-olds identified physical activity and friendship as important dimensions of school, but found that school increasingly restricted activity. These two boys recalled the social world of the infants:

Bob: In the infants it was more fun. Because you weren't sat down all the time, you were doing things, like painting.
Fred: Now you don't do painting. In the infants we built the Great Wall of China. We made it go right round the room. With the big bricks.
I: You liked doing that?
Fred: We did then! We're not allowed to do it now. We did this big thing: we made a big catapult, across both classrooms and –
Bob: – we made it, it [joint laughter], it didn't work in the end!
I: Whereas now?
Fred: We're doing more of: sit down, write down, write up!
Bob: The teacher reckons we're too big to do running around, because we hardly ever do. We hardly ever go out. We usually work.

And Dan outlines a common complaint about teacher control:

Dan: . . . when the teacher keeps on talking and she keeps on telling you over and over again and she doesn't let you go and get on with it.

Formal exercise sessions were appreciated by both girls and boys: especially swimming, gym and games – rounders, cricket and football. Observation of gym classes suggested that children enjoyed both individual achievement and collaborative activities such as following a leader round a 'shipwreck' course. When a boy talked of playing football at playtime, a girl explained the advantages of games organized for everyone to join in, 'Kickball rounders – it's fun. It's a change from being in the classsroom and it's nice when everyone's playing, not just a few people.'

Out of school, opportunities in time and space for exercise and play are mediated through adult agendas and the character of adult social worlds. Adults have created social environments they regard as too dangerous for unsupervised children, whom they then debar from streets and parks. Social policies have put a price-tag on swimming pools and sports centres. Among the

Greenstreet 9-year-olds, almost all described physical exercise positively as part of their life outside school (8 of 9 girls and 14 of 16 boys); this included formal sports such as swimming, running, tennis; and less formal activities such as football and bike-riding. They noted that they had to enlist parents as escorts and to pay. The children drew contrasts between their activities out of school, compared to restriction in school.

> *I:*   What do you like doing?
> *Chris*: Swimming. I go nearly every day after school. It's fun and it gives
>   you exercise, more than at school, where you don't get any
>   exercise, except in the playground. They make you sit down all the
>   time.

Children's play and exercise, therefore, is hedged about with limitations of place, time and adult agendas and control. Play is legitimate at home, but home lacks peers and access to them depends on adult permission. At school play is legitimated through psychological schemas within the curriculum for younger but not for older children. Playtimes are designated according to school custom and the curriculum; free play with peers in the playground is structured by resource allocation which determines numbers of children and the size and character of the playground. In the neighbouring area, children's access to space and time for exercise depends on adult allocation of resources for facilities, and on adult – mostly parental – time and willingness: to accompany, to pay. Children are thus faced with a paradox: play is sanctioned at home, and in its neighbourhood, but restricted by adult agendas. At school, play is sanctioned and valued for younger but not for older children. Exercise is controlled by adults at home and at school. In particular it may be devalued in the school curriculum, and symbolically through the facilities available (Titman 1994), though it is valued in health education messages.

Health maintenance

Time to stay healthy and time to be ill are the topics here. At home, children's time is subject to both parental and school timetables. Children are aware that their time at home is determined by parental routines, and that mothers have responsibility for getting the family off the ground in the morning.

> When I get up, my dad wakes up and I, when my mum's awake she
> makes my dad sandwiches for work, then he goes to work. My mum has
> a cup of tea and when she's finished her cup of tea, then we have
> breakfast and then we watch the video. Then we dress ourselves for
> school and Mum puts our shoes on and we go to school.
>
> (Jean, aged 5)

School timetables require adjustment at home of sleep and leisure patterns, nutrition and exercise. Home time and school time are interlinked for mothers and for children, and management of these linkages forges working partnerships between mothers and children. School demands that children organize home time to fit in with school timetables. This includes getting up and getting organized, on time; remembering to take books, food, clothes back and forth to school as required. Children work in alliance with mothers to meet school demands: preparing packed lunches, cooking and dress-making for school events. Children act as liaison workers between home and school: making sure mothers provide them, on time, with the right belongings (food, money, swimming clothes, written replies to school requests, sickness notes). Mothers identified links between school timetables and children's social development:

I: Does he look after himself more [or less] nowadays?
Mother: He would never brush his teeth or his hair, or get dressed unless you told him to do it. But now he has to; there are limits on his time; he's expected to be places on time, so he has to do these things. If he's going out, to school, he'll get his shoes on and tie them, so he's got into that at school, because you have to do it at school, so I suppose in that way . . .

But school timetables also control mothers' and children's time-use in less agreeable ways:

Mother: It's this rush and hurry.
I: To get them there?
Peter: Yeah –
Mother: – the whole thing. It doesn't matter what time you get up, even if I get up half an hour earlier, we still end up with this rush, and it's like 'Come on, hurry up, hurry.' And it's one of the things that, when it's half-term or weekends, you think, Oh, you don't have to rush.

And mothers are required to act as subordinates to the social norms of school (Smith 1988: ch. 5; Ribbens 1993; Mayall 1994a: ch. 7). This includes ancillary work: helping in class, accompanying on trips and to swimming lessons, mending books, washing cushions, and helping with fundraising. It includes the work intrinsic to presenting their children in good physical shape each day. It may include helping the school reach academic targets, by teaching the child at home. It includes accepting school definitions of good motherhood, and modifying their socializing behaviour to suit these.

Time present and time future are implicated in how schools respond to children's sickness bids. Alan Prout (1986) has described both parental and teacher suspicion of these in the context of curriculum demands. Top juniors' success in sickness bids was affected by school priorities: when the heat was on (before secondary school transfer decisions), recorded numbers of illness absence from school were fewer than when these decisions had been made (Prout 1992). In the Greenstreet study, which looked across the school years, it seemed that legitimation of illness was easier for the younger than for the older children. Whilst teachers of younger children aimed to train children to discount minor discomfort as part of socialization, they also worked closely with mothers to ensure children's well-being, and recognized tensions between school agendas and timetables and the children's biological timetables. Teachers of older children, whose top concern was to 'deliver' the formal curriculum, also indicated their suspicion that children had learned to work the system.

Within school, both curriculum demands and socialization agendas condition children's ability to go sick. As Pia Haudrup Christensen (1993) notes, staff tend to say 'Let's wait and see how you go; meanwhile do your best to work.' For children, the time present of feeling ill and wanting time now to be ill sometimes has to give way to adult emphasis on time future: learning for adult life. A Greenstreet example where socialization agendas took precedence over pain, was when a reception class child cut her lip badly in a playground collision at the end of the morning; her teacher asked her to take part in dinner-time, play and the afternoon session. In discussing this event, the teacher explicitly placed socialization above 'fussing unnecessarily over a child'. But there were also instances in both the reception class and class 5 where children who complained of feeling ill were told to lie down on the carpet with cushions, and just read, or sleep; teachers, as caring people, thought this was the best (and instrumentally most effective) course of action. Alternatively, teachers sent children to the non-teaching staff for diagnosis, care and treatment. However, teachers of older children wrote off frequent and regular complainers as just that: 'the regulars' who tried it on; and they got short shrift. In one case a mother finally came to confirm that her daughter really did have the health problem she complained of. Indeed teachers noted that their own ignorance of health matters could make diagnosis and judgement difficult.

Children's understanding of the process of going sick at school was that the social world of school was not always sympathetic or responsive. They perceived that their bodily experience was not respected, as this boy suggests:

> Miss X – she shouts all the time. One day I was ill, really sick and sitting down, and she comes up to me and stands next to me, and starts to shout at me: 'Where's your book, why are you sitting next to the window? Only people who are sick can sit by the window.'

Among the older Greenstreet children, gender differences in health-related behaviour were evident: girls were more likely than boys to ask for help about accidents or ill-health. They also discussed each other's health conditions with each other and with their class teacher. Boys had learned that boys don't cry (Askew and Ross 1988). In fact, several boys in conversation with me, as a non-official adult, referred to, and displayed, minor injuries for which they did not intend to seek help at school. Mothers also reported gender differences: girls, but not boys had sought help at school. One mother cited an extreme case: her son had fallen at school, had not complained (he 'never' would), but his injury (a broken arm) was spotted by the head teacher.

The legitimation of sickness in teachers' eyes was a function not only of acute and obvious distress, but also of parental information and request. In cases of chronic conditions (such as asthma) or specific conditions 'under the hospital' or merely if the mother requested care or management, teachers agreed without question. Teachers assigned to mothers responsibility for children's physical health and regarded themselves as the experts on psychological health. In the eyes of the school, the division of labour for child health care was between parents and school staff; children themselves were not responsible for their own health. A graphic indicator of this is the demand that parents legitimate school absence with a note or phone call. This understanding of the division of labour contrasts with the children's own understanding (as discussed on pp. 91–5) that they themselves were responsible for self-care at school, though constrained by school agendas.

Neglect by the education service of the time present of children's health is shown in the SSRU national survey of 620 primary schools. In 36 per cent of schools, no member of the teaching staff had any health-care training, and a further 37 per cent had done only a short first-aid course (fewer than six sessions or three days). Slightly more of the non-teaching staff had some training – mostly short first-aid courses. In 13 per cent of schools no adult had any training (SSRU 1994: 20–2). In addition, only 58 per cent of schools had written guidelines for the management of ill children, 58 per cent for accidents and 25 per cent had written guidelines for neither eventuality (p. 25). Furthermore, the provision of a place where children could rest and be cared for was patchy. Only 10 per cent had a sole use first-aid room, and another 7 per cent a room shared just with the school health service. In nearly half the schools (46 per cent) ill children shared space with the supervisors, secretary, head or another person or function. In 37 per cent of schools there was no space designated as space for first aid at all (p. 26). These data indicate that health care has low priority for the education service. It relies instead on women's willingness and ability to add caring on to whatever job they are formally paid to do: secretarial, administrative, teaching.

In sum, like adults, children are subject to demands that their bodily rhythms are subordinated to the social order. As a social group they have particular difficulties about making their voices heard, about finding a time for their bodies in the context of school agendas. Health care is not formally recognized as a component of school agendas, if we judge by policies on training and space to meet health-care needs. An important feature of children's subordination is the alliance constructed between adults across school and home. Thus, on absence for sickness, school accepts parental not child statements; and it is mothers' negotiations with teachers about the management of chronic conditions (such as asthma, eczema) that ensure school compliance.

The school health service

The provision of formal health services within the education system has been described earlier (pp. 23–4), where it was suggested that historical factors, current fears about duplication of service within the NHS and models of childhood served to structure the present, threatened low-key school health service (SHS). This is a service which has traditionally worked in the public health tradition, monitoring health through routine inspections and referral. It has only recently begun to think in terms of the children as its clients. Here it is considered as a service to children.

The most striking feature of the SHS is the low provision of staff time and its consequent inability to serve children well. Again the SSRU national survey (1994) provides some data. Frequency of staff visits varied widely. In 25 per cent of schools, the nurse visited up to once a term, in 50 per cent two or more times a term, and in 17 per cent once a week. The doctor was more rarely sighted: in 19 per cent schools s/he came once a year, in 37 per cent two or three times a year, and in only 2 per cent once a week. The dentist generally (71 per cent) came once a year.

For children, there are two principal implications of the service: poor access to a trained health professional and poor opportunity during consultations for raising their own agendas. Traditionally, children as a class file through, perhaps once a year, to be inspected by the doctor, nurse or dentist. Presumably this is thought adequate for defect-spotting. So children do not have access to a health professional as and when they need it. As a social event, filing through for inspection is not conducive to children's raising their own health agendas. Conversely, children have no choice about submitting to inspection: informed consent plays no part in a service designed for universalist defect-spotting.

The SHS is not structured and operationalized to serve children directly. Thus in our survey only 30 per cent of schools had a sole use room for health staff – so most children have no access to a private health consultation (SSRU 1994: 41). The Greenstreet school nurse told me that children would grab her in the corridor – presumably only the more daring would do so. Turnover of nurses is high – the poor pay and conditions of work are implicated, according to nurses, so children will lack familiarity with the nurse. The rarity of visits, and the fact that children are meant to be always under the eye of teacher or playtime supervisor, make access difficult. And finally, it is not suggested to children that they might make use of the service themselves. Things are changing slightly, probably under the influence of the children's rights movement: some schools now offer 'health interviews', a more leisurely meeting (half an hour at Greenstreet), where the nurse is taught to give children space and time to discuss any issue (HVA 1988).

In the Greenstreet study, no child mentioned consulting the nurse or doctor. However, mothers, asked whether they valued the SHS, thought children should have access to professional health care, and that schools should be staffed to deal with child illness and accident. Mothers argued in terms of confidentiality, convenience and children's rights for an accessible health service in school. They gave examples of occasions when the school had failed to diagnose conditions, and where their primary schoolchildren had wanted and in some cases sought help on their own, for instance about stomach pains, difficulties in class, fears about cancer. As mothers said, there were health issues, including school-related health issues, which children might prefer to raise with an independent person, rather than with teacher or parent. The school nurse mentioned menstruation, body shape and body image, headaches, difficulties with reading and hearing. As she said 'It's easier in secondary school, because the nurses are based there, they're there all the time, so the children know they'll be in the medical room the majority of the time, so they can come when they like.' In the health authority area where she worked, a nurse was based in each secondary school; it is not known how general this is nationally. Presumably nurse : child ratios favour the basing of a nurse in secondary, but not in primary schools.

Finally, the education service and the health service have no formal links which might benefit children's health and welfare. As the head teacher at Greenstreet said, now as in the past, 'the school health service's main *raison d'être* was to keep health and education separate, you know. What is health is health, and you have no right to look at the records; this is confidential to us . . .'

Liaison at school level, as she and other teachers noted, was a matter for personal initiative by teacher and nurse (the doctor did not figure in these conversations). The national survey data (SSRU 1994) indicate that 53 per cent of heads had an agreed procedure for liaison with the SHS, but liaison between class teachers and the SHS was informal in 53 per cent of schools. SHS liaison with parents was through agreed procedures in 54 per cent of schools, and informally in 29 per cent; 8 per cent of respondents said there was no liaison and a further 9 per cent did not reply on this. In sum, the SHS is a good example of a service which by tradition has been adult-oriented: designed to collect data for adults. The time-allocation of health staff has reflected this design. Recent moves towards offering a child-oriented service are hampered by the costs allocating staff time within a health service that has no tradition of conceptualizing children as people in their own right.

Children's time?

That children's time is organized by adults in adult interests, is well attested; a particular problem for children is that adult timetables often conflict with body time. Children, like adults, seek time where they have control over activity. For children, as for the onlooking adult, there is a tension between control in adult-free domains, and control during participation in adult-ordered domains.

The evidence is that children at primary school age have little freedom from parental supervision, based on fear. Colin Ward has documented the narrowing of opportunities for children to roam freely, under both urban (1990) and rural conditions (1988). Hillman and colleagues (1991) have shown how children's mobility has decreased in recent years. Robin Moore (1986) described how, nevertheless, some children identify and colonize urban spaces: waste ground, spaces between buildings, garage-lots; though these may lie within sight of adults or not far away, they offer children the space to develop time-honoured activities – making homes, inventing games.

Further evidence is provided by a study of children's out-of-school activities. Pat Petrie and Penny Logan (1984) collected data from all 7- and 10-year-olds and their mothers living in a small multi-ethnic area of London. They found, not surprisingly, that more of the older children, especially boys, were allowed some freedom to spend time out of the house unsupervised. (On a freedom scale of 1 to 8, juniors averaged 6.2: boys 6.6, girls 5.9; and infants 2.6: boys 2.8, girls 2.5.) Mothers had rules about roads, strangers and distance away from home; and these were understood by the children. Children themselves reported playing mainly on the street or estate (49 per cent), with fewer playing in gardens (23 per cent) or public parks (14 per cent). Playing in the colonized urban spaces identified by Moore's sample was rare. It was also notable that children mentioned traffic danger and 'scarey' places most frequently as problems in their area, and that the main attraction of their neighbourhoods was the presence of friends (30 per cent), and facilities such as parks and shops (25 per cent).

The Greenstreet study bore out these accounts. Mothers set limits on spatial mobility according to their perception of their children's sense, and of their fears about adults' behaviour (in cars, as abductors and abusers). Limits on spatial mobility led to limits on children's own use of time. At 5 all children were accompanied to and from school; at 9 some were allowed to walk with friends. The older Greenstreet children valued space and time relatively free of adult control: though they understood it as permitted within the limits of overall supervision. As Viola notes, getting to the park involves adult escort:

I: What's life like out of school?
Viola: Much better! I go to my friend's house. And they take us up the park. And that's better than running about the playground because – I don't know.
Billy: It's much better. Because there's no one to tell you off. You've got more space. It's crowded in school.

The 9-year-olds were mostly allowed out with friends, in the street, on the estate, near home, or in the local park (6 of 8 girls; 13 of 14 boys). Only two (boys) talked about going further afield, on buses. The ability to make some choices, and above all not to be under the immediate control of parent or teacher was valued.

Ben: I like playing tennis, being with friends.
I: Do you prefer being with friends to parents?
Dean: Easily! You can do what you like, go where you like. Buy crisps. Where, with parents, they go 'NO!' It's true, isn't it?
I: Last week [half term] did you enjoy that?
Dean: Yes, really good. I went out every day with my friends. My parents just picked me up at the end of the day.

The achievement of time and space out of sight of parents (if not out of their minds) probably constitutes a small but valued component of children's daily lives. However, children construct social worlds of their own within and across the worlds of home and school. Their friendship groups constitute arenas for the development of their own interests. Judging by Greenstreet children's accounts, interacting with computers both at home and school provided intellectual stimulation without adult control. They did not refer to TV in these terms – it seemed to be a fall-back when nothing else offered; but others have noted children's constructive interpretations of what they see on TV (Buckingham 1994). The media revolution is providing children in advanced societies with new means of achievement and control. They regard interaction with computers as fun; learning and enjoyment are linked as not, for many, most of the time, at school. 'Children learn more outside the classroom than in it, in a world where they're increasingly used to computers in their bedroom, cable TV, satellite television and computer games' (Chapman 1994). Arguments such as these suggest that education as conventionally provided through books and teacher talk may be increasingly inadequate and inappropriate for children (Gardner 1993). However, both gender and social class inequalities are implicated in the brave new technological world.

The idea of children's own domains has traditionally, and certainly in reminiscences, included space and time where they are free to control activity. As suggested at the beginning of this chapter, this idea rests partly on the belief that children as developing individuals should be free to learn creatively and to enjoy activity, unhampered by the responsibilities and constraints that adults face. So investigators have studied whether, when and where children can squeeze out their own domains, for the exercise of traditional activities. Whilst such concerns focus on an important aspect of children's rights and freedoms, and on the quality of their daily life, it is equally important to consider how far children can participate in social life. For children's accounts strongly suggest that whilst, like adults, they value free time and space to use as they choose, there is an equally strong current in their thought, which values participation.

Children value highly creative, active learning of skills and knowledge, and participation in issues relating to social life. As I have tried to suggest in this and the previous chapter, children engage with the construction of relationships, consideration of moral dilemmas and the maintenance of the social order of the home. The children's conversations with each other indicate their delight in discussion. The argument that education is about preparing children for future adult life fits only partly with how children talk and act: they are engaged now in the moral enterprise of living during childhood. This argument suggests one reason why some children find time at school less rewarding than time at home, free time, and interaction with friends and computers. These offer better opportunities for interactive and creative learning and participation in the construction of knowledge and social relationships.

In this chapter, four main aspects of children's experience have been considered: food, play and exercise, health management, and the school health service. The effects of certain interlocking factors on children's experience have been explored: adult timetables and agendas, adult remits with children, and models of childhood. At school, children experience the devaluing of their body clocks and bodily experience, in the face of adult timetables and constructions of childhood; for the time future of children predominates over their time present. At home, adult agendas constrain children's play, but encourage children to participate in household maintenance and family relationships. Children experience both control over activity and valuation of their bodily and social identities, in time present and for time future.

seven

Children and childhoods revisited

This book seeks to contribute to understandings of childhood. Through studying the social conditions within which childhood is lived, it has explored the idea of children as a social group within society. This enterprise has structured the book, which has dealt, in turn, with large-scale policies and practices, with adults' knowledge, with the home and school as social contexts for children's daily lives, and with children's own accounts of their experiences. Thus in Chapter 2, aspects of child-related policies and practices were outlined: child health policies; the status of health in the social world of education; the knowledge adults bring to childcare and the division of labour in health care between adults and children; the designation of women as responsible for childcare; and finally the allocation and restriction of resources to enable children to live healthy lives. Chapter 3 explored the knowledge that adults bring to their constructions of children and childhood, with particular emphasis on psychological and sociological traditions of thinking about children. In Chapter 4 the discussion moved on to consider the home and the school as social environments in which children live. A principal topic here was the knowledge and experience women bring to their daily lives with children, in tension with social expectations of what their activities should comprise. These three chapters thus constitute an attempt to consider social and economic forces that provide structures within which children live and with which they engage in interaction. Chapters 5 and 6 start from the perspectives of children themselves in order to explore their experiences of the home and the school, and in particular their relationships during life lived with the adults in the two settings.

Of central importance in reconsidering childhood through the knowledge adults and children acquire is the status of both bodies and minds, and linkages between the two. The evidence is that most psychology and most sociology has focused on the mind, and attempted to relegate the body to the natural and to the private. It is women's theoretical work in this area, building on their experience of managing their bodies and minds in both the private and public domains, that has been a major determinant in exposing deficiencies in theories which aim to separate the two and devalue the physical. In this book, it has been critical to respond to what children themselves say and to recognize how in their daily lives at home and at school the civilizing, regulating and constructing of their bodies is managed and negotiated. These two social contexts operate with distinctive evaluations of the body. For mothers at home, their children's well-being depends on the care and comfort of bodies and minds, seen as interlinked and interactive. For teachers at school, children's physical well-being is subordinated to cognitive activity, and the division of labour serves to reinforce divisions in adults' activities and children's experience. So children learn at home that physical and mental well-being are interlinked, but are asked at school to subjugate the first to the second.

These explorations of childhood have required consideration of the gendered character of knowledge, which in turn bears upon children's experience. For in both psychology and sociology, malestream theories have been developed to complement and support the lives lived by men. The interest of male theorists in adult activities in the public worlds of work fits neatly with the construction of children as merely developing non-persons, of the home as the site of socialization, with women as its natural agents, and of the school similarly as taking forward socialization within a group setting, with women acting as agents of state enterprises. It has been important in this book to consider the sources of knowledge held by women, and the ways in which this knowledge serves to reconstruct our ideas about the status of children. This chapter builds on earlier discussions to consider how children may be incorporated into sociology, and how incorporating children must lead to reconsideration of sociological frameworks.

Children as a social group

Childhood emerges from macro analysis in the Childhood as a Social Phenomenon (CSP) project as a period of subjection to adult interests, and of exclusion from adult social worlds. In the industrialized countries where the project was conducted, children's incompetence in the highly specialized differentiated worlds of adult activity provides an explanation for children's exclusion, and the protectiveness which accompanies it. The social and physical environment constructed by adults is understood not only as ignoring children's interests, but as hostile to them. Within the framework of these propositions children as a social group have little say in how they live through their childhoods. Their voices are muted and disregarded. Their daily lives are structured through adults' organization of time and place, and the management of children's bodies and minds. The importance of pointing to these features of modern childhood in industrialized countries is clear. It counteracts the notion that children are indisputably the objects of benevolent adult attention, acting in children's interests, and protected from a hostile world by social and economic provisions.

The CSP work has been immensely useful in presenting a large view and identifying themes to be pursued in each country in the light of local conditions. In considering the work, we have to note that an important impetus for the project was the deliberate institutionalization of children in some Scandinavian countries, in complement to high rates of parental employment. Whilst Scandinavia presents a unique combination of concern for children's welfare, and of massive interventions which have, for better or worse, changed the condition of childhood, neither of these trends are evident in Britain as simple parallels. Commentators here note the general hostility to children's welfare (e.g. Ennew 1993; Kumar 1993; Oppenheim 1993) and to their rights (Rosenbaum and Newell 1991; Lansdown 1994); and, whether as victims or as threats to the social order, they are (like women) commonly defined as a social problem (Hendrick 1994). The social condition of childhood in the UK is characterized by hostility and neglect; and commentary on children and parents is characterized by individualistic victim-blaming rhetoric about such moral panics as changes in family structures, educational achievement, child abuse and youth crime (see Ennew 1993). Though more mothers now go out to work, we have not provided daycare places for children; the private market, friends and relations have continued to help out. UK policies ensure that, compared to children in some countries, they spend less time in nursery care, longer hours in formal schooling, and less time in out-of-school centres than in some countries; time at home with a parent may take up a larger proportion of their time. But time under their own control may be decreasing in most countries.

Theories derived from large-scale considerations provide a framework within which to consider how childhood is lived. But because the policies and practices in place will be specific to any one country, it is appropriate to use the concepts developed in the CSP project with caution, as tools to think about the UK circumstances of children, rather than as precepts. Currently we lack large-scale studies of childhood in Britain, and have few small-scale ones. We need more studies, to throw light on how children and their parents understand contemporary childhood; whether for parents, childhood has changed and for the worse or better; and whether children regard childhood as a problem to be escaped from, as adult tyranny, or as offering more in the way of opportunities than of constraints and frustrations.

The Greenstreet study indicated that children share points of view on their social positioning. It was clear that both age-groups recognized adult–child power relations as operating both at home and at school, though negotiation was legitimized at home. They understood the dual functions of the education system – skill-provision and childminding – to provide them with the skills to function in the adult world, and to protect them during the day while their parents worked. They were fully aware of the need for adult protection in a dangerous adult-constructed world. Within that context, it was evident that, as a social group, they were like other people in desiring some space and time to choose their own activities. The data also indicate the importance for children of personal relationships, in particular relationships they played a part in developing at home, and relationships with friends at school and in the neighbourhood. The value of achievement ran through their accounts, and so did enjoyment of participation, both in learning and in social interaction.

There are other pointers in the Greenstreet data to children's understanding that they constitute a social group, with its own interests in and perspectives on the social world, a group whose members are subject in specific ways to social forces. Children's conversations strongly suggest identification with other children and with the childhoods they experienced in common. When one girl or boy introduced a theme, others acknowledged it, picked it up and ran with it, and discussed the detail of the general proposition, with each contributing a view. For instance, they discussed: power relations at home; the character of life at home from a child's point of view; the control exercised by adults over their free time; how children's daily lives at school were organized and controlled by teachers; and their opportunities for activities and social groupings outside the immediate control of adults. Undoubtedly, as a social group, children saw themselves as actors whose position required them to negotiate with, and occasionally fight against parents and school teachers.

The agency of children as a group has to be seen in tension with the understandings of childhood held by adults; and these in turn vary according to social context. Thus children's ability to negotiate through interaction is modified by structural factors. I have suggested that at home, the framework of social norms was permeable. Mothers' emotional identification with their children allowed them to negotiate the social order of the home both for specific instances – whether or not they had to clean their room today; and in accordance with individual development: as a child acquired knowledge and competence, the socially expected activities were gradually altered. The school presented a much less permeable normative framework, within which teachers acted more closely in accordance with notions of child development and with prevailing social norms; so children found it more difficult to negotiate. When they felt ill, tired or in need of a drink, it often required more than a statement of need to secure teacher acceptance that they break through the regime. However, teachers themselves were aware of the tensions between the pull of the regime and of their caring dispositions, and sometimes allied themselves with the children. An example was where a teacher stopped work early and read the children a story, because she could see they were exhausted and restless. In more general terms, then, it seems that children's agency is conditioned by the interacting strength of the social norms and of adult responses to those norms and to the children's bids.

Framing the daily lives of children, and adult attitudes and behaviours towards them, are large-scale policies and practices. Here the UK stands in contrast to some other 'advanced' industrialized countries, for children come low on the political agenda. As was outlined in Chapter 2, children are poorly served in a number of critical respects: through the package of services and financial resources impacting on their lives via the severe rationing of resources for the public daycare and education service; through policies on health, housing, transport and leisure facilities; and through hostility to children's rights. Children have no power to change these policies, the adults closely concerned with and for them have very little power, and adults vary in the extent to which they endorse these policies. As actors, therefore, children can make some headway at micro level in negotiating their social position, in particular at home, where the intergenerational contract has some flexibility and respect for childhood and children. But they have no power to work towards modifying social policies that affect them as a social group.

Bodies and minds: health and education

The designation of children as pre-social objects of adult attention compounds with the designation of mothers as their carers within the private domain, to construct a model of society where the private, natural and bodily are contrasted with the public, civilized and cognitive. Mothers' natural task in the privacy of the home is to deal with the bodily, to prepare children for the world of the cognitive, and to hand them over to that world in due course. This model breaks down in the face of interpenetration of the cognitive and bodily across the domains: thus mothers are required to work across the private and public domain, in co-operation with arbiters of child social and cognitive development. And the public world of school, in taking children into its 'care' is thereby forced to take account of caring for the bodily alongside the cognitive.

However, in the study of childhood there is a problematic grey area between the idea of children as natural and bodily, and the idea of adults as civilized and cognitive: that is, how and through what agencies the transition takes place towards adulthood. Furthermore, children inhabit triple personhood: they are persons now, are in process towards another version of personhood, and are too the persons they will become. In this book relationships, tensions and conflict between body and mind have constituted an appropriate arena for exploring where children are socially positioned and how adults recognize, manage and manipulate children's social positioning in the light of their ambiguous social and generational status.

One of the main themes emerging from these explorations is tension between integration and separation. It seems that mothers regard bodies and minds as integrated: in theory and in practice the care of one cannot be divorced from the care of the other, since they are mutually influential. This view is likely to be held also by some health and welfare professionals, and within pre-school settings, such as day nurseries, childminding, play centres. Nursery schools and classes provide a bridge between home and school, between the integrated view and the separated: for staff will strive, at least for an hour or two a day, to socialize the children into restraining and downgrading their bodies in favour of cognitive activities. At primary school the process continues, with designated play and exercise periods gradually reduced, in favour of the formal academic curriculum. Of particular interest in this process is the perceived role and actual behaviour of school teachers, who are largely women. They are caught within, and to some extent endorse, a system which requires them to deliver the curriculum and manage large groups of children, and which moreover aims to socialize children into adherence to group codes. Yet there were many instances in the Greenstreet data where teachers put the bodily well-being of children first, if only temporarily, and if only because the cognitive would be served by attention to the bodily and emotional.

But children learn at school that adults make a conceptual distinction between the bodily and the cognitive, implement the distinction in practice, and ascribe relative values to each. This is indicated to children through the timetabling of the day, with its work and recreation periods clearly demarcated, and through the complementary delegation of supervision and of care to non-teaching staff at playtime, dinner-time and in case of illness and accident. Here the division of labour between adults frames children's experience. Play is endorsed as a proper part of education in infant but not junior classes. Children, keen to be active, find the amount of time teachers allot to physical education is small. The physical care of children is largely in the hands of non-teachers: the supervisors/helpers, dinner ladies, secretary. Health education is likely to be a cognitive classroom topic, conceptually and practically separated from the provisions in the education system for attending to children's bodily well-being. Thus children are likely to absorb the message that the bodily is a separate consideration from the cognitive and that the cognitive is more highly valued by teachers. Within the school enterprise the time future of children is more highly valued than the time present.

Children learn that both age and gender are implicated in the social construction of their bodies and minds. As they get older they are meant to subdue their bodies. Yet in many schools boys will be allowed greater latitude for activity: the domination of playgrounds by boys is well documented (Blatchford and Sharp 1994). Iris Young (1980) has discussed how girls learn to restrict bodily movement, and to operate in smaller spaces than boys. An exploration in one primary school of how school staff responded to sickness bids (Prout 1986) found that the secretary judged these in terms of both gender and age: she thought younger children more often feigned illness than older, but older girls more than older boys. Paradoxically, as children reach the top of the primary school, they are likely to find a sudden classroom focus on their bodies, in the shape of sex education. Yet it appears that schools do not provide for the day-to-day implications of puberty: menstruating girls are poorly served at school (Prendergast 1992); this is particularly relevant at secondary schools, but primary schools too are increasingly faced with the educational and practical implications of lower ages of menarche.

A further important theme concerns children's independent control over their bodies. I have suggested that at school children have to unlearn what they learn at home. Learning to manage one's own body at times to suit its needs is valued at home, but that learning has to give way to having one's body managed to suit the school timetable. This very broad statement immediately needs qualification: homes too demand that children's own clocks give way to adult-run home routines: in terms of meal-times, bed-times, playtimes. But the value assigned to children's self-care actions is high at home compared to school. At a practical level, the state primary school day seems ill-suited to the wishes of children for physical activity. Perhaps the timetable at prep schools and in Scandinavian schools, where academic work is concentrated in a short time-span each day, are better suited to children. It is an open question.

I have noted earlier (Chapters 2 and 6) the separation of health from education at all levels from ministerial to school staff level. Collaboration is not structured into health and education services, but depends on individual initiative. The division of labour, whereby health and education services employ separate sets of staff with discrete remits, serves to show children that their bodies and minds are separated in the adult mind. Currently the idea of the health-promoting school is receiving some research, policy and practice attention across Europe with the aim of working towards a whole-school approach to health promotion – in the physical, social and educational environment. The World Health Organization (WHO) (1993) document '*The European Network of Health Promoting Schools*' emphasizes that encouragement to adopt healthy life-styles requires a health-promoting physical environment and a social environment which promotes people's self-esteem and enables them to fulfil their physical, psychological and social potential. We have yet to see whether or how this broad programme will be implemented in the UK. Health promotion is a phrase commonly used in the UK to suggest a more integrated approach to health in schools. However, it seems from documentation so far (HEA 1993; NFER 1994; Northern Ireland Curriculum Council 1994) that the movement is concerned mainly with improving the quality of health education within the formal and informal curriculum, rather than with improving children's access to good health through the provision of a health-promoting social and physical environment. Indeed, given the split responsibility for health and education and the current squeeze on school spending, it is unlikely that many UK schools will proceed beyond the goal of improving children's behaviour (cf. Morton and Lloyd 1994 for discussion).

So this exploration of the construction of children's lives at home and school points to evaluations of bodies and minds and of links between these as a key to understanding how children experience their daily lives. The integrated approach intrinsic to care at home progressively breaks down in the education system as children proceed through it. The division between health and education services both parallels and reinforces the separation of bodies from minds. Children experience the demand to subjugate their bodies in the interests of education. The current policy interest in health education points up tensions in the UK education system: the unequal status of bodies compared to minds conflicts with curriculum and whole school policies to link the two.

Gender and generation

Study of children as agents requires consideration of the interacting forces of gender and generation. These are both relational concepts where subordination of one group to the other is systematically structured (Alanen 1994): females to males and young to old. I have explored how these relationships are operationalized, and what resistances children and women can and do make to them. For most children, the principal adult in their lives is their mother, and study of gendered and generational issues in child–mother relationships probably constitutes the best hope for understanding the construction of children's lives and the character of their experience of childhood.

As discussed in Chapter 6 (pp. 115–16), whilst women at home are required to socialize their children to fit them for the wider world, women propose the home as a free zone where publicly unacceptable behaviours are, under some circumstances, permitted. Within the home, Greenstreet girls and boys indicated that they regarded both mothers and fathers as authority figures and as controllers of their social lives. But it is women rather than men who work across the private and public domains to both regulate and enable children; and so it is children and their mothers who may collaborate to resist the public world of male adults. Yet these intergenerational relationships are cross-cut by gender: the girls were more closely involved in daily activities with their mothers. The Greenstreet children's accounts of home and school provided some evidence that girls had closer identification with the relational world of the home: they talked more about participation in activities such as preparing packed lunches, and doing housework; they also talked and wrote more about relationships with and activities with their mothers. Fewer boys talked about these, but their writing did address such topics. It may be that the social construction of boyhood inhibited their talking about relationships.

Gender differences at school in experience and scholastic achievement (e.g. Tizard *et al.* 1988: 7), can be further understood through consideration of how children's bodies as well as their minds are managed by the regime and by the specifics of teacher behaviour. The Greenstreet regime seemed to offer girls (compared to boys) a more sympathetic package: they were less irked by physical restriction at school, and perhaps were better at pacing the day; school emphases on cognitive activity complemented girls' interest and achievement in reading and writing. Boys found physical restriction disabling and a disincentive to conforming to the official curriculum of 'sitting down and writing up'. So there may be gendered differences for children in the body–mind conflict. The amount of physical activity included in the curriculum at individual schools will depend on both governmental emphases and direction, and on the interests of staff; for instance, women teachers, who predominate in primary schools, may give low priority to PE. Playtime was clearly a gendered experience: the culture of the playground, as has been documented elsewhere, requires boys to engage in 'gross motor' activity; 5-year-olds found this daunting, older boys varied. For girls, playtime involves finding companions to act as physical and psychological buffers in the crowded active playground.

Gender and generation are implicated in children's caring work. By the age of 5, girls have already learned at their mother's knee that girls may and should care for people, and that it is legitimate to seek help from adults at school for illness and accident. Boys seemed less active in caring work and less likely to seek help. It is not only that norms of children's behaviour were gendered, but that these were reinforced through the gendered structure of the school; not only the teachers, but also the class helpers/supervisors – who were the principal carers – were women. So the world of caring is presented to girls and boys as female: both within and across generations. Having observed that, however, we have to cross-cut the cake once again: children at school respond to the generational order: in a social world with relatively strange adults, it is up to children to make out as best they can; and both girls and boys form alliances to help each other (Haudrup Christensen 1993).

There is a long tradition of work suggesting forcibly that schools are hostile to girls: they denigrate girls' ability and connive at teaching girls to fail academically and socially and to accept traditional gendered roles (Deem 1980; Walkerdine 1989; Connell 1994; Wajcman 1994). Such work has been undertaken as a component of the women's movement, but also specifically to explain girls' academic failure, especially in areas traditionally commandeered by boys: mathematics and technology. The suggestions (which need much more study) arising out of the Greenstreet study, based on consideration of children's social and bodily experience, may help to explain some boys' rejection of school. If the social environment of the school, staffed mainly by women, provides a more sympathetic environment for girls than for boys this may result from empathy between girls and women, but also from the time-allocation to exercise. Where physical activity is recognized as important by school staff, we may see more contented boys and girls; but girls seem better able to bear restriction. Possibly these reflections on the bodily experience of children at school, in relation to academic work may serve, along with possible increases in girls' self-esteem, as one basis for further work exploring why it is that, during the later school years, girls are apparently maintaining their advantage in academic achievement over boys (Grant 1994a).

It would seem that just as the embodied identities of girls and boys at home and at primary school are structured in interaction with mothers' and teachers' knowledge and remits, so children's learned gendered behaviour is reinforced through participation in peer groups to further differentiate girls' from boys' activities and daily experiences.

The division of labour

The study of children's experiences and understandings, although at an early stage, already begins to point to ways in which sociological thought needs modification. It is clear that the way opened up by feminists to challenge traditional sociological frameworks should be further explored through incorporating children's perspectives. In the first place, constituting children as a social group requires exploring the impact of social and economic forces on that group. This was done at a macro level in the Childhood as a Social Phenomenon project. At the level of everyday life, studies are beginning to show the detail of how children's lives are structured by divisions of adult labour in social policies and practices, as well as through specific adult understandings. I gave some examples earlier, citing nutrition, play and exercise, health care and the school health service (Chapter 6). For instance, the character and quality of food available at school is determined by nutritional policies with a long history, by educational thinking about the care of children's bodies, and by the remits and behaviours of adults who immediately provide and supervise dinner-times. Both space and time play their parts in structuring children's daily experience – at home, at school and locally.

In particular, women and children can increase knowledge of how social relations between people are mediated through understandings of their bodies; and as suggested in Chapter 5, the study of early mother–child interactions is illuminating. Since the care of young children demands loving attention to the interactions of their bodies and minds, children learn to value both at home; and to experience links between the two. At school social relations are based on different adult views on the inter-relatedness of bodies and minds. Understanding how children interact with adults at home and school requires putting their bodily experience and perception into the equation. A related topic is the management of emotion, for, as Arlie Hochschild (1979) argues, people are required to do emotion work in connection with the specific role or work they are engaged in – that is, to construct emotional behaviour acceptable to their superiors. The requirement on children is very strong to behave in certain ways, and to adopt specific emotional relationships according to social context. Adults also, within the context of socialization work, act to manage, control and construct children's emotions, both at home and at school.

Constituting children as social actors also requires reconsidering both their contribution to work, and the nature of work itself. Children are best regarded not as costly objects of attention by parents and teachers, but as contributors to the division of labour. Many do paid and unpaid work at home and locally (Ennew 1993; Morrow 1994). Their work at school contributes to the wealth of society; adult work in education is outweighed by children's work in self-capitalization: acquiring literacy, numeracy and skills required for adult social life (Oldman 1994). These contributions are framed within traditional definitions of work: that is, contributions towards production, towards the gross national product. However, building on Stacey's work (1980), we should, as suggested in this book, widen definitions of work to include the people work that both women and children, from their earliest years, engage in. This includes caring for themselves and for others, and contributing to the production and reproduction of the social order of the home, through the activities of home maintenance and the construction of family relationships. Children's competence and engagement in these activities suggests children as net contributors to the division of labour at home.

Children engage in socially useful work, too, through the contribution they make to learning. It is well documented that women are allocated responsibility for teaching children at home and later on at school; and that negotiations about the division of labour take place in an intermediate domain between the private and the public (Stacey and Davies 1983; Wyke and Hewison 1991; David *et al.* 1993). Less fully documented has been children's own part in this early learning enterprise, and in liaison between the public and the private domains; and one function of this book has been to lay out some data on this topic, in order to show at micro level that children participate in learning, and that mothers welcome children's acquisition of knowledge and skill and their assumption of responsibility. Indeed children are teachers: teaching adults how best to be parents. Socialization, therefore, as commonly understood – a top–down enterprise – is a misnomer. Collaborative learning might be a more accurate term. These viewpoints are not new, since psychological study of children's early interactions has recently focused on their abilities rather than their deficiencies (e.g. Dunn 1988). But the concept of children as active participants in early learning at home has been slower to feed into sociological thinking.

The feminist proposition that both women and children should be seen as oppressed, includes for some commentators the further proposition that women should be regarded as oppressors of children, in league with the psy complex (Smith 1988). Whether willingly or not, mothers learn to control and manipulate their children in the interests of social norms. These two propositions seem to offer only a partial fit with what we know of children's experiences. Both propositions deny children agency and suggest that they form part and parcel of women's lives, and are inseparable conceptually from women's lives. But constituting children as a social group requires extracting them from that positioning; it requires considering what is the specific set of relationships they experience with the social order, working out what are the structures of oppression that specifically affect them, and whether there are mitigating characteristics of their social position. Thus, as the next generation of adults, they perhaps have some privileges that are denied to women; and though boys may be granted more respect than girls in most areas of life, the social institution of the school may favour girls more than boys (as discussed earlier). The very considerable weight attached to children's duty to acquire social and educational skills has to carry with it (even for the most rigid top–down educators) some latitude in time and space for children to learn, rather than be taught. If childhood in modern societies is a condition of oppression, it is also one of limited opportunity. On the other hand, compared to women children have even less power to modify their lived experience, including little recognition of their rights. They have to rely on parents to speak for them across the boundaries of the home and the public education and health insitutions which participate in childcare.

Alliances

It is clear that, given their social positioning and their relative lack of experience and knowledge, children cannot make much headway alone in fighting for improved social status. The work of political activists, sociological commentators, national and local pressure groups may slowly begin to dent the massive prevailing denigration and subjection of childhood. Meanwhile children need allies on the ground, on a day-to-day basis. I explore here the argument that women, especially mothers, constitute the natural allies of children, in helping them face the world.

Here we have to take account first of the requirement that women, as child-rearers, socialize children to suit public social norms. It seems from the available evidence that mothers and children recognize both this requirement, and the tension between that ascribed task and the protective, enabling activities of mothers, based on attentive love (Ruddick 1990: 119). Indeed there is no necessary conflict (at all points) between the two kinds of work, for intrinsic to the preparation – including regulation – of children to face the world is giving them the emotional strength and stability to do so.

The character of girls' and boys' relationships with their mothers are relevant here. As ever, we need both theoretical and empirical studies, for we know little about how girls and boys experience these relationships or about how they understand child–parent relationships in general. Such evidence as we have indicates that children of both sexes identify closely, through the primary years, with family relationships, which in most cases includes or comprises child–mother relationships. At a day-to-day level, detailed information from mothers of 5- and 9-year-olds in the Greenstreet study provides evidence of mothers' collaborative work with their children: how mothers prepare their children for school; soothe them at the end of a tiring day; work through with their children problems faced at school; discuss and sort out such problems with teachers; and provide complementary care to fit with the school day. From the children's accounts (see Chapter 6), we learn that children, especially the older boys, save up their grazed legs and their aches and pains, to refer them to their mothers' care at the end of the day. As I have tried to indicate, it seems that girls and boys both regard their mother as the central figure in the home, and they value and contribute to the construction of relationships at home.

The Newsons' (1978) research with mothers of 7-year-olds provides some relevant data. In response to the question 'Would you say he's closer now to you or to his daddy?' – 40 per cent of mothers reported no difference, 40 per cent thought their son or daughter was closer to them, and only 19 per cent to his/her father. Overall class and sex differences were negligible, but in middle-class homes, mothers tended to report no difference, possibly a function of the prevailing ideology of shared parenting (Newson and Newson 1978: 293–4, table 28). In reply to a further question on children's displays of affection (i.e. to parents) three-quarters said their child showed a lot of affection, with no sex or class differences. It seemed too that parental and child behaviour to some extent matched: among the 9 per cent of the children who were 'very reserved', 58 per cent did not receive frequent hugs and kisses, whereas among the highly demonstrative children 95 per cent did so; these data suggest some kind of interaction between adult and child willingness to display affection (pp. 305–10, table 32).

These pieces of information obviously do not provide a full account of the quality of child–adult relationships, but they do suggest that at the age of 7, girls and boys, across the social classes, received much the same quality of emotional care, though there were individual differences between mothers, and in return children gave much the same affection, with again individual, probably interacting, differences. Judging by the mothers' quoted accounts, most of these displays of affection took place within the privacy of the home, a point which links with the earlier one (p. 148) about the home as a free zone, where behaviours not sanctioned in public have currency.

Studies from Scandinavia also show us not to make sweeping generalizations according to sex and age. Anne Solberg (1990, 1995) has analysed data on contributions made by 10- to 12-year-olds to housework, and found that the traditional division of labour between adults held as regards children: women did most and men least; between these two extremes girls came second and boys third, but the difference between girls and boys was smaller than that between women and men, which suggests either that social norms are changing or that boys do less as they become men, or both. She then went on to look in more detail at the out-of-school lives of 12-year-olds and found that these girls and boys (whose school day is shorter than in the UK) were spending considerable periods in charge of the home, and in the process were taking over the home-staying role, while their parents were out at work. That is, they were carrying out activities such as cooking, entertaining their friends, looking after themselves. In turn, mothers regarded their children as competent and independent. Through these changes in the ways in which children and adults use the home, children's social age is increased; and they become collaborators with their mothers in home management.

Some data on these topics for the UK scene is available from the Petrie and Logan (1984) study referred to in Chapter 6. Very few of their 7- and 10-year-olds looked after themselves before or after school (with no person over the age of 14 with them); they constituted 7 per cent of the children of mothers who were students or in paid employment. But self-supervision during the holidays was more common, with 34 per cent of the juniors caring for themselves at some time. Data were collected on children's independence skills (whether they could wash and bath themselves, get a snack, use a sharp knife and tin opener, use a cooker and phone, travel on public transport). Though the findings are complicated, a general point is that children in one-parent families tended to supervise themselves more than those in two-parent families, and tended to have higher domestic skills scores. As Petrie and Logan say (1984: 101), this may be a combination of necessity and of higher value attached by both parents and children to children's independence. And one could say that children granted some independence grow up a bit faster.

How children live their daily lives, and their relationships with their mothers, have been explored in a nordic study (Denmark, Finland, Norway and Sweden) on children in families headed by one adult, the mother. Twenty-five children aged 9 to 13 years were studied in each of the four countries. The general framework for analysis has been worked out cross-nationally, but at present detailed data are available only for the 25 Finnish children (Alanen 1992: 114–36). The study was concerned with the extent to which the child's life was integrated or autonomous in relationship to the mother's life: that is, how far did they share free time, friends and relatives, discussion of problems and daily events. The numbers are small, but there was no clear age difference, and only a slight sex difference: more boys were 'autonomous'. A second dimension studied was organization: how far the child, or mother, or both jointly, organized resources for the child, such as time, space, money, people, and social and commercial services. Again age was only weakly related to child organization; but there were slightly more boys than girls among the co-organized and self-organized groups than among the mother-organized. Cross-tabulation of the two dimensions indicates a range of kinds of relationships between child and mother, and these are structured by the availability of resources and opportunities for choice.

These Scandinavian studies of the complex inter-relationships between children as actors and mothers suggest that in most social circumstances children in these age-groups lead lives that are closely tied in with those of their mothers, so that one can understand their daily lives as collaborative integrated enterprises. Possibly girls are closer to their mothers than boys are. Other data point to gender differences in views on intergenerational relationships. Gunilla Halldén (1994) asked Swedish girls and boys aged 8 and 9 to write about their future families, and the complex data suggest that whilst girls presented a familiar picture of homes headed by a strong mother figure in control of the children, boys tended to omit this figure; no one was in charge, except possibly a child. Gunilla Halldén suggests that the girls took account of relationships, including power relationships, in the home, in the light of their own future status as powerful women at home; whereas the boys seemed to be trying to by-pass power issues, and implicitly to ascribe the mother a subordinate role as fosterer of boys.

These studies provide some interesting pointers to gender similarity and difference in children's relationships with their mothers; they also point to the importance of studies of that most difficult topic: the home, and relationships within it. Understanding of how childhood is negotiated at home in relationship to adults has been gained through detailed accounts of 'yesterday' by children and their parents, collected over spaced visits; these show the gradual intricate transition from being supervised to caring for oneself, and to social competence (Gulbrandsen 1995). Reminiscence is another way in. Mary Field Belenky and her colleagues asked women to reflect on their lives so far; their alliances with their own mothers in some cases carried through to adulthood. Study of the character of these women's knowledge led to the development of the idea of connected knowing: arising out of the experience of intimate, equal relationships, where the goal is understanding (Belenky *et al.* 1986: 183–6). The ideas developed in that project resonate with those of Carol Gilligan and her colleagues, who propose mothers as allies, helping their daughters maintain their own voice, in the face of the male-dominated social order (Brown and Gilligan 1992: 222–32; Gilligan 1993: xxii–xxvii).

The current state of knowledge on the fostering or encouragement by mothers of children's independence and strength within the context of mother–child alliances is very partial, and particularly weak as to how children see this topic. But conceptualizing children as people who participate in the construction of their social worlds through relationships does allow for further study of it – more research is needed!

The public and the private: children as citizens

The above discussion of the division of labour has begun to feed into a principal theme addressed in this book: the position of children as a social group in and across the public and private domains. Essentially the concept of the public and the private, developed in order to describe and discuss how the social order functions, has served the theoretical and experiential interests of those men who developed it. Feminist re-analyses of the history of political thought have sufficiently drawn our attention to the association of the private with the feminine and the subjection of women within that association (e.g. Friedan 1963; Mitchell 1971; Firestone 1972). Jean Bethke Elshtain (1993) reflects on the more extreme early requirements of the women's liberation movement and notes (p. 320) that some visionaries and revolutionaries aimed not to throw the baby out with the bathwater, but to throw the baby out instead of the bathwater. Their demand for the conceptual and policy separation of the biology of childbearing from the social role of mothering has been modified more recently, where analysts have, possibly in the wake of their own acquired status as mothers, sought to link the private and the public by pointing to the character of maternal thinking (Ruddick 1990) and more generally of women's moral thinking (Brown and Gilligan 1992) as bases for the development of a more humane social order. Thus Elshtain (1993: ch. 6) proposes the experiences and social relationships developed in the private domain, including the activities integral to mothering, both as essential to what it is to be human, and as a necessary basis for adequate social and political life. She is calling for the 'redemption of everyday life': for public recognition and acceptance of the complexity of human social life, including experiences gained in the private and public domains.

As many have pointed out, it is not mothering, but the social isolation, denigration and political exclusion of women as mothers that needs to be fought. And that fight includes working towards a voice for women in reconstructing the public order to take account of the values taught and learned in human relationships within the private domain. Similarly, it is not childhood but the condition of childhood that is at stake. Women theorists have fought mainly for women. Elshtain glances at children; she says the young, the old, the infirm may be included as citizens: included 'on terms of an equality guaranteed by their humanness'; they may gather together with others in the name of acting together in common towards ends they debate and articulate in public (Elshtain 1993: 348). But she leaves it to Martin Luther King to give rhetorical force to a dramatic example of implementation:

> A non-violent army has a magnificent universal quality. To join an army that trains its adherents in the methods of violence you must be of a certain age. But in Birmingham, some of the most valued foot soldiers were youngsters ranging from elementary pupils to teen-age high school and college students. For acceptance in the armies that maim and kill, one must be physically sound, possessed of straight limbs and accurate vision. But in Birmingham, the lame and the halt and the crippled could and did join up. Al Hibbler, the sightless singer, would never have been accepted in the United States Army or the army of any other nation, but he held a commanding position in our ranks.
>
> (Martin Luther King quoted in Elshtain 1993: 349)

Indeed if we look for examples where children have participated in movements for social and political change, we find them mainly in respect of overwhelmingly large issues, such as racism in the United States and South Africa, where the boundaries of institutionalized denial of children's knowledge and right to participate are broken by the sheer scale of the problem they, alongside adults, confront. If in the UK we aim to conceptualize children as citizens with the right to participate in the shaping of the social order and their own lives within it, in both the public and private domains, then clearly there is a long way to go.

The Children's Rights Development Unit (1994) provides a comprehensive compilation of the wrongs done to children in the UK. Their report sets out the policies and practices necessary to comply with the UN Convention on the Rights of the Child in the areas of personal freedom, care, physical and personal integrity, standards of living, health and health services, the environment, education, play and leisure, justice, work, immigration and nationality, violent conflict, abduction, and international obligations to promote children's rights. In all these areas of life, UK children are subordinated to adult interests, not only to serve those interests, but because their own interests are regarded as relatively unimportant. They are denied a voice, not only because adult interests are at stake, but also in some areas, because the best interests of the child are defined by adults, and in others because they are deemed incompetent. As Gerison Lansdown (1994) argues, the two most important rights, which need to be enforced in conjunction, are the right (Article 12) to express an opinion and have it taken into account in matters affecting the child, and the right (Article 3) that all actions concerning the child should take full account of her or his interests. Concern for neglect of children's rights in the UK has been expressed by the UN Committee on the Rights of the Child (1995), with a particular focus on the absence of any effective co-ordinating mechanism for implementation of economic, social and cultural rights. Among the UN Committee's many strictures on policy and practice in the UK, the disregard for Articles 3 and 12 comes in for particular criticism. The points the Committee makes are taken up in a Save the Children report (Save the Children 1995) which identifies six key factors implicated in the invisibility of children in planning and policy making: failure to collect child-specific information; lack of recognition of children's productive contribution; exclusion of children from participation in decision making; a standard (Western) model of childhood; the pursuit of adult interests; and the impact of generational and gender factors on children's childhoods. The report calls for action on all these factors with the aim of 'putting children at the heart of policy-making', in line with the principles set out in the UN Convention.

These recent investigations of the status of children's rights show that the idea of children as citizens does not have common currency, at least in the UK. Again we have to turn to feminism – to historians of civil rights – to help us understand this. The history of ideas about citizenship in the UK indicates the increasingly strong link developed over the last 300 years between citizenship and concepts of rationality and independence: through their free status and power of knowledge, rational individuals were independent of other men's [*sic*] will or influence (Davidoff 1990). Integrity – isolation from subjection to others – allowed for the free exercise of reason. Only the rational individual was fitted to be a citizen. Women, subject to men, irrational by nature, were clearly not so fitted. Similarly unfitted were, and are, children, who have not yet attained rationality. In their case, the battle against designating them as irrational and in favour of recognizing their rights, has only just begun.

The designation of a social group as inferior is accomplished and maintained on the basis of their assigned characteristics, which may include physical or biological as well as socially ascribed characteristics. In the case of children, their inherent vulnerability – requiring protection, care and education – is frequently confounded with structural vulnerabilities (Lansdown 1994). Call a person of any age a child, and the inherent vulnerabilities of early childhood will be stretched to include her. In the UK, at 17 people need protection, at 18 they are capable of independent life. Conversely, protection may be withdrawn on the basis of age: many children in care move on their 16th birthday from the status of childhood to a limbo status, from council protection to independent life on the streets (CRDU 1994: 38). Children also suffer under the ascription of irrationality. And this is backed by the massive enterprise of cognitive psychology, which argues for progression towards the adult ideal of mature rationality. There are by now considerable bodies of work which take up these themes. The structural vulnerabilities of children have been exposed through considerations of the education system: (Oldman 1994); family life (Walkerdine and Lucey 1989), welfare (Ennew 1993) and child abuse (Kitzinger 1990; La Fontaine 1990); paid work (Morrow 1994); and leisure (Hillman 1993).

The question of children's rationality has been tackled through the re-examination of cognitive theories about their incompetence (Siegal 1991), and through detailed study of children's abilities to discuss issues of importance to them, and to participate in managing their own lives. Some of the earliest of these studies concerned children 'in care', where adults collected children's views on their daily lives now, their experiences so far and their hopes for the future (Page and Clark 1977). The work has extended to practical politics: the formation of pressure groups to give them a say in the disposition of their lives (Black and in Care; National Association of Young People in Care). It is not by chance that these children first attracted adult interest in their rights: the combination of critical decisions to be made (where to live, with whom) and the fact that many of them have no parent to speak for them, made it obvious they need a forum to express their views. At a policy level, the Children Act 1989 has, at least on paper, recognized children's right to be attended to on matters affecting them. However, the claim (in the official guide to the Act) that it strikes a new balance between the autonomy of the family and the protection of children can readily be interpreted as giving weight to parental responsibilities rather than to children's rights (Hendrick 1994: 281).

Children's competence in analysing and discussing issues that are of importance to them has been revealed in another area where critical issues are at stake: health care. Myra Bluebond-Langner (1978) studied how children find out what adults would rather they did not know, in the particular case: that the child is dying of cancer. She demonstrates children's abilities to read the social scene in hospital and to relate what they see and experience to their own circumstances. Children observed how the care given changed when the health condition deteriorated; they understood their parents' fears and anxieties on their own behalf and for their children. Using this information, children were able to discuss their condition and the treatments and care now and in the future, to make their own preparations for death, and to help their parents bear it. In a further study of the experiences and views of children whose sib had cystic fibrosis, Myra Bluebond-Langner found that the children went through a series of reactions to living in a family where a sib is mortally ill;

this series was related not to age, but to the stages in the progress of the sib's illness (Bluebond-Langner 1994); their knowledge was gained experientially. In another hospital study, Priscilla Alderson (1993) studied children's, parents' and staff's ideas about whether and when children should take part in decisions about surgical treatment. Her study demonstrates children's knowledge about their condition, and their willingness to take part, with their parents, in reaching a decision. The study illustrates how children's competence is linked to experience rather than to chronological age and examines the value of shared, relational decision making (rather than isolated autonomous rationality). Though staff varied in their attitudes to children's rights, some did respect them. These studies provide important ways forward in thinking about children's rationality. Experience rather than age is crucial in providing children with relevant knowledge. Participatory discussion, based on trusted relationships, constitutes an appropriate way of reaching difficult moral and practical decisions, and dealing with important relational crises.

The idea of competence, rather than age, as a marker of people's ability and right to have a say in decisions affecting them has been put on the legal agenda through the Gillick case and subsequent decisions, though granting children a say still meets resistance in some court decisions (Montgomery 1994). Priscilla Alderson (1992) builds on her work on competence to challenge the traditional linkage between rationality and rights. Instead, she argues, we should ground rights in needs; people of whatever age may be competent through experience to voice their needs and demand their rights. Further, all of us are both emotional and rational, and both these qualities are relevant to claiming rights; the division between the rational, autonomous, unemotional man and others is a false one.

Perhaps it is because the implications of decisions for children 'in care' and in hospital are not just critical but immediate, that children's rights command higher respect than in other areas. The education service also critically influences children's lives now and in the future, yet here children in the UK have no effective rights. I suggest that this is because the time present of children is subordinated to time future. Typically children have no say in the running of the school, in determining the curriculum, in how it is delivered, in the health and social aspects of school life (playtime, dinner-time, length of the day and so on). If we want explanations it is easy to find them. Firstly, the state instrumentally wants a return for the huge expenditure on education. Secondly, educationalists at all levels have been specifically instructed that children lack reason. Thirdly, and partly because of this, adults in schools are reluctant to share control (Cowie 1994). Fourthly, any serious attention to children's rights in education would require rethinking important aspects of the social order: such as adults' hours of work and teacher authority.

At ministerial levels, there appear to have been no UK moves to ratify the 1989 UN Convention on the Rights of the Child in respect of education. Allegedly, ministers have claimed that no action was needed since the UK complied with it by providing an educational service and rights to attend

(Lansdown 1994). The emphasis in recent Education Acts and such documents as the Parents' Charter [*sic*] is on parental rights, rather than children's. Children are denied rights to be heard, across the whole range of issues, including equality of access, equality of educational and social experience within the school, and their civil rights within the school system. These include having a voice in matters such as exclusion, truancy, special needs provision, racism and sexism; participation in decisions affecting themselves individually and collectively and in decision making on the running of the school. The UN Committee on the Rights of the Child (1995) referred to above (p. 157) drew particular attention to UK shortcomings in education; it urged 'that children are provided with the opportunity to express their views on matters of concern to them in the running of the schools', and that trainee teachers and children should be taught about children's rights; teaching methods should be inspired by the Convention and notably by Article 29: development of children's potential, and of respect for human rights and freedoms, for cultural identity, and preparation of children for responsible life in a free society.

The education service offers a paradoxical twist to debates on children's civil rights. The Education Reform Act 1988 proposes (ch. 1, para. 1) that pupils be prepared for citizenship. Further guidance has been issued (National Curriculum Council (NCC) 1990b), but whilst it suggests allowing children some experience (at Key Stage 1) of discussing school-related issues (p. 21), the main emphasis is on preparatory teaching and learning. Participation in decision-making is low on the agenda, and indeed the school, the obvious arena for such experience, is down-played as a social setting children might study. Thus the school is not problematized and the time future of children is the focus: they are to be taught how, as adults, to take their place as citizens. Yet, it is through participation that children will learn about the rights and responsibilities of citizenship (Cowie 1994). Rosemary Chamberlin (1989: ch. 10) argues that education for participation in a democracy requires three components: teaching children relevant skills and knowledge to engage in debate; giving them specific knowledge about political issues and institutions; and giving them practice within schools of participation in a democratic institution. For as John Stuart Mill says, 'We do not learn to read or write, to ride or swim, by being merely told how to do it, but by doing it, so it is only by practising popular government on a limited scale that the people will ever learn how to exercise it on a larger' (quoted in Chamberlin 1989: 123). Just as women have had to fight to be recognized as citizens – for they lacked reason; so too do children. There is a remorseless circularity about children's subjection: they have no voice because they are deemed to have no voice. The turning point in the battle for women's rights – at least in the formal sense – was the belated recognition that women can be as rational as men. Recognition also needs to be given to the point that rationality, competence to think about an issue, is not a prerogative of age; experience is a great teacher. And competence includes understanding of relational issues.

There is indeed scope for interplay between the traditionally ascribed virtues of the public domain and those of the private domain. As feminists have pointed out, women provide a challenge to the rational, impersonal world of the public domain by taking both their bodies and their minds into it; so too do children. So, of course, do men, but theoretically this point is likely to meet with male resistance. Specifically as regards children, we may argue that their agency in essential knowledge acquisition takes place in both the private and public domains, and is contributive in both. Women take the knowledge they gain from people work at home into the public domain, where it provides one basis (often unacknowledged) for their work: the middle-aged secretary-cum-mother is a classic example. Women argue that the affective and the personal should be recognized as contributing to the success of work (e.g. Hochschild 1979) and this proposition is one that is increasingly recognized in the study of organizations (e.g. Handy 1985: *passim*, esp. chs 2 and 3). The rationality of the public domain cannot now be asserted in the face of what such studies have shown about how organizations work.

In more general terms, we may assert that the separation of the personal and the political is untenable. As feminists say, the personal is the political, in that how people live their lives is shaped and constrained by political forces. But the personal also feeds into the political: in particular through the acquisition and deployment of knowledge. What people learn through experience of child–adult relations provides the basis for their later learning, and for their contribution to the political. Children's own agency in acquiring essential knowledge both before they go to school and during their school years is an important case in point.

Changing childhood, changing sociology

As children's accounts stress, what they lack most is not freedom apart from adult social worlds, but the opportunity to participate in them, and in so doing to reconstitute those social worlds to take account of people of all ages. In practice children do not live lives separate from those of adults; for the social worlds of home, school and the spaces and times between are, as they recognize, constructed by adults. Further, even if once upon a time their knowledge was bounded by what parents and school teachers chose to tell them, it certainly is not so now. Television and computers give them access to the knowledge bank adults use. Yet their knowledge and interest in partici-pating is rarely recognized. On the rare occasions when children's concerns have been canvassed it is evident that they are intensely concerned about important issues. Barbara Tizard (1984), for instance, found children anxious about nuclear disasters. A 1994 conference of primary schoolchildren in Lothian identified for discussion a list of topics including AIDS, education, vandalism, sport and safety; Lothian Education Department is aiming to incorporate children's views into the development of the Lothian Children's Family Charter, and to ensure that the principles of the charter are embedded into the curriculum (*West Lothian News*, 25 May 1994). Young people faced with decisions on major surgery have provided evidence of the complexity of their moral thinking (Arnott and Hammond 1994). The Children's Rights Development Unit's consultation with 40 groups of children and young people aged 8 to 18, was important in developing the discussion of children's rights set out in the final report (CRDU 1994: xv).

Undoubtedly children's social positioning requires that adults take action to upgrade the status of children and childhood. This action includes resourcing of equal opportunities for children, investment in education, collecting child-related data and increasing children's participation in decisions that affect them (Save the Children 1995: ch. 4). Rosenbaum and Newell (1991) have made out a strong case for a children's rights commissioner: they argue that children are particularly disadvantaged in the democratic process as a social group with no vote; they are a vulnerable group, and are the object of poorly co-ordinated services; they are also important as a social group. Numerically important (about a fifth of the population) they have their lives to live now and as adults. The commissioner would tackle the rights and wrongs of childhood through three main functions: to influence policy and practice to take account of children's rights; to promote compliance with the UN Convention; and to ensure effective means of redress in the case of complaints. The times are not right for promoting the rights of children, but then there never was a golden age of childhood. The worst of times and the best of times are equally times to work for children.

The enterprises of changing childhood and changing sociology are linked. Changing childhood in practice requires recognition at theoretical levels that children are an important social group, whose present matters, as well as their future as adults: they are people first, children second. As a social group, a point stressed throughout this book, their daily lives (as well as their future prospects) are constructed through the specific impacts of the social order and social policies on them. They are not simply part of families. Thus a social order which allows individual and group poverty has specific impacts on children – whose opportunities for a flourishing daily life now and for establishing firm foundations for their future will be importantly diminished. Most obviously, poverty will also diminish their parents' ability to offer them a healthy, constructive, productive, even a loving, environment, to strengthen them to face the world. Health and education policies obviously impact directly on children's present and cast shadows forward to their future. Changing childhood therefore requires a number of activities. It requires documenting the impact of social policies on children, both through macro studies and through micro studies of children's own experiences. It also requires taking account of children's own needs and wishes, as they define them, and their rights as laid out in the 1989 Convention. And it requires justice and equal opportunities as dominant values in the allocation of resources to children.

Within this enterprise of putting children on the political agenda, sociology has a part to play. Just as women have had to fight to get themselves recognized as a social group within sociology, so too, the fight has begun in respect of children. It is commonplace to find that children are simply omitted from consideration in academic sociology, a recent example being the fashionable sociology of the body and the emotions, where, if anywhere, one might think consideration of children was relevant. Through taking account of the social group children, sociological discourse can play a part in upgrading the condition of childhood as a suitable topic for adult consideration. In particular, work is needed at both theoretical and empirical levels on the impact of social and economic forces on children's lives, as distinct from families' lives or parental lives.

The sociological enterprise probably has to go through the same two main stages as in the case of feminist academic work. Initially, women forced feminist approaches on to the academic and political agenda, by insisting as a first stage that women be added on. Gender has now become an essential component of any research on adults that aims for respectability. The second main stage, still being tackled, is to challenge the male assumptions built into sociological concepts, through exploration of how consideration of gender modifies such concepts. Similarly, we have to work first to ensure that children be added on as a group to be fitted into prevailing notions. The more important second step is to consider how sociological thought needs modification under the impact of accepting children as a social group. Some suggestions have been canvassed in this book, on some central topics: the social construction of knowledge; understandings of work; concepts of the public and the private; and the division of labour. A lot more work remains to be done.

Bibliography

Dates given in square brackets refer to the first edition.

Acker, S. (1990) Teachers' culture in an English primary school, *British Journal of Sociology of Education*, 11: 257–73.

Adelman, C. (1989) The context of children's learning: an historical perspective, in G. Barrett (ed.) *Disaffection from School: The Early Years*. London: Falmer Press.

Alanen, L. (1992) *Modern Childhood? Exploring the 'Child Question' in Sociology*, Research Report 50. University of Jyvaskyla.

Alanen, L. (1994) Gender and generation: feminism and the 'child question', in J. Qvortrup, M. Bardy, G. Sgritta and H. Wintersberger (eds) *Childhood Matters: Social Theory, Practice and Politics*. Aldershot: Avebury Press.

Alderson, P. (1992) Rights of children and young people, in A. Coote (ed.) *The Welfare of Citizens: Developing New Social Rights*. London: Institute for Public Policy Research/ Rivers Oram Press.

Alderson, P. (1993) *Children's Consent to Surgery*. Buckingham: Open University Press.

Alderson, P. and Montgomery, J. (1995) *Young People's Right to be Heard in Health Care Decisions*. London: Institute for Public Policy Research.

Aldridge, J. and Becker, S. (1993) 'Children who Care: Inside the World of Young Carers', unpublished report of research. Department of Social Science, Loughborough University.

Armstrong, D. (1981) *The Political Anatomy of the Body*. Cambridge: Cambridge University Press.

Arnott, C. and Hammond, L. (1994) Accepting and refusing treatment for short stature, in P. Alderson and B. Mayall (eds) *Children's Decisions in Health Care and Research*, Consent Conference Series No. 5. London: Social Science Research Unit.

Aronsson, K. and Rundström, B. (1988) Child discourse and parental control in pediatric consultations, *Text*, 8: 159–89.

Askew, S. and Ross, C. (1988) *Boys Don't Cry: Boys and Sexism in Education*. Milton Keynes: Open University Press.

Audit Commission (1994) *Seen but not Heard: Co-ordinating Community Child Health and Social Services for Children in Need*. London: HMSO.

Backett, K.C. and Alexander, H. (1991) Talking to young children about health: methods and findings, *Health Education Journal*, 50: 34–7.

Bardy, M., Qvortrup, J., Sgritta, G. and Wintersberger, H. (eds) (1990–3) *Childhood as a Social Phenomenon: A Series of National Reports*, Eurosocial Reports 1–16. 36/1 Norway; 36/2 Italy; 36/3 Denmark; 36/4 USA; 36/5 Israel; 36/6 Canada; 36/7 Finland; 36/8 Ireland; 36/9 Scotland; 36/10 Federal Republic of Germany; 36/11 Switzerland; 36/12 Greece; 36/13 Yugoslavia; 36/14 Czechoslovakia; 36/15 Sweden; 36/16 England and Wales. Vienna: European Centre.

Barrett, G. (1989) A child's eye view of schooling, in G. Barrett (ed.) *Disaffection from School: The Early Years*. London: Falmer Press.

Barton, L. and Meighan, R. (eds) (1978) *Sociological Interpretations of Schooling and Classrooms: A Re-appraisal*. Driffield: Nafferton Books.

Belenky, M.F., Clinchy, B.M., Goldberger, N.R. and Taryule, J.M. (1986) *Women's Ways of Knowing: The Development of Self, Voice and Mind*. New York: Basic Books.

Bellaby, P. (1992) Broken rhythms and unmet deadlines: workers' and managers' time perspectives, in R. Frankenberg (ed.) *Time, Health and Medicine*. London: Sage.

Bendelow, G. and Oakley, A. (1993) *Young People and Cancer*. London: Social Science Research Unit and Women's Nationwide Cancer Control Campaign.

Bernardes, J. (1985) Do we really know what 'the family' is?, in P. Close and R. Collins (eds) *Family and Economy in Modern Society*. London: Macmillan.

Bernardes, J. (1988) Founding the new 'Family Studies', *Sociological Review*, 36, 1: 57–86.

Bishop of Salisbury, White, P., Andrews, R., Jacobsen, B and Tizard, B. (1984) *Lessons Before Midnight: Educating for Reason in Nuclear Matters*, Bedford Way Paper no. 19. London: Institute of Education.

Björklid, P. (1986) *Schoolchildren and Joint Influence: Participation or Pseudo-democracy?* Stockholm: Institute of Education.

Blatchford, P. and Sharp, S. (eds) (1994) *Breaktime and the School: Understanding and Changing Playground Behaviour*. London: Routledge.

Bluebond-Langner, M. (1978) *The Private Worlds of Dying Children*. Princeton: Princeton University Press.

Bluebond-Langner, M. (1991) Living with cystic fibrosis: the well sibling's perspective, *Medical Anthropology Quarterly*, 5, 2: 133–52.

Bluebond-Langner, M. (1994) Children living with a sibling with cystic fibrosis. Paper presented at Childhood and Society Seminar, Institute of Education, University of London, 24 June.

Blyth, A. (1980) Children's social experience: a framework for primary education and primary teacher education, in C. Richards (ed.) *Primary Education: Issues for the Eighties*. London: A. and C. Black.

Blyth, W. (1965) *English Primary Education*, vols 1 and 2. London: Routledge and Kegan Paul.

Board of Education (1931) *Report of the Consultative Committee on the Primary School* (The Hadow Report). London: HMSO.

Boulton, M.B. (1983) *On Being a Mother: A Study of Women with Pre-school Children*. London: Tavistock.

Bourdieu, P. (1978) Sport and social class, *Social Science Information*, 17: 819–40.

Bradley, B.S. (1989) *Visions of Infancy: A Critical Introduction to Child Psychology*. Cambridge: Polity Press.

Bradshaw, J. (1990) *Child Poverty and Deprivation in the UK*. London: National Children's Bureau.

Brannen, J., Dodd, K., Oakley, A. and Storey, P. (1994) *Young People, Health and Family Life*. Buckingham: Open University Press.

Bray, S. (1991) Health-related physical activity in the primary school, in N. Armstrong and A. Sparkes (eds) *Issues in Physical Education*. London: Cassell.

British Paediatric Association (1993) *Community Child Health Services: An Information Base for Purchasers*. London: BPA.

British Paediatric Association (1995) *Health Needs of School Age Children: Report of a Joint Working Party*. London: BPA.

Bronfenbrenner, U. (1971) *Two Worlds of Childhood: US and USSR*. London: Allen and Unwin.

Bronfenbrenner, U. (1979) *The Ecology of Human Development: Experiments by Nature and Design*. Cambridge, MA: Harvard University Press.

Brook, E. and Davis, A. (eds) (1985) *Women, the Family and Social Work*. London and New York: Tavistock.

Brown, L.M. and Gilligan, C. (1992) *Meeting at the Crossroads: Women's Psychology and Girls' Development*. Cambridge, MA and London: Harvard University Press.

Bryder, L. (1992) 'Wonderlands of buttercup, clover and daisies': tuberculosis and the open-air school movement in Britain, 1907–38, in R. Cooter (ed.) *In the Name of the Child: Health and Welfare, 1880–1940*. London: Routledge.

Buchner, P. (1990) Growing up in the eighties: changes in the social biography of childhood in the FRG, in L. Chisholm, P. Buchner, H.-H. Kruger and P. Brown (eds) *Childhood, Youth and Social Change: A Comparative Perspective*. London: Falmer Press.

Buckingham, D. (1994) Television and the definition of childhood, in B. Mayall (ed.) 1994b op cit.

Burgess, H. and Carter, B. (1992) 'Bringing out the best in people': teacher training and the 'real' teacher, *British Journal of Sociology of Education*, 13, 3: 349–59.

Burman, E. (1994) *Deconstructing Developmental Psychology*. London: Routledge.

Carlen, P., Gleeson, D. and Wardaugh, J. (1992) *Truancy: The Politics of Compulsory Schooling*. Buckingham: Open University Press.

Chamberlin, R. (1989) *Free Children and Democratic Schools: A Philosophical Study of Liberty and Education*. London: Falmer Press.

Chapman, K. (1994) Opinion: Education Superhighway. BBC Radio 4, 6 October.

Children's Rights Development Unit (1994) *A UK Agenda for Children*. London: CRDU.

Chodorow, N. (1978) *The Reproduction of Mothering*. Berkeley, CA: University of California Press.

Claxton, G., Swann, W., Salmon, P., Walkerdine, V., Jacobsen, B. and White, J. (1985) *Psychology and Schooling: What's the Matter?*, Bedford Way Paper no. 25. London: Institute of Education.

Coles, A. and Turner, S. (1992) *Catering for Healthy Eating in Schools*. London: Institute of Education.

Collins, R. (1994) *Four Sociological Readings*. Oxford: Oxford University Press.

Connell, R.W. (1994) Gender regimes and the gender order, in Polity Press (ed.) *The Polity Reader in Gender Studies*. Cambridge: Polity Press.

Conner, C. with Lofthouse, B. (eds) (1990) *The Study of Primary Education: A Source Book*, vol. 1: Perspectives. London: Falmer Press.

Cooter, R. (ed.) (1992) *In the Name of the Child: Health and Welfare, 1880–1940*. London: Routledge.

Cowie, H. (1994) Ways of involving children in decision-making, in P. Blatchford and S. Sharp (eds) *Breaktime and the School: Understanding and Changing Playground Behaviour*. London: Routledge.

Cox, C. and Boyson, R. (eds) (1975) *Black Paper 75*. London: Dent.

Craib, I. (1992) *Modern Social Theory: From Parsons to Habermas*, 2nd edn. Hemel Hempstead: Harvester Wheatsheaf.

Cullingford, C. (1991) *The Inner World of the School: Children's Ideas about Schools*. London: Cassell.

Cunningham, H. (1991) *The Children of the Poor: Representations of Childhood since the Seventeenth Century*. Oxford: Blackwell.

Curry, W.B. (1947) *Education for Sanity*. London: Heinemann.

Danziger, K. (1971) *Socialization*. Harmondsworth: Penguin.

David, M.E. (1985) Motherhood and social policy – a matter of education? *Critical Social Policy*, 12: 28–43.

David, M., Edwards, R., Hughes, M. and Ribbens, J. (1993) *Mothers and Education: Inside Out? Exploring Family-education Policy and Experience*. London: Macmillan.

Davidoff, L. (1990) 'Adam spoke first and named the orders of the world': masculine and feminine domains in history and sociology, in H. Corr and L. Jamieson (eds) *Politics of Everyday Life: Continuity and Change in Work and the Family*. London: Macmillan.

Davies, B. (1982) *Life in Classroom and Playground: The Accounts of Primary School Children*. London: Routledge and Kegan Paul.

Davies, B. (1990) Agency as a form of discursive practice: a classroom scene observed, *British Journal of Sociology of Education*, 11, 3: 341–61.

Davin, A. (1978) Imperialism and motherhood, *History Workshop*, 5: 9–65.

Davin, A. (1990) When is a child not a child? in H. Corr and L. Jamieson (eds) *Politics of Everyday Life: Continuity and Change in Work and the Family*. London: Macmillan.

Davis, A. and Brook, E. (1985) Women and social work, in Brook, E. and Davis, A. (eds) *Women, the Family and Social Work*. London: Tavistock.

Dearden, R.F. (1967) The concept of play, in R.S. Peters (ed.) *The Concept of Education*. London: Routledge and Kegan Paul.

Deem, R. (ed.) (1980) *Schooling for Women's Work*. London: Routledge and Kegan Paul.

Dencik, L. (1989) Growing up in the post-modern age: on the child's situation in the modern family, and on the position of the family in the modern welfare state, *Acta Sociologica*, 32, 2: 155–80.

Denzin, N.K. (1977) *Childhood Socialization*. San Francisco, CA: Jossey-Bass.

Department for Education (1991) *The Parent's Charter: You and Your Child's Education*. London: Department for Education.

Department for Education (1994) *Our Children's Education: The Updated Parent's Charter*. London: HMSO.

Department of Education and Science (1967) *Children and their Primary Schools*, a report of the Central Advisory Council for Education (The Plowden Report). London: HMSO.

Department of Education and Science (1972) *Movement: Physical Education in the Primary Years*. London: HMSO.

Department of Health (1991) *Family Support, Day Care and Educational Provision for Young People*, vol. 2 of the Children Act Series. London: Department of Health.

Department of Health (1992) *The Health of the Nation*. London: HMSO.

Department of Health and Social Security (1989) *The Diets of British School Children*. London: HMSO.

Department of Social Security (1994) *Households below Average Income*. London: HMSO.

Department of Transport (1992) *Road Accidents Great Britain 1991*. London: HMSO.

Dewey, J. (1956 [1938]) *Experience and Education*. New York: Macmillan.

Donaldson, M. (1978) *Children's Minds*. London: Fontana.

Donzelot, J. (1980) *The Policing of Families: Welfare versus the State.* London: Hutchinson.

Dowson, T. and Hewison, J. (1990) The effects of mothers' employment on child health care management, in S. Lea, P. Webley and P. Young (eds) *Applied Economic Psychology in the 1990s.* Exeter: Washington Singer Press.

Doyal, L. (1983) *The Political Economy of Health.* London: Pluto Press.

Dunn, J. (1977) *Distress and Comfort.* London: Fontana.

Dunn, J. (1984) *Sisters and Brothers.* London: Fontana.

Dunn, J. (1988) *The Beginnings of Social Understanding.* Oxford: Blackwell.

Durkheim, E. (1961[1912]) *Moral Education: A Study in the Theory and Application of the Sociology of Education.* New York: Free Press of Glencoe.

Elias, N. (1978 [1939]) *The Civilising Process,* trans. Edmund Jephcott. Oxford: Blackwell.

Elshtain, J.B. (1993 [1981]) *Public Man, Private Woman,* 2nd edn. Princeton, NJ and Chichester: Princeton University Press.

Engelbert, A. (1994) Worlds of childhood: differentiated but different: implications for social policy, in J. Qvortrup, M. Bardy, G. Sgritta and H. Wintersberger (eds) *Childhood Matters: Social Theory, Practice and Politics.* Aldershot: Avebury Press.

Ennew, J. (1993) *Childhood as a Social Phenomenon: National Report England and Wales,* Eurosocial Report 36/16. Vienna: European Centre.

Ennew, J. (1994) Time for children or time for adults, in J. Qvortrup, M. Bardy, G. Sgritta and H. Wintersberger (eds) *Childhood Matters: Social Theory, Practice and Politics.* Aldershot: Avebury Press.

Epstein, C.F. (1990) Strong arms and velvet gloves: the gender difference model and the law, in *The Invisible Majority,* papers from the Mellon Colloquium, Graduate School of Tulane University, New Orleans, Louisiana.

Farquhar, C. (1989) *Exploring AIDS-related Knowledge amongst Primary School Children.* London: Thomas Coram Research Unit.

Finch, J. (1984) *Education as Social Policy.* London: Longman.

Finch, J. and Groves, D. (eds) (1983) *A Labour of Love: Women, Work and Caring.* London: Routledge and Kegan Paul.

Fine, G.A. and Sandström, K.L. (1988) *Knowing Children: Participant Observation with Minors.* London: Sage.

Firestone, S. (1972) *The Dialectic of Sex.* London: Paladin.

Fortes, M. (1970) Social and psychological aspects of education in Taleland, in J. Middleton (ed.) *From Child to Adult: Studies in the Anthropology of Education.* Austin, TX: University of Texas Press.

Foucault, M. (1979) *Discipline and Punish: The Birth of the Prison.* Harmondsworth: Penguin.

Foucault, M. (1980) Truth and power, in Gordon, C. (ed.) *Power/Knowledge: Selected Interviews and Other Writings 1972–1977 Michel Foucault.* Brighton: Harvester Press.

Frankenberg, R. (1992) 'Your time or mine' temporal constructions of bio-medical practice, in R. Frankenberg (ed.) *Time, Health and Medicine.* London: Sage.

Freund, P. (1990) The expressive body: a common ground for the sociology of emotions and health and illness, *Sociology of Health and Illness,* 12, 4: 454–77.

Friedan, B. (1963) *The Feminine Mystique.* London: Victor Gollancz.

Galton, M., Simon, B. and Croll, P. (1980) *Inside the Primary Classroom.* London: Routledge and Kegan Paul.

Gardner, H. (1993) *The Unschooled Mind: How Children Think and How Schools Should Teach.* London: Fontana Press.

Gavron, H. (1966) *The Captive Wife*. Harmondsworth: Penguin.

Giddens, A. (ed.) (1972) *Emile Durkheim: Selected Writings*. Cambridge: Cambridge University Press.

Giddens, A. (1979) *Central Problems in Social Theory: Action, Structure and Contradiction in Social Analysis*. London: Macmillan.

Giddens, A. (1993) *Sociology*, 2nd edn. Cambridge: Polity Press.

Gilligan, C. (1993) *In a Different Voice: Psychological Theory and Women's Development*, new edn. Cambridge, MA and London: Harvard University Press.

Gipps, C. (1992) *What We Know about Effective Primary Teaching*. London: The Tufnell Press.

Glauser, B. (1990) Street children: deconstructing a construct, in A. James and A. Prout (eds) *Constructing and Reconstructing Childhood: Contemplating Issues in the Sociological Study of Childhood*. London: Falmer Press.

Goodnow, J. and Burns, A. (1985) *Home and School: A Child's Eye View*. Sydney and London: Allen and Unwin.

Gosse, E. (1949 [1907]) *Father and Son: A Study of Two Temperaments*. Harmondsworth: Penguin.

Graham, H. (1983) Caring – a labour of love, in J. Finch and D. Groves (eds) *A Labour of Love: Women, Work and Caring*. London: Routledge.

Grant, L. (1994a) First among equals, *Guardian*, 22 October.

Grant, L. (1994b) Deadlier than the e-mail, *Guardian*, 30 November.

Greer, G. (1970) *The Female Eunuch*. London: McGibbon and Kee.

Grimshaw, J. (1986) *Feminist Philosophers*. Brighton: Harvester Wheatsheaf.

Gulbrandsen, M. (1995) *Becoming a Nine-year-old in Modern Norway: Empirical Approaches and Analytical Perspectives on Development as Contextually Embedded Processes*, paper presented at ESRC-funded seminar, *Childhood and Society*, 24 March. London: Institute of Education.

Gullestad, M. (1988) Children's care for children, *Social Analysis*, 23, 8: 38–52.

Hall, D.M.B. (ed.) (1992) *Health for All Children*, 2nd edn. Oxford: Oxford University Press.

Hall, G.S. (1904) *Adolescence: Its Psychology and its Relations to Physiology, Anthropology, Sociology, Sex, Crime, Religion and Education*, vols 1 and 2. New York: Appleton.

Halldén, G. (1991) The child as project and the child as being – parents' ideas as frames of reference, *Children and Society*, 5, 4: 334–46.

Halldén, G. (1993) Reproduction the essence of family life? in B. Mayall (ed.) *Family Life and Social Control: Discourses on Normality*, proceedings of conference, 18 March. London: Social Science Research Unit.

Halldén, G. (1994) The family – a refuge from demands or an arena for the exercise of power and control – children's fictions on their future families, in B. Mayall (ed.) *Children's Childhoods: Observed and Experienced*. London: Falmer Press.

Handy, C.B. (1985) *Understanding Organizations*. Harmondsworth: Penguin.

Harding, S. (1992 [1986]) The instability of the analytical categories of feminist theory, H. Crowley and S. Himmelweit (eds) *Knowing Women: Feminism and Knowledge*. Cambridge: Polity Press in association with Open University Press.

Hardyment, C. (1984) *Dream Babies*. Oxford: Oxford University Press.

Hargreaves, D.W. (1978) Whatever happened to symbolic interactionism? in L. Barton and R. Meighan (eds) *Sociological Interpretations of Schooling in Classrooms*. Driffield: Nafferton Books.

Harré, R. (1986) The step to social constructionism, in M. Richards and P. Light (eds) *Children of Social Worlds*. Cambridge: Polity Press.

Harre, R. (1993) Reappraising social psychology: rules, roles and rhetoric, *The Psychologist*, January: 24–8.

Haudrup Christensen, P. (1993) The social construction of help among Danish children, *Sociology of Health and Illness*, 15, 4: 488–502.

Haugli, A. (1993) Muted actors – children in court, in B. Mayall (ed.) *Family Life and Social Control: Discourses on Normality*. London: Social Science Research Unit.

Head, D. (ed.) (1974) *Free Way to Learning: Educational Alternatives in Action*. Harmondsworth: Penguin.

Health Education Authority (1993) *Childhood Diseases Haven't Died; Children Have: Immunisation: the Safest Way to Protect Your Child*, new edn. London: HEA.

Health Education Authority (1995) *Background to the European Network of Health Promoting Schools Project*. London: HEA.

Health Visitors' Association (1988) *Meeting Schoolchildren's Health Needs: The School Nurse's Role*. London: HVA.

Health Visitors' Association (1994) *Health Visitor Staffing and Training in England 1988–94: An Interim Analysis*. London: HVA.

Hearnshaw, L.S. (1964) *A Short History of British Psychology, 1840–1940*. London: Methuen.

Heiliö, P.-L., Lauronen, E. and Bardy, M. (1993) *Politics of Childhood and Children at Risk: Provision, Protection and Participation*. Vienna: European Centre.

Hendrick, H. (1994) *Child Welfare: England 1872–1989*. London: Routledge.

Henriques, J., Hollway, W., Urwin, C., Venn, C. and Walkerdine, V. (1984) *Changing the Subject*. London: Methuen.

Henshall, C. and McGuire, J. (1986) Gender development, in M. Richards and P. Light (eds) *Children of Social Worlds*. Cambridge: Polity Press.

Hillman, M. (ed.) (1993) *Children, Transport and the Quality of Life*. London: Policy Studies Institute.

Hillman, M., Adams, J. and Whitelegg, J. (1991) *One False Move: A Study of Children's Independent Mobility*. London: Policy Studies Institute.

Hochschild, A. (1979) Emotion work, feeling rules and social structure, *American Journal of Sociology*, 85, 3: 551–75.

Hochschild, A. (1983) *The Managed Heart: Commercialization of Human Feeling*. Berkeley, CA: University of California Press.

Hockey, J. and James, A. (1993) *Growing Up and Growing Old: Ageing and Dependency in the Life Course*. London: Sage.

Hoggart, R. (1959) *The Uses of Literacy*. Harmondsworth: Penguin.

Holcombe, L. (1973) *Victorian Ladies at Work: Middle-class Working Women in England and Wales 1850–1914*. Newton Abbot: David and Charles.

Holt, J. (1975) *Escape from Childhood: The Needs and Rights of Children*. Harmondsworth: Penguin.

Hoyles, C. (ed.) (1988) *Girls and Computers: General Issues and Case Studies of Logo in the Mathematics Classroom*, Bedford Way Papers no. 34. London: Institute of Education.

Howson, A. (1994) Book review: Chris Shilling *The Body and Social Theory*, *Sociology of Health and Illness*, 16, 3: 403–5.

Hughes, M. (1986) *Children and Number*. Oxford: Blackwell.

Hughes, M., Mayall, B., Moss, P., Perry, J., Petrie, P. and Pinkerton, G. (1980) *Nurseries Now*. Harmondsworth: Penguin.

Huizinga, J. (1976) Play and contest as civilising functions, in J. Bruner, A. Jolly and K. Sylva (eds) *Play: Its Role in Development and Evolution*. Harmondsworth: Penguin.

Hurt, J.S. (1979) *Elementary Schooling and the Working Classes, 1860–1918.* London: Routledge and Kegan Paul.

Ingleby, D. (1986) Development in social context, in M. Richards and P. Light (eds) *Children of Social Worlds.* Cambridge: Polity Press.

Jackson, M. (1987) Making sense of school, in A. Pollard (ed.) *Children and their Primary Schools.* London: Falmer Press.

Jacobsen, B. (1985) Does educational psychology contribute to the solution of educational problems? in G. Claxton, W. Swann, P. Salmon, V. Walkerdine, B. Jacobsen and J. White *Psychology and Schooling: What's the Matter?,* Bedford Way Paper no. 25. London: Institute of Education.

James, A. (1993) *Childhood Identities: Social Relationships and the Self in Children's Experiences.* Edinburgh: Edinburgh University Press.

James, A. and Prout, A. (1990a) Re-presenting childhood: time and transition in the study of childhood, in A. James and A. Prout (eds) *Constructing and Reconstructing Childhood: Contemporary Issues in the Sociological Study of Childhood.* London: Falmer Press.

James, A. and Prout, A. (eds) (1990b) *Constructing and Reconstructing Childhood: Contemporary Issues in the Sociological Study of Childhood.* London: Falmer Press.

Jenks, C. (1982) Introduction: constituting the child, in C. Jenks (ed.) *The Sociology of Childhood: Essential Readings.* London: Batsford.

Jensen, A.-M. and Saporiti, A. (1992) *Do Children Count? Childhood as a Social Phenomenon: A Statistical Compendium.* Vienna: European Centre.

Josefson, I. (1988) The nurse as engineer – the theory of knowledge in research in the care sector, in B. Goranzon and I. Josefson (eds) *Knowledge, Skill and Artifical Intelligence.* Berlin: Springer Verlag.

Kalnins, I., McQueen, D.V., Backett, K.C., Curtice, L. and Currie, C.E. (1992) Children, empowerment and health promotion: some new directions in research and practice, *Health Promotion International,* 7: 53–9.

Kärrby, G. (1990) Children's conceptions of their own play, *Early Child Development and Care,* 58: 81–5.

Kennedy, I. (1983) *The Unmasking of Medicine.* London: Paladin.

Kessen, W. (ed.) (1965) *The Child.* New York: John Wiley and Sons.

Kessen, W. (1975) *Childhood in China.* New Haven, CT: Yale University Press.

Kessen, W. (1983) The child and other cultural inventions, in F.S. Kessel and A.W. Siegel (eds) *The Child and Other Cultural Inventions.* New York: Praeger Publishers.

King, M. and Piper, C. (1990) *How the Law Thinks about Children.* Aldershot: Gower.

King, R.A. (1978) *All Things Bright and Beautiful? A Sociological Study of Infants' Classrooms.* Chichester: John Wiley and Sons.

King, R.A. (1989) *The Best of Primary Education? A Sociological Study of Junior Middle Schools.* London: Falmer Press.

Kirk, D. (1988) *Physical Education and Curriculum Study.* London and New York: Croom Helm.

Kirk, D. and Tinning, R. (1994) Embodied self-identity, healthy lifestyles and school physical education, *Sociology of Health and Illness,* 16, 5: 600–25.

Kitzinger, J. (1990) Who are you kidding? Children, power and the struggle against sexual abuse, in A. James and A. Prout (eds) *Constructing and Reconstructing Childhood: Contemporary Issues in the Sociological Study of Childhood.* London: Falmer Press.

Kumar, V. (1993) *Poverty and Inequality in the UK: the Effects on Children.* London: National Children's Bureau.

La Fontaine, J. (1986) An anthropological perspective on children in social worlds, in M. Richards and P. Light (eds) *Children of Social Worlds*. Cambridge: Polity Press.

La Fontaine, J. (1990) *Child Sexual Abuse*. Cambridge: Polity Press.

Langan, M. (1985) The unitary approach: a feminist critique, in E. Brook and A. Davis (eds) *Women, the Family and Social Work*. London: Tavistock.

Lansdown, G. (1994) Children's rights, in B. Mayall (ed.) *Children's Childhoods: Observed and Experienced*. London: Falmer Press.

Lawn, M. and Grace, G. (eds) (1987) *Teachers: The Culture and Politics of Work*. London: Falmer Press.

Leder, D. (ed.) (1990) *The Absent Body*. Chicago and London: Chicago University Press.

Lewis, J. (1986) Anxieties about the family and relationships between parents, children and the state in twentieth century England, in M. Richards and P. Light (eds) *Children of Social Worlds*. Cambridge: Polity Press.

Liljeström, R. (1983) The public child, the commercial child and our child, in F.S. Kessel and A.W. Siegel (eds) *The Child and Other Cultural Inventions*. New York: Praeger.

McCullers, J.C. (1969) G. Stanley Hall's conception of mental development and some indications of its influence on developmental psychology, in *American Psychologist*, 24: 1109–14.

McGuire, J. (1991) Sons and daughters, in A. Phoenix, A. Woollett and E. Lloyd (eds) *Motherhood: Meanings, Practices and Ideologies*. London: Sage.

Mackay, R.W. (1991) Conceptions of children and models of socialisation, in F.C. Waksler (ed.) *Studying the Social Worlds of Children: Sociological Readings*. London: Falmer Press.

Maclure, S. (1984) *Educational Development and School Building: Aspects of Public Policy 1945–73*. London: Longman.

McMillan, M. (1923[1907]) *Education through the Imagination*, 2nd edn. London: Allen and Unwin.

McMillan, M. (1930) *The Nursery School*. London: Allen and Unwin.

Mandell, N. (1991) The least-adult role in studying children, in F.C. Waksler (ed.) *Studying the Worlds of Children: Sociological Readings*. London: Falmer Press.

Manicom, A. (1984) Feminist frameworks and teacher education, *Journal of Education*, 166, 1: 77–89.

Martin, E. (1989) *The Woman in the Body*. Milton Keynes: Open University Press.

Matterson, E. (1969 [1965]) *Play with a Purpose for the Under-Sevens*. Harmondsworth: Penguin.

Mauthner, M., Mayall, B. and Turner, S. (1993) *Children and Food at Primary School*. London: Institute of Education.

Mayall, B. (1986) *Keeping Children Healthy*. London: Allen and Unwin.

Mayall, B. (1991) Researching childcare in a multiethnic society, *New Community*, 17, 4: 553–68.

Mayall, B. (1994a) *Negotiating Health: Children at Home and Primary School*. London: Cassell.

Mayall, B. (ed.) (1994b) *Children's Childhoods: Observed and Experienced*. London: Falmer Press.

Mayall, B. and Foster, M.-C. (1989) *Child Health Care: Living with Children, Working for Children*. Oxford: Heinemann Educational.

Mayall, B. and Petrie, P. (1983) *Childminding and Day Nurseries: What Kind of Care?* London: Heinemann.

Mayall, B., Bendelow, G., Barker, S., Storey, P. and Veltman, M. (in press) *Health in Primary Schools*. London: Falmer Press.

Meighan, R. (1986) *A Sociology of Educating*, 2nd edn. London: Holt, Rinehart and Winston.

Melhuish, E.C. and Moss, P. (eds) (1990) *Day Care for Young Children: International Perspectives*. London: Routledge.

Mitchell, J. (1971) *Woman's Estate*. Harmondsworth: Penguin.

Montgomery, J. (1994) The Retreat from Gillick, in P. Alderson and B. Mayall (eds) *Children's Decisions in Health Care and Research*, Consent Conference Series no. 5. London: Social Science Research Unit.

Moore, H.C. (1983) *Feminism and Anthropology*. Cambridge: Polity Press.

Moore, R.C. (1986) *Childhood's Domain: Play and Place in Child Development*. London: Croom Helm.

Morgan, D.H.J. (1975) *Social Theory and the Family*. London: Routledge and Kegan Paul.

Morgan, D.H.J. (1985) *The Family, Politics and Social Theory*. London: Routledge and Kegan Paul.

Morgan, D.H.J. (1994) *Family Sociology and the Sociology of Childhood: Potentialities for further Collaboration*, paper presented at ESRC-funded seminar, *Children and Society*, June. London: Institute of Education.

Morrison, M. (1995) Researching food consumers in school: recipes for concern. *Educational Studies*, 21, 2: 239–63.

Morrow, V. (1994) Responsible children? Aspects of children's work and employment outside school in contemporary UK, in B. Mayall (ed.) *Children's Childhoods: Observed and Experienced*. London: Falmer Press.

Morss, J.R. (1990) *The Biologising of Childhood: Developmental Psychology and the Darwinian Myth*. Hove and London: Lawrence Erlbaum Associates.

Morton, R. and Lloyd, J. (eds) (1994) *The Health-Promoting School*. London: David Fulton Publishers.

Moss, P. (1990) *Childcare in the European Community 1985–1990*, report to the European Commission Childcare Network. London: Commission of the European Communities, 8 Storey's Gate, London SW1 3AT.

Moyles, J.R. (ed.) (1994) *The Excellence of Play*. Buckingham: Open University Press.

Näsman, E. (1994) Individualisation and institutionalisation of childhood in today's Europe, in J.Qvortrup, M. Bardy, G. Sgritta, and H. Wintersberger (eds) *Childhood Matters: Social Theory, Practice and Politics*. Aldershot: Avebury Press.

National Confederation of Parent–Teacher Associations (1991) *The State of Schools in England and Wales*. Gravesend: NCPTA.

National Curriculum Council (1990a) *Curriculum Guidance 5: Health Education*. York: NCC.

National Curriculum Council (1990b) *Curriculum Guidance 8: Education for Citizenship*. York: NCC.

National Foundation for Educational Research (1994) *Evaluation of the European Network of Health Promoting Schools*. Slough: NFER.

Neill, A.S. (1937) *That Dreadful School*. London: Herbert Jenkins.

Neill, A.S. (1976 [1962]) *Summerhill*. Harmondsworth: Penguin.

Newson, J. and Newson, E. (1970) *Four Years Old in an Urban Community*. Harmondsworth: Penguin.

Newson, J. and Newson, E. (1978) *Seven Years Old in the Home Environment*. Harmondsworth: Penguin.

Northern Ireland Curriculum Council (1994) *The Health Promoting School: A Guide for Teachers*. Belfast: NICC.

Oakley, A. (1984) *The Captured Womb: A History of the Medical Care of Pregnant Women*. Oxford and New York: Blackwell.

Oakley, A. (1985a [1972]) *Sex, Gender and Society*, revised edn. Aldershot: Gower.

Oakley, A. (1985b) *Taking it Like a Woman*. London: Fontana.

Oakley, A. (1994) Women and children first and last: parallels and differences between children's and women's studies, in B. Mayall (ed.) *Children's Childhoods: Observed and Experienced*. London: Falmer Press.

Office for Standards in Education (1993) *Physical Education: Key Stages 1, 2 and 3: First Year, 1992–3*. London: HMSO.

Oldman, D. (1994) Childhood as a mode of production, in B. Mayall (ed.) *Children's Childhoods: Observed and Experienced*. London: Falmer Press.

Opie, I. (1993) *The People in the Playground*. Oxford: Oxford University Press.

Opie, I. and Opie, P. (1959) *The Lore and Language of Schoolchildren*. Oxford: Clarendon Press.

Opie, I. and Opie, P. (1969) *Children's Games in Street and Playground*. Oxford: Clarendon Press.

Oppenheim, C. (1993) *Poverty: The Facts*. London: Child Poverty Action Group.

Page, R. and Clark, G.A. (eds) (1977) *Young People's Working Group: Who Cares? Young People in Care Speak Out*. London: National Children's Bureau.

Parton, C. and Parton, N. (1989) Women, the family and child protection, *Critical Social Policy*, 24: 38–49.

Parton, N. (1985) *The Politics of Child Abuse*. London: Macmillan.

Parton, N. (1991) *Governing the Family: Child Care, Child Protection and the State*. London: Macmillan.

Paterson, F.M.S. (1989) *Out of Place: Public Policy and the Emergence of Truancy*. London: Falmer Press.

Peters, R.S. (1969) 'A recognisable philosophy of education', in R.S. Peters (ed.) *Perspectives on Plowden*. London: Routledge and Kegan Paul.

Petrie, P. (1994) *Play and Care Out of School*. London: HMSO.

Petrie, P. and Logan, P. (1984) *Out of School Study*, Final Report. London: Thomas Coram Research Unit.

Pollard, A. (1982) A model of classroom coping strategies, *British Journal of Sociology of Education*, 3: 19–37.

Pollard, A. (1985) *The Social World of the Primary School*. London: Holt, Rinehart and Winston.

Prendergast, S. (1992) *This is the Time to Grow Up: Girls' Experiences of Menstruation in School*. Cambridge: Centre for Family Research.

Prout, A. (1986) 'Wet children' and 'little actresses': going sick in primary school, *Sociology of Health and Illness*, 8, 2: 111–36.

Prout, A. (1988) 'Off school sick': mothers' accounts of school sickness, *Sociological Review*, 36, 4: 765–89.

Prout, A. (1992) Work, time and sickness in the lives of schoolchildren, in R. Frankenberg (ed.) *Time, Health and Medicine*. London: Sage.

Prout, A. and James, A. (1990) A new paradigm for the sociology of childhood? Provenance, promise and problems, in A. James and A. Prout (eds) op cit.

Qvortrup, J. (1985) Placing children in the division of labour, in P. Close and R. Collins (eds) *Family and Economy in Modern Society*. London: Macmillan.

Qvortrup, J. (1987) Introduction in the sociology of childhood, *International Journal of Sociology*, 17, 3: 3–37.

Qvortrup, J. (1991) *Childhood as a Social Phenomenon: An Introduction to a Series of National Reports*. Vienna: European Centre.

Qvortrup, J. (ed.) (1993) *Childhood as a Social Phenomenon: Lessons from an International Project*. Vienna: European Centre.

Qvortrup, J., Bardy, M., Sgritta, G. and Wintersberger, H. (eds) (1994) *Childhood Matters: Social Theory, Practice and Politics*. Aldershot: Avebury Press.

Rapoport, R.N., Fogarty, M.P. and Rapoport, R. (eds) (1982) *Families in Britain*. London: Routledge and Kegan Paul.

Ribbens, J. (1993) Standing by the school gate: the boundaries of maternal authority, in M. David, R. Edwards, M. Hughes and J. Ribbens *Mothers and Education: Inside Out? Exploring Family Education Policy and Experience*. Basingstoke: Macmillan Educational.

Rich, A. (1977) *Of Woman Born: Motherhood as Experience and Institution*. London: Virago.

Richards, M.P.M. (ed.) (1974) *The Integration of a Child into a Social World*. Cambridge: Cambridge University Press.

Richards, M. and Light, P. (eds) (1986) *Children of Social Worlds*. Cambridge: Polity Press.

Richman, S. and Miles, M. (1990) Selective medical examinations for school entrants – the way forward, *Archives of Disease in Childhood*, 65: 1177–81.

Roberts, A. (1980) *Out to Play: The Middle Years of Childhood*. Aberdeen: Aberdeen University Press.

Robson, P. (1986) The development of health visiting in north-east England: a case study in social policy, in A. While (ed.) *Research in Preventive Community Nursing Care: Fifteen Studies in Health Visiting*. Chichester: John Wiley and Sons.

Rogers, A. and Pilgrim, D. (1994) *Rational Non-Compliance with Childhood Immunisation: Personal Accounts of Parents and Primary Health Care Professionals*. London: Health Education Authority.

Rose, H. (1986) Women's work: women's knowledge, in J. Mitchell and A. Oakley (eds) *What is Feminism?* Oxford: Blackwell.

Rose, H. (1994) *Love, Power and Knowledge*. Cambridge: Polity Press.

Rose, N. (1985) *The Psychological Complex: Psychology, Politics and Society in England 1869–1939*. London: Routledge and Kegan Paul.

Rosenbaum, M. and Newell, P. (1991) *Taking Children Seriously: A Proposal for a Children's Rights Commissioner*. London: Calouste Gulbenkian Foundation.

Rowbotham, S. (1973a) *Woman's Consciousness, Man's World*. Harmondsworth: Penguin.

Rowbotham, S. (1973b) *Hidden from History: 300 Years of Women's Oppression and the Fight Against It*. London: Pluto Press.

Royal College of General Practitioners (1982) *Healthier Children: Thinking Prevention*. London: RCGPs.

Royal Society for the Prevention of Accidents (1993) *Care on the Roads*. London: RoSPA.

Rubinstein, D. and Stoneman, C. (eds) (1970) *Education for Democracy*. Harmondsworth: Penguin.

Ruddick, S. (1990) *Maternal Thinking: Towards a Politics of Peace*. London: The Women's Press.

Saunders, A. (1989) Creativity and the infant classroom, in G. Barrett (ed.) *Disaffection from School: The Early Years*. London: Falmer Press.

Save the Children (1995) *Towards a Children's Agenda: New Challenges for Social Development*. London: Save the Children.

Scarr, S. and Dunn, J. (1987) *Mother Care/Other Care*. Harmondsworth: Penguin.

Scheper-Hughes, N. and Lock, M.M. (1987) The mindful body: a prolegomenon to future work in medical anthropology, *Medical Anthropology Quarterly*, 1, 1: 6–41.

Sharp, I. (1993) *Nutritional Guidelines for School Meals*, Report of an Expert Working Group. London: The Caroline Walker Trust.

Sharp, R. and Green, A. (1975) *Education and Social Control*. London: Routledge and Kegan Paul.

Shilling, C. (1993) *The Body and Social Theory*. London: Sage.

Siegal, M. (1991) *Knowing Children: Experiments in Conversation and Cognition*. Hove and London: Lawrence Erlbaum Associates.

Silverman, D. (1987) *Communication and Medical Practice: Social Relations in the Clinic*. London: Sage.

Skolnick, A. (1975) The limits of childhood: conceptions of child development and social context, *Law and Contemporary Problems*, 39, 3: 38–77.

Sluckin, A. (1981) *Growing Up in the Playground*. London: Routledge and Kegan Paul.

Smith, D.E. (1988) *The Everyday World as Problematic: A Feminist Sociology*. Milton Keynes: Open University Press.

Smith, P.K. (1994) Play and the uses of play, in J.R. Moyles (ed.) *The Excellence of Play*. Buckingham: Open University Press.

Social Science Research Unit (1994) *Health in Primary Schools: Report on a Postal Questionnaire*. London: SSRU.

Solberg, A. (1990) Negotiating childhood: changing constructions of age for Norwegian children, in A. James and A. Prout (eds) *Constructing and Reconstructing Childhood: Contemporary Issues in the Sociological Study of Childhood*. London: Falmer Press.

Solberg, A. (1995) *Doing Age: Methodological Challenges in Studying how Age is made Relevant in the Everyday Life of Twelve-year-olds*, paper presented at ESRC-funded seminar, *Childhood and Society*, 24 March. London: Institute of Education.

Sparkes, A.C. (1992) The changing nature of teachers' work: school governors and curriculum control in physical education, in N. Armstrong (ed.) *New Directions in Physical Education. Vol. 2: Towards a National Curriculum*. Leeds: Human Kinetics Publishers.

Stacey, M. (1980) The division of labour revisited or overcoming the two Adams, in P. Abrams, R. Deem, J. Finch and P. Roch (eds) *Practice and Progress in British Sociology 1950–1980*. London: Allen and Unwin.

Stacey, M. and Davies, C. (1983) *Division of Labour in Child Health Care, Final Report to the SSRC 1983*. Department of Sociology, University of Warwick.

Stacey, M. and Olesen, V. (1993) Introduction, Women, Men and Health, *Social Science and Medicine*, 36, 1: v–vii.

Stainton Rogers, R. and Stainton Rogers, W. (1992) *Stories of Childhood: Shifting Agendas of Child Concern*. Hemel Hempstead: Harvester Wheatsheaf.

Statham, J. (1986) *Daughters and Sons: Experiences of Non-Sexist Childraising*. Oxford: Blackwell.

Steedman, C. (1982) *The Tidy House: Little Girls Writing*. London: Virago.

Steedman, C. (1986) *Landscape for a Good Woman: A Story of Two Lives*. London: Virago.

Steedman, C. (1988) 'The mother made conscious': the historical development of a primary school pedagogy, in M. Woodhead and A. McGrath (eds) *Family, School and Society: A Reader*. London: Hodder and Stoughton.

Stoppard, M. (1990) *New Baby Care Book: A Practical Guide to the First Three Years*, 2nd edn. London: Dorling Kindersley.

Strauss, A. (ed.) (1964) *George Herbert Mead on Social Psychology*. Chicago and London: Chicago University Press.

Tattum, D. and Tattum, E. (1992) *Social Education and Personal Development*. London: David Fulton Publishers.

Thompson, F. (1973) *Lark Rise to Candleford*. Harmondsworth: Penguin.

Thorne, B. (1993) *Gender Play: Girls and Boys in School*. New Brunswick, NJ: Rutgers University Press.

Thorne, B. and Yalom, M. (1982) *Re-Thinking the Family: Some Feminist Questions*. New York and London: Longman.

Titman, W. (1994) *Special Places; Special People: The Hidden Curriculum of School Grounds*. Godalming, Surrey: World Wide Fund for Nature/ Learning through Landscapes.

Tizard, B. (1984) Problematic aspects of nuclear education, in Bishop of Salisbury, P. White, R. Andrews, B. Jacobsen and B. Tizard *Lessons Before Midnight: Educating for Reason in Nuclear Matters*, Bedford Way Paper no. 19. London: Institute of Education.

Tizard, B. and Hughes, M. (1984) *Young Children Learning: Talking and Thinking at Home and School*. London: Fontana.

Tizard, B., Blatchford, P., Burke, J., Farquhar, C. and Plewis, I. (1988) *Young Children at School in the Inner City*. Hove: Lawrence Erlbaum Associates.

Townsend, P. and Davidson, N. (1982) *Inequalities in Health: The Black Report*. Harmondsworth: Penguin.

Travers, T. (1995) The council tax crunch again, *Guardian*, 4 February: 24.

Turnaturi, G. (1987) Between public and private: the birth of the professional housewife and the female consumer, in A.S. Sassoon (ed.) *Women and the State*. London: Hutchinson.

Turner, B.S. (1992) *Regulating Bodies: Essays in Medical Sociology*. London: Routledge.

United Nations Committee on the Rights of the Child (1995) *Concluding Observations of the Committee on the Rights of the Child: United Kingdom of Great Britain and Northern Ireland*. New York: United Nations.

Urwin, C. (1984) Power relations and the emergence of language, in J. Henriques, W. Hollway, C. Urwin, C. Venn and V. Walkerdine *Changing the Subject*. London: Methuen.

Wajcman, J. (1994) Technology as masculine culture, in Polity Press (ed.) *The Polity Reader in Gender Studies*. Cambridge: Polity Press.

Waksler, F.C. (1991a) Dancing when the music is over: a study of deviance in a kindergarten classroom, in F.C. Waksler (ed.) *Studying the Social Worlds of Children: Sociological Readings*. London: Falmer Press.

Waksler, F.C. (1991b) Studying children: phenomenological insights, in F.C. Waksler (ed.) *Studying the Social Worlds of Children: Sociological Readings*. London: Falmer Press.

Walkerdine, V. (1984) Developmental psychology and the child-centred pedagogy: the insertion of Piaget into early education, in J. Henriques, W. Hollway, C. Urwin, C. Venn and V. Walkerdine *Changing the Subject*. London: Methuen.

Walkerdine, V. (1985) Psychological knowledge and educational practice: producing the truth about schools, in G. Claxton, W. Swann, P. Salmon, V. Walkerdine, B. Jacobsen and J. White (eds) *Psychology and Schooling: What's the Matter?*, Bedford Way Paper no. 25. London: Institute of Education.

Walkerdine, V. (1989) *Counting Girls Out*. London: Virago.

Walkerdine, V. and Lucey, H. (1989) *Democracy in the Kitchen: Regulating Mothers and Socialising Daughters*. London: Virago.

Ward, C. (1988) *The Child in the Country*. London: Robert Hale.

Ward, C. (1990 [1978]) *The Child in the City*, new edn. London: Bedford Square Press.

Webster, C. (1983) The health of the school child during the depression, in N. Parry and D. McNair (eds) *The Fitness of the Nation – Physical and Health Education in the Nineteenth and Twentieth Centuries*. Leicester: History of Education Society.

Whitehead, M. (1987) *The Health Divide: Inequalities in Health in the 1980s*. London: Health Education Council.

Wilkinson, R.G. (1994) *Unfair Shares: The Effects of Widening Income Differences on the Welfare of the Young*. Ilford: Barnardos.

Wilkinson, S.R. (1988) *The Child's World of Illness: The Development of Health and Illness Behaviour*. Cambridge: Cambridge University Press.

Williams, A. (1980) Intention versus transaction – the junior school physical education curriculum, *Physical Education Review*, 3: 96–104.

Williams, T., Wetton, N. and Moon, A. (1989) *A Picture of Health: What Do You Do that Makes You Healthy and Keeps You Healthy?* London: Health Education Authority.

Wilson, E. (1977) *Women and the Welfare State*. London: Tavistock.

Wilson, P. and Pahl, R. (1988) The changing sociological construction of the family, *Sociological Review*, 36, 2: 233–66.

Wintersberger, H. (1994) Costs and benefits – the economics of childhood, in J. Qvortrup, M. Bardy, G. Sgritta and H. Wintersberger (eds) *Childhood Matters: Social Theory, Practice and Politics*. Aldershot: Avebury Press.

Wohl, A.S. (1983) *Endangered Lives: Public Health in Victorian Britain*. London: Methuen.

Woodhead, M. (1990) Psychology and the cultural construction of children's needs, in A. James and A. Prout (eds) *Constructing and Reconstructing Childhood: Contemporary Issues in the Sociological Study of Children*. London: Falmer Press.

World Health Organization (1993) *The European Network of Health Promoting Schools*. Copenhagen: WHO.

Wright Mills, C. (1967 [1959]) *The Sociological Imagination*. Oxford: Oxford University Press.

Wyke, S. and Hewison, J. (eds) (1991) *Child Health Matters: Caring for Children in the Community*. Milton Keynes: Open University Press.

Young, I.M. (1980) Throwing like a girl: a phenomenology of feminine body comportment motility and spatiality, *Human Studies*, 3, 137–56.

Index